ARCHAEOLOGICAL
APPROACHES
ⲧⲟ medieval europe

ARCHAEOLOGICAL
APPROACHES
to medieval europe

edited by

KATHLEEN BIDDICK

Studies in Medieval Culture, XVIII
MEDIEVAL INSTITUTE PUBLICATIONS
Western Michigan University
Kalamazoo, Michigan–1984

Library of Congress Cataloging in Publication Data
Main Entry under title:

Archaeological approaches to medieval Europe.

(Studies in medieval culture ; 18)
Papers presented at the Sixteenth International
Congress on Medieval Studies, Medieval Institute,
Western Michigan University, May 6-9, 1981.
Includes bibliographical references.
1. Archaeology, Medieval—Congresses. 2. Land
Use—Europe—History—Congresses. 3.
Agriculture—Europe—History—Congresses. 4. Excavations
Archaeology)—Europe—Congresses. I. Biddick, Kathleen. I.
International Congress on Medieval Studies (16th :
1981 : Kalamazoo, Mich.) III. Series.
CB351.S83 vol. 18   940.1'7 s   84-14759
[D125]   [940.1]
ISBN 0-918720-53-2
ISBN 0-918720-52-4 (pbk.)

Cover Design by Cynthia Tyler
Printed in the United States of America

To Mary Gordon
"all these infinitely obscure lives remain to be recorded"
(V. Woolf, *A Room of One's Own*)

CONTENTS

ACKNOWLEDGEMENTS

Numerous colleagues have provided support and critical assistance to bring this project to fruition.

Professor Suzanne Wemple, Barnard College, encouraged me to pursue my idea of assembling medieval archaeologists and historians here in North America and suggested the International Congress on Medieval Studies as the ideal setting for such a meeting.

Professor Otto Gründler, Western Michigan University, Director of the Medieval Institute, supported the experiment wholeheartedly, and I am particularly grateful for the warm hospitality which he extended to our European visitors.

Professor Ambrose Raftis of the Pontifical Institute of Mediaeval Studies was, unfortunately, unable to attend and chair our first meeting, but his longstanding concern for interdisciplinary communication has served, and continues to serve, as an inspiration.

The Institute for Research in History offered crucial assistance during the early planning stages of this volume, and Dr. William Zeisel of the Institute provided invaluable help with the first stages of editing.

Dr. Thomas H. Seiler, Managing Editor, Juleen Eichinger, Editorial Assistant, and Marcia Blaustein of Medieval Institute Publications, have labored long to solve a range of technical problems.

My debt to fellow archaeologists and historians continues to increase. Their enthusiastic response to our first meeting has made possible further sessions in 1982 and 1984.

Finally, a generous donation from my dear friend Mary Gordon helped defray the travel expenses of English colleagues. I am most grateful to her and to all those who worked on this volume for their dedication to "all these infinitely obscure lives [that] remain to be recorded."

K. B.

INTRODUCTION

A good deal of the rough pioneering has been done. . . . An admitted need of the present day is the methodical exploration of the social unit on a more expansive scale than has been normal in the past. The phase of the sondage or isolated trial pit, however skillfully executed, is now to a large measure past. What we need now is horizontal excavation on an extensive scale.[1]

In his Rhind lectures of 1951, Sir Mortimer Wheeler recounted the history of the first generation of archaeological excavation. He foresaw that the discipline was on the verge of transformation as new fields of investigation shifted its basic methodologies and criteria of interpretation. As archaeology moved out of the trial pit onto the open-area site, it redefined itself. Its purpose as a discipline was no longer simply the study of past culture; its subject matter expanded to incorporate the interaction between material cultures, human behavior, and ideas through space and time, even into the present.[2] These concerns are now recognized as central ones in all the historical sciences. It is not surprising, therefore, that the idea of the open-area archaeological site has become a powerful metaphor in contemporary critical thought.

Over the past thirty years, historians have also come to embrace archaeological modes of thought. In their own studies of material life, they have been confronted with complexities that have recast the meaning of continuity and change. In recognizing that the history of the commonplace and of everyday life embraces processes of long duration, and in trying to distinguish change in such deep strata, history has become closely bound with archaeology.

1

This new union—or mature reunion—is especially welcome for the study of the Middle Ages. The convention of bracketing off this period from the classical and early modern worlds has hampered the study of the formative processes of the medieval period, the roots of which lie in prehistory.[3] Likewise, studies of the development of the early modern world system, in particular the formation of specialized farming regions in northwestern Europe, would profit from a longer perspective.[4] Questioning our chronological compartments is certainly not new in history, but the chance to re-evaluate them through an archaeological perspective is.

As fruitful as cooperation in medieval archaeology and history might be at this stage of disciplinary development, its realization requires that we deal with the practical and often awkward issue of what specialists have to say to each other and how they can say it. Shared concerns and subject matter do not automatically translate into a common language. Historians and archaeologists of the medieval period who wish to work together are faced with the challenge of developing a discourse. This is an especially difficult task in North America, where no institutional base for medieval archaeology exists and where no academic institution offers a coherent program of courses devoted to the study of the material culture of medieval Europe. Nevertheless, there is a growing number of North American scholars, especially younger ones, working in the field of medieval archaeology or with archaeological approaches to historical documentation.

In 1978, the Center for Mediaeval Studies, University of Toronto, made a pioneering effort to improve communication in North America by inviting archaeologists and historians to participate in a conference on the material foundations of medieval village life.[5] In conjunction with the conference, John Hurst, Principal Inspector of Ancient Monuments for the Department of the Environment, England, and founder, along with Maurice Beresford, of the Wharram Percy Medieval Village Excavation, offered a series of lectures devoted to medieval archaeology. In order to provide a much needed continuity for this first effort at communication, a series of sessions devoted to archaeological approaches to medieval Europe was held at the Sixteenth International Congress on Medieval Studies (Medieval Institute, Western Michigan University, May 6-9, 1981). It was hoped that this meeting would bring together North American scholars working in medieval archaeology and related fields and broaden their contacts with European colleagues.[6] The setting of the Congress was ideal for interdisciplinary contact.

The papers presented at the 1981 sessions and collected in this volume are striking for their diversity of approaches and subject matter.

2

They reflect the spirit of an open area excavation where specialists from many disciplines with diverging methodologies meet and work side by side. No paper is specifically devoted to an excavation report, although the majority of contributors made use of data from such reports. Field survey, a technique commonly employed by prehistorians and now adopted by medieval archaeologists, emerges here as a powerful research tool. It also serves as a methodological model for the new approaches to historical documentation which are rooted in regional reconstructions of material culture. Medieval documents from a local area, such as account and court rolls, charters, wills, and tax lists, when set side by side, can be systematically explored for information about agricultural arrangements, resource organization, settlement, social complexity, and human behavior.

In bringing together these papers, I have a further hope that their publication will emphasize the need for active participation of different disciplines in formulating questions about and interpretations of material culture in the Middle Ages. Past collaboration has been marred by dependent "borrowing" of often outmoded explanatory structures or choked off by unfair application of inappropriate criteria of proof to pioneering undertakings. As Professor Raftis commented in one planning session, we need to build "new bridges" if we wish to achieve some interdisciplinary coherence.[7]

In a broader perspective, this volume celebrates the coming of age of historical archaeology, of which medieval archaeology is a subdiscipline. Historical archaeology is now developing both an archaeology of complex "historical" societies and an anthropology.[8] A past resentment at having to ask traditional historiographical questions can be set aside, since historical archaeology is no longer a "handmaiden" but a field of inquiry in its own right.

This collection is intended primarily as a sampler; nonetheless, a thematic unity emerges. Certainly, the potential of archaeological approaches to contribute to a political ecology of the medieval period is a major one. By "political ecology" is meant "the system of relationships between groups possessed of differential access to resources, power, and symbols."[9] The allocation of resources, critical to the agrarian-based communities of medieval Europe, indeed critical to all societies, is in great need of exploration. The early *Annalistes* were working in this direction, but, without the full use of modern archaeological techniques and, in particular, the application of the natural sciences to archaeology, there were real limitations to their undertakings. These need no longer apply, as the approaches presented here suggest.

The political ecology of the multiple estate is reconstructed by

3

Glanville Jones from medieval Welsh texts. The territorial organization of resources and labor, which he describes, is analogous to arrangements in complex chiefdom societies as studied by anthropologists. How these territories break up and grow incoherent is an important study of social change. David Hall's contribution, which combines field survey and topographical reconstruction from documents, introduces evidence for the deliberate organization of field lay-outs in the English Midlands in the early medieval period (c. eighth century). These findings question some of the traditional technological and demographic explanations for the development of field systems. Kathleen Biddick explores the relation between the changing complexity of social organization and control over access to pastoral resources. In an ecological interpretation of historical documents, Harold Fox turns discussion of the English Midland system of two-and three fields away from a traditional focus on cereals by emphasizing also the role of pastoral resources in these arrangements. His approach and materials complement the theory of simulation modeling of traditional agricultural systems presented by William Cooter. Computer simulation, used extensively by historical demographers as well, can help researchers in judging how important observed change actually is within dynamic systems.

The use of time-depth is critical to the study of how resources are patterned by communities. By combining archaeological and historical evidence with a botanical survey of historical woodlands, Oliver Rackham is able to trace the history of woodland management in England for four millennia. Pamela Crabtree uses time-depth comparison of Iron Age, Roman, and Later Saxon bone samples excavated from British archaeological sites to elucidate patterns of continuity and change in animal husbandry at the Early Saxon rural site of West Stow, Suffolk. William TeBrake explores the question: how do communities adjust to environmentally sensitive areas where the scope for subsistence strategies is limited—barring large-scale man-made alterations to the environment? As an historian, he draws upon environmental and archaeological data in a case study of a Dutch coastal zone to describe an ecological tradition of subsistence which had its roots in the Bronze Age (second millennium B.C.) and continued up to the period of reclamation in the tenth century A.D. This long-term adaptation offers an excellent opportunity for future study of diversity of social organization and settlement within one subsistence tradition.

Much may be learned about the changing internal and external social and economic relations among communities by studying settlement patterns through time. The field survey and excavation programs in southwestern Burgundy and in the area of the Roman *Ager Cosanus*,

4

north of Rome, as described by Carole Crumley and Walter Berry and by Stephen Dyson, respectively, are good illustrations of this archaeological methodology. Some of the ways in which archaeologists trace the external relations between different areas are presented in the papers of Richard Hodges and Janet Buerger. Hodges' reconstruction of North Sea exchange in the seventh through ninth centuries revolutionizes the traditional historical model and powerfully demonstrates what can happen when archaeology, rather than conjecture, fills in the blanks left by the absence of adequate historical documentation. The complex interrelationships between material and symbolic exchange are tackled by Buerger in her study of medieval fine pottery trade in the Mediterranean. Her work also underlines the fact that, despite a long tradition of classical archaeology in the Mediterranean, its medieval archaeology is poorly known.[10]

Walter Janssen's overview of medieval archaeology in West Germany is a sampler within a sampler and places the development of the discipline in its historical context. He reminds us in his conclusions that medieval archaeology is a young discipline just facing its trying years of theoretical and methodological growth. We concur with his closing wish that the problems raised about early European development by research in medieval archaeology be explored in as broad an interdisciplinary setting as possible. We hope that our ongoing plans for meetings at the International Congress on Medieval Studies will provide one forum for this interdisciplinary exploration.

Kathleen Biddick
University of Notre Dame

NOTES

[1] Sir Mortimer Wheeler, *Archaeology from the Earth* (Harmondsworth, England, 1954), p. 224.

[2] William Rathje, "Modern Material Culture Studies," in *Advances in Archaeological Method and Theory*, vol. 2, ed. Michael Schiffer (New York, 1979), pp. 1-37.

[3] This topic was explored in a series of six sessions at the International Congress on Medieval Studies at Kalamazoo in May 1984, in a symposium entitled "Europe under Development: A Critical Millennium, B.C 200 - 800 A.D."

[4] Plans are underway to explore this later development at the Twenty-Third International Congress on Medieval Studies in 1988: Europe Under Development II: 800 A.D. - 1600 A.D.

[5] For papers from the conference, see *Pathways to Medieval Peasants*, ed.

5

J. A. Raftis, Papers in Medieval Studies, no. 2 (Toronto, 1981).

[6] For instance, we were very happy to make contact with Elisabeth Zadora-Rio of the Centre de Recherches Archéologiques Médiévales who observed the conference and has encouraged our work since 1981.

[7] From a discussion at a meeting held at the 1982 sessions on "Beyond Urban and Rural Archaeology: Connecting Town and Country," Seventeenth International Congress on Medieval Studies, May, 1982.

[8] For parallel developments in anthropology, see: John W. Cole, "Anthropology Comes Part-Way Home: Community Studies in Europe," in *Annual Review of Anthropology*, 6 (1977), 349-78.

[9] The concept of political ecology and its application is explored in some detail in: John W. Cole and Eric R. Wolf, *The Hidden Frontier: Ecology and Ethnicity in an Alpine Valley* (New York, 1974.) Quotation cited from p. 286.

[10] Medieval archaeology in the Mediterranean will constitute the theme for sessions in archaeology and history at the Twenty-First International Congress on Medieval Studies in 1986.

PART I:
ORGANIZING SPACE AND MANAGING RESOURCES

THE MULTIPLE ESTATE: A MODEL FOR TRACING THE INTER-RELATIONSHIPS OF SOCIETY, ECONOMY, AND HABITAT

GLANVILLE R. J. JONES

Introduction

The laws of a people are at once a mirror and a mold. They reflect that people's way of life and also help to shape it. Such is the case with the lawbooks of medieval Wales, the handbooks of practitioners of customary law.[1] These Welsh lawbooks were lawyers' text books, patched together from a variety of sources, some old, some new. They were "collections which in their day were always evolving, always emerging,"[2] for, like custom itself, customary law was not immutable.

These Welsh lawbooks were not the mandatory pronouncements of royal lawgivers, and, as a result, they were neither sufficiently complete nor sufficiently systematic to be designated as codes. It is true that in various ways they do record the substance of a great deal of the Welsh law that was current in medieval Wales, but, at the same time, they took for granted that there was a great mass of Welsh law that lay outside their pages. Accordingly, they prompt recollection of Maitland's shrewd observations about the Anglo-Saxon laws:

If we owe to these laws a certain sum of assured knowledge, we owe to them also—and this is hardly less valuable—a certain sum of assured ignorance. When they do not satisfy they, at all events, stimulate a rational curiosity; and where they do not give us intelligible answers they prompt us to ask intelligent questions.[3]

The Model

The lawbooks of Wales prompt a rational curiosity and questioning about the nature of territorial organization and, within that framework, the interrelationships of the trilogy of society, economy, and habitat. Particularly is this true of the law-texts relating to north-west Wales, an area where lawyers appear to have inspired much of the state-building aspirations of the princes of Gwynedd during the late twelfth century and the thirteenth century.[4] A group of related law texts of the thirteenth century, known collectively as the *Book of Iorwerth*, presents an elaborate, if highly schematized, model of territorial organization.[5]

So precise are the beginnings of this model that we dare hardly say *de minimis non curat lex*; for the *Book of Iorwerth* recalls that they made the measure of the legal acre by the barleycorn. Thus three lengths of a barleycorn made an inch, nine inches a foot, and sixteen feet a long yoke used for laying out an acre, whose dimensions in statute measure appear to have been twelve statute yards in breadth by 120 in length, so that the Iorwerth acre contained a mere 1,440 statute square yards. The main components of this model, giving the legal acreage, as specified, are presented in simplified form as follows:

4 acres	= 1 homestead (*tyddyn*)		
4 homesteads	= 1 shareland (*rhandir*)	=	16 acres
4 sharelands	= 1 holding (*gafael*)	=	64 acres
4 holdings	= 1 vill (*tref*)	=	256 acres
4 vills	= 1 multiple estate (*maenol*)	=	1,024 acres
12 multiple estates + 2 vills (= 50 vills)	= 1 commote (*cwmwd*)	=	12,800 acres
2 commotes (100 vills)	= 1 hundred (*cantref*)	=	25,600 acres

Table 1
The Iorwerth Model for Territorial Organization

Despite the obviously idealized nature of this model, the lawyers reiterate their claim that "the number of acres in the hundred is twenty-five thousand and six hundred, neither more nor less."[6] In reality, however, it is likely that the acreages cited in the Iorwerth model, apart probably from some of the lands contained within the homestead or messuage site, referred to lands in regular arable cultivation.

In this model the territorial unit which contained four vills was known as a *maenol* (plural *maenolau*). Clearly the *maenol* contained a multiplicity of settlements, and, for this reason, this term has been translated for convenience as "multiple estate." The term *maenol* itself is a later dialectical variant of the South Welsh *maenor*, a term probably originally used for the stone-girt residence of a lord and used later, by extension, for the territorial unit from which rents and services were contributed to this residence. The term "composite estate," sometimes used of the *maenol* or *maenor*, in the sense of a territorial unit, is here deliberately eschewed, for all estates, even lesser ones, are likely to have been composite units comprising such varied resources as arable, pasture, and meadowland.

By the thirteenth century the commote appears to have supplanted the hundred in importance. Consequently it is for the commote rather than the hundred that the *Book of Iorwerth* provides a further model for the territorial subdivison of a hierarchy of estates, as shown in Table 2:

For the king:

maerdref land	= 1 vill	
waste and summer pasture	= 1 vill	
4 multiple estates of bond vills	= 16 vills	= 26 vills
1 multiple estate of the greater reeve	= 4 vills	
1 multiple estate of the royal bailiff	= 4 vills	

For the free notables:

6 multiple estates	= 24 vills

50 vills

Table 2

The Iorwerth Model for the Sub-Division of a Commote

In this model, pride of place was accorded to the estate of the king. Within each commote, there were two vills or townships said to be for the use of the king: "one of them to be *maerdref* land for him and the other to be the king's waste and summer-pasture land (*hafod dir*)."[7] The

11

maerdref, literally the vill (*tref*) of the reeve (*maer*), contained the king's mensal land (*tir bwrdd*) for the provisioning of his table and the sustenance of the royal court (*llys*). The reeve was "to regulate the king's court, and what may pertain to it, such as ploughing, sowing, tending the king's cattle, his summer pastures (sic), and other things which may be necessary."[8]

The king's mensal land was cultivated, in part, by the bond tenants of the reeve's vill (*maerdref*), working under the direction of a reeve. In addition, however, recourse was made to the services of other bondmen said to belong to the king. In accordance with the mnemonic purposes of the Iorwerth model these bondmen were deemed to reside on four estates, each of which contained four vills. The king's bondmen who occupied the four multiple estates of bond vills in each commote were of a very lowly status, like the tenants of the reeve's vill (*maerdref*). Men without pedigree and bound to the soil, their rights in land were determined by the king's officers. Within any one vill the land they held was shared out equally among all adult males, save the youngest in each household, and accordingly was known as reckoned land (*tir cyfrif*). In the reeve's vill (*maerdref*) this sharing was done by the local land reeve, known pejoratively as the "reeve of the dung-heap." In the other vills of the king's bondmen, however, the sharing of reckoned land was done by two superior officers, the greater reeve and the royal bailiff, who, significantly, were also obliged to keep the king's waste. The king's bondmen, in return for their lands, cultivated the mensal land and erected the buildings of the royal court. They furnished the king with pack-horses for the armed hosts, and, to make the encampments for these hosts, they provided one axe-man from each bond vill. In addition, they contributed to the king in every year two food-gifts made up of the products of cultivation and those of pastoral farming. Once a year, also, they provided the queen with food and drink. Furthermore, these same heavily-burdened tenants provided maintenance and entertainment for various royal retainers and servants when on circuit. Those supported by the bondmen included the greater reeve, the royal bailiff, the falconers, the huntsmen with their dogs, and, not least in importance for martial purposes, young freemen on military training.

One multiple estate was said to be attached to the office of the greater reeve, and, since the latter had to be supported during his term of office, the four vills in the multiple estate were probably occupied by bond under-tenants. The same was undoubtedly true of the multiple estate attached to the office of the royal bailiff. Since the two offices of the greater reeve and the bailiff were in the gift of the king, the multiple estate attached to each office should probably be regarded as detachable por-

12

tions of the royal estate. Viewed in this wider sense, the royal estate in the ideal commote of the Iorwerth model would have contained no fewer than twenty-six vills.

There would have remained in the commote six multiple estates, each containing four vills. These vills, totalling twenty-four out of the fifty vills in the commote (or half hundred), were said to be held by notables, freemen of pedigree. The notables held hereditary land (*tir gwelyog*), the tenure taken for granted in the lawbooks.[9] The essential features of this kind of land were that the rights to it passed to male descendants in equal shares. By the time of the compilation of the extant lawbooks, equal shares, *per stirpes*, were normally inherited by brothers on their father's death. Provision, however, was made for a re-partition under certain circumstances; this occurred within an agnatic lineage, comprising the surviving male members of a four-generation inheritance group extending vertically backwards as far as the great-grandfather and horizontally outwards as far as second cousins.[10] Earlier it is likely that all hereditary land had been held by members of such four-generation groups and that rights over land were shared equally among members of these groups, with a re-allocation occurring with the passage of each generation. The idea was that each heir should be provided with a standard holding or shareland, but, with any marked growth of population, this might well become impossible. In practice, sharing by the four-generation agnatic lineage came to be displaced by equal division among brothers as the normal inheritance custom. As a result, the rule that a kindred must split up with each generation appears to have atrophied. Consequently the typical agnatic lineage expanded from one generation to the next and became a large kindred to which the name *gwely*, meaning bed, or *lectus* was applied. The same term, *gwely* (plural *gwelyau*), came to be applied to the permanent stake in the soil, or "resting-place," of this large kindred. In return for their patrimonies, the heirs of hereditary land owed to the king various dues, including food rents, diverse obligations, and, above all, military service for a limited period during each year.

The presence of under-tenants further increased the complexity of social organization. The heirs of expanding lineages, like those of earlier four-generation inheritance groups, could have their own under-tenants who held small plots of land, including gardens, by a variant of hereditary-land tenure.[11]

No matter what the tenure, however, on hereditary land as on reckoned land, an infield-outfield system of cultivation appears to have been adopted. The well-manured infield, usually located near the permanent settlement, was cultivated year in, year out. The outfield was normally used as a common pasture, but from time to time, particularly when there was pressure of population, parts of it would be dunged and cultivated for as long as they would bear a worthwhile crop.[12]

The Evidence: Extents and Surveys

As might be expected, in Gwynedd, during the Middle Ages, there were in practice both parallels with and deviations from the Iorwerth model. This can be clearly demonstrated in the extents or surveys compiled after the English conquest of Gwynedd in 1282-83.[13] The testimony of these extents is in part supported by the fragmentary evidence of a papal taxation return for the period before the conquest and, at least for a few localities, by the detailed evidence of local lay subsidy rolls for 1292-93.

Malltraeth Commote in the Anglesey Hundred of Aberffraw provides an instructive and appropriate example, for here was located a royal court, the ancient principal seat of Gwynedd (see Fig. 1 at end of essay). As is evident from the extents of 1294, 1306, and 1352 as well as other sources, the kind of social organization which existed within this commote in the late thirteenth century had long antedated the English conquest.[14]

The *maerdref* land for the sustenance of the court was located to the west of the surviving nucleated village of Aberffraw. It comprised five carucates of arable land, each probably of sixty acres; of these, four carucates adjoined the village and the fifth was in the outlying hamlet of Trecastell.[15] The king's waste and summer pasture of the Iorwerth model were less clearly evident in the extents, but they probably lay in Dindryfwl, a vill containing the largest expanse of poorly-drained land in the interior of the commote but land which could be readily grazed during the drier months of summer. Dindryfwl and the Manor of Aberffraw proper contained the largest areas of royal bond land in the commote, and between them there were close links. If one of the two chapels of the medieval parish of Aberffraw was Eglwys y Beili, in the royal court itself, the second chapel, Capel Mair, was at Dindryfwl. Moreover, in what was described in 1294 as the Manor of Aberffraw there were three mills: one was near Aberffraw proper; the second was at Dindryfwl; and the third near Treruffydd, a hamlet in the parish of Llangwyfan, itself, anciently, a chapelry of Aberffraw.[16]

The king's bond vills of the Iorwerth model were most clearly in evidence within the Manor of Aberffraw, as can be seen in Figure 1. The tenants of the hamlet of Maerdref, near the royal court, held their lands by reckoned-land tenure in return for heavy rents and services. Their obliga-

14

tions, before commutation, had included food rents, among them contributions to the royal store for the king when on progress, and others for circuits of royal officers. These tenants of Maerdref also performed transport and building duties associated with mill construction and, not least, heavy labor services for the cultivation of the royal demesnes. In addition they owed suit of mill, that is, were obliged to grind their corn at either the lord's mill at Aberffraw or that near Treruffydd. All the other exclusively bond hamlets of the manor, such as Treberfedd and Dinllwydan, like the outlying hamlet of Trecastell, were inhabited by reckonedland bondmen owing similar rents and services. But these were not the only bondmen in the Manor; for, at the hamlet called Garthau (Gardens), part of Aberffraw proper, there were fourteen small gardens occupied by bondmen who in return paid rents, contributed part of the store, performed transport duties, and also owed suit of mill at the lord's mill at Aberffraw.[17]

The remaining royal bondmen in the commote held land by hereditary land tenure. Such was the case in the exclusively bond township of Rhosmor and its hamlet of Treruffydd. These bondmen, besides paying rents, did their share of the works of the Manor of Aberffraw, but, whereas they owed mill suit at the royal mill near Treruffydd, it was for the royal mill at Dindryfwl that they performed transport and construction duties.[18] The other royal bondmen of Malltraeth occupied vills or hamlets which were also held in part by freemen and are therefore designated as mixed settlements. The occupants of these vills and hamlets, whether bond or free, normally held by hereditary-land tenure. Among such bondmen were the occupants of the five bond *gwelyau* (resting places) of Dindryfwl.[19]

Clearly, therefore, as far as royal bond vills were concerned, the regularities of the Iorwerth model, if they had ever existed, had long since disappeared. Yet the survival of a group of reckoned-land hamlets near Aberffraw proper suggests that a *maenor* of bond settlements of the kind recorded for South Wales had once existed there. It is possible also, that near the summer pastures of Dindryfwl there had once been a similar group of reckoned-land settlements before these had been deliberately transformed into hereditary-land settlements in order to promote colonization.[20]

The presence in Malltraeth Commote, after the conquest, of a number of vills as well as *gwelyau* bearing the names of royal officers points to the former existence of a system of support for free notables based on land, hence Trefwastrodion (The Vill of the Grooms) in which there were six free *gwelyau*, including Gwely Meilyr ap Gwalchmai (Meilyr son of Gwalchmai) and also the Gwely of the Falconers.[21] The heirs of these free *gwelyau*, according to the 1352 extent, paid rents to the king, owed suit at Dindryfwl mill, and also made their part of the prince's chamber at Aberffraw. But the heirs of the one *gwely* of bond land in this vill owed much heavier rents and services; these included the circuits of the falconers, of the otter-hounds, and the king's warhorse, as well as the duty of making part of each house of the lord prince's manor at Aberffraw.[22]

The neighboring Trefddisteiniaid (The Vill of the Stewards) contained two *gwelyau* of free land. Their obligations, according to the 1352 extent, were lighter than those of the freemen of Trefwastrodion; yet most of the heirs of one *gwely* still paid for the circuit of the king's warhorse and worked on the chamber at Aberffraw. Far more privileged, however, were the heirs of a second lineage, Gwely Wyrion Einion ap Gwalchmai, that is, the Lineage of the Descendants of Einion son of Gwalchmai. These heirs, who had their own mill, appear also to have had bond under-tenants and owed suit, that is attendance, at the bi-annual tourns of the lord prince. Otherwise, apart from suit of court at the county court once a month and at the hundred court every three weeks, they owed nothing to the lord prince, not even relief on the inheritance of their lands or the customary fine paid on the loss of a daughter's virginity.[23] Originally the office of steward, though an honorable one in the courts of Welsh kings, was lower in rank that that of chief of the warband. With the state-building activities of the rulers of Gwynedd, however, the office developed special characteristics, and the steward emerged as the leader of the armed forces with an enhanced status. It is therefore significant that part of an Anglesey vill named after such stewards, whose very title was a borrowing from the Anglo-Saxon *discpegn*,[24] should have held their lands on privileged terms.

Land was sometimes alienated on privileged terms in return for increased military service. Thus in the hamlet of Grugor, which had been carved out of the lands of Dindryfwl, there was a holding (*gafael*) of free land whose heirs, according to the extent of 1352, rendered "nothing thence annually except suit to the county and hundred and except that they go with the lord prince to his war at their own cost for forty days and afterwards at the lord prince's cost for all other services."[25] Again the only heir of the 1½ carucates in the free vill of Bodffordd in 1352 was Llywelyn ap Dafydd Fychan, and he rendered nothing thence to the lord prince in annual rent apart from suit at the county and hundred courts. He owed neither relief nor virginity fine, but he went "with the lord prince to his war at the lord prince's cost."[26] It is clear, also, that grants of bond settlements had been made to members of an aristocracy. Thus, in what was described in the 1352 extent as the free vill of Lledwigan Llan, one

Hywel ap Madog ap Llywelyn was the only heir, and he rendered nothing thence except suit to one county court each year. In addition, he claimed that "he and his bondmen" were free to mill wherever they wished, and for all other services he and his bondmen did suit to the two great tourns of the lord prince.[27]

Other, different services to the Welsh rulers of Gwynedd also brought rewards. Among them were the services of Gwalchmai ap Meilyr, the noted court poet who flourished at the close of the twelfth century. As a result, Gwalchmai, himself the son of a court poet, was the eponym of a number of lineages including the privileged Gwely Wyrion Einion ap Gwalchmai in Trefddisteiniaid. At Trewalchmai (The Vill of Gwalchmai), yet another free hamlet carved out of Dindryfwl, there were three other *gwelyau* named after three other sons of this poet.[28] One of these was the Gwely Meilyr ap Gwalchmai, which was also represented at Trefwastrodion, and in Lledwigan Llys there was yet another *gwely* named after Einion ap Gwalchmai. More lowly servants of the king were similarly endowed. Thus, among the four free *gwelyau* in the Manor of Aberffraw was Gwely Porthorion (The Gwely of the Doorkeepers) whose obligations included the duty of making and repairing part of the wall on either side of the door of the manor.[29]

As might be expected, vills were also alienated to the church. One such vill was Heneglwys (Old Church), which was free and said in 1352 to be held of Saints Faustinus and Bacellinus. Apart from one heir, the occupants of the three *gwelyau* there owed nothing to the lord prince save suit at the royal mill of Dindryfwl and suit at the bi-annual tourns of the lord prince.[30] The vill of Eglwys Ail (Wattled Church) also was said in 1352 to be free and to be held of Saint Cadwaladr the King. The occupants of the two *gwelyau* there owed even less to the lord prince, apart from suit at the two great tourns, for they claimed that they were free to mill in their own houses; presumably they had enough under-tenants or servants to undertake the laborious task of hand-milling.[31] Since the tenure of this vill was named after a seventh-century ruler of Gwynedd, there is an implication that this monastic vill had once been a royal possession alienated to the Church at a very early date, after its almost complete severance from the multiple estate of Aberffraw proper.

In contrast, Bodgedwydd was alienated by the rulers of Aberffraw to the Cistercians of Aberconwy only in the twelfth century.[32] The most numerous of the alienations made to the Church by the rulers of Gwynedd, however, were the vills and hamlets which had passed into the possession of the Bishop of Bangor. Although located in various parts of Malltraeth, they formed a noteworthy cluster, especially on the south-eastern fringe of the Manor of Aberffraw within the area which came to form part of the parish of Llangadwaladr. At Llanfeirian, a chapelry of Llangadwaladr, six bondmen in 1306 held in villeinage one carucate of land in return for rents in cash and oats as well as for light labor services. At Bodorgan a group of six free tenants held "in common" (*in communi*) one carucate of land in return for rents and suit at the Bishop's court. At Bodeon more complex conditions prevailed; for, besides the seven bond tenants of the Bishop here, there were other tenants who held some land of the Bishop and other land of the lord prince. Thus four tenants, including one Iorwerth ab Elidyr, who held two parts of one free carucate of the Bishop in return for various rents and services, also held freely one carucate of the prince in return (*inter alia*) for going in the army with him.[33] These four free tenants of the prince constituted the group known as Gwely Conws who in 1352 occupied one *gwely* (resting place) in the hamlet of Tregornor which was "called Bodeon in the account roll."[34] This *gwely*, which contained only one carucate of arable land, was obviously a small unit. As such, like many another *gwely* on church land, it appears to have been more akin to the joint holding of the members of a four-generation inheritance group than to the larger and more widely ramified joint holding of an expanding lineage.

Clearly the typical small *gwely* which had survived into the fourteenth century on church land was typical of an earlier and simpler stage of development than the characteristically larger and more complex *gwely* on lay land, of the kind which, for example, was occupied in Trewalchmai and Trefwastrodion by the lineage claiming descent from Meilyr ap Gwalchmai. Such *gwelyau* as the latter, which had expanded probably during the twelfth and thirteenth centuries, were no doubt associated with the colonization and development of land which had either come to be under-utilized or had remained so. The social structure of Malltraeth as portayed in medieval extents was, therefore, far more complex than that envisaged in the models presented in the lawbooks. This was in large measure a consequence of the alienation of lands to aristocrats as well as to the Church.

Despite the devastation caused by the wars of 1277 and 1282-83, the detailed local assessment roll for the taxation of personal property which has survived for Malltraeth Commote conveys a good impression of the complexity of the social structure of pre-conquest Gwynedd.[35] This local roll, the greater part of which has neither been published nor hitherto analyzed, suffers from the limitations of this class of record in that it is concerned only with movables—possessions which could be moved from place to place—and, as Father Raftis has emphasized, these lists were in no sense an inventory of the resources of the community.[36]

According to the instructions which were issued to royal officials in Gwynedd in 1292-93, the assessment of movable goods was to be confined to the more important domestic animals and to the main crops.[37] In practice these were nominally valued as follows: a horse, a mare, or an ox at 5s.; a foal, a three-year old affer, or draught animal, or a cow at 3s. 4d;[38] a two-year old affer or a calf at 2s., and a sheep normally at 6d. Crops were measured by the crannock which contained the standard London measure of four bushels. A crannock of wheat was nominally valued at 2s. 6d, one of ground oats at 2s., one of barley or peas at 1s. 4d. It is likely that in any taxable household most of the important domestic animals were recorded, but the crops represented for any such household a surplus beyond that needed for sustenance.[39] Although the tools of a trade were believed to have been exempt from taxation of this kind, utensils of an unspecified kind were included among movables assessed in Malltraeth. Moreover, for the fifteenth of 1292-93, those households whose movables were valued at less than 15s., in theory at least, paid no tax at all. For Gwynedd, the untaxed population was estimated to lie between one-sixth and one-half of those assessed and probably at a third of the total number of families.[40]

The territorial unit used for the purpose of assessment varied. In most cases it was a single vill, with or without constituent hamlets. The "vill of Aberffraw with its hamlets" was one such unit.[41] The omission, however, of any reference to Eglwys Ail, earlier recorded as a church in the *Valuation of Norwich* in 1254, and also the absence of any reference to the parish of Llangadwaladr, which was later served by Eglwys Ail,[42] suggests that this area, adjoining the Manor of Aberffraw and embracing vills alienated to the Bishop of Bangor, was included for assessment purposes under the rubric of Aberffraw with its hamlets. Certainly the status of Eglwys Ail as a monastic vill does not appear to have led to its exclusion, for Heneglwys, a similar monastic vill, was chosen as the name of one assessment unit. Heneglwys was named as a church in the *Valuation of Norwich* and was undoubtedly the focus of the parish of the same name. This parish of Heneglwys embraced a number of lay vills and hamlets which are quite unlikely to have escaped the attention of the tax-gatherer in 1292-93. Clearly, therefore, problems abound with the interpretation of the taxation roll for 1292-93; yet its analysis, within the context of other social and economic sources, does serve to identify real people with places and to illuminate the way of life of the community.[43]

The mean or average assessment of the 313 taxpaying households recorded for the whole of Malltraeth Commote was 3s. 4⅞d.[44] The mean or average is not very meaningful, however, whether for the commote as a whole or for its constitutent assessment units. The mean can be readily distorted by the presence of a few wealthy individuals, and within the

ASSESSMENT UNIT	TAX-PAYING HOUSE-HOLDS	VALUE OF FIFTEENTH	MEAN ASSESS-MENT	HIGHEST ASSESS-MENT	MEDIAN ASSESS-MENT	LOWEST ASSESS-MENT
Heneglwys	17	£ 2 9s 3¾d	2s 10¾d	7s 2½d	2s 4½d	1s 0½d
Lledwigan Llan	30	£ 3 19s 7d	2s 7⅝d	10s 10d	2s 4d	11d
Lledwigan Llys	30	£ 4 4s 6½d	2s 9⅞d	6s 4d	2s 7½d	11d
Trefddisteiniaid	56	£11 16s 7¾d	4s 2¾d	13s 0d	3s 1d	1s 0½d
Rhosmor	30	£ 3 12s 1¾d	2s 4⅞d	4s 6d	2s ¾d	1s 1d
Aberffraw	68	£12 12s 7d	3s 8½d	£1 2s 9d	2s 11d	1s 0d
Dindryfwl	48	£ 8 8s 3¼d	3s 6⅛d	13s 4½d	2s 7d	1s 2½d
Trefwastrodion	34	£ 6 2s 0¼d	3s 7⅛d	13s 4d	2s 7¾d	1s 0½d
Malltraeth Commote	313	£53 5s 1¼d	3s 4⅞d	£1 2s 9d	2s 6¾d	11d

Table 3

Returns of the Assessments of the Fifteenth
on Movables for Malltraeth Commote, 1292-93

various units of assessment there was a far from even spread of possessions among taxpaying households. Thus, use of the median gives a far better impression of social distributions as measured in terms of taxable goods. The assessment of the median household, of the 313 taxpaying households recorded for Malltraeth Commote as a whole, was 2s. 6¾d.

Aberffraw with its hamlets exhibited the greatest extremes; one Iorwerth Foel was assessed at no less than 22s. 9d; and one Madog ap Bleddyn was assessed at the lowest taxable threshold of 1s. The former, the wealthiest taxpayer in the whole commote, had in taxable possessions no fewer than five horses, eight affers, twenty oxen, a herd of sixteen cows, a flock of twenty sheep, twenty crannocks of wheat, forty of ground oats, and six of peas and barley, valued *in toto* at £17 1s. 3d. The latter, the poorest, had in taxable possessions only one mare, one affer, two cows, and half a crannock of wheat valued altogether at a mere 14s. 11d, so that, although strictly speaking his goods were valued at less than the minimum threshold, he did not escape the tax-gatherer's net. At Aberffraw with its hamlets, despite the former presence of the court, the average assessment was only 3s. 8½d and the median assessment only 2s. 11d.

The Iorwerth ab Elidyr, assessed in Aberffraw with its hamlets for 7s. 1d, can probably be identified with the freeman of the same name who, in 1306, shared one carucate of lay land at Bodeon with three other freemen and also shared, with the same three freemen, two parts of one carucate of church land.[45] Iorwerth's taxable goods, valued in 1292-93 at £5 6s. 3d, were three horses, two affers, four oxen, six cows, ten sheep, six crannocks of wheat, nine of ground oats, and two of peas and barley, together with utensils deemed to be worth 80 d; indeed the latter were worth more than the utensils of any of the other thirteen taxpaying households in Aberffraw recorded as having utensils. After the conquest, freemen with more than four bovates, or sixteen acres, of arable land who owed suit of court at the county court are considered to have formed an elite. On the basis of an analysis of the subsidy rolls for other parts of North Wales, it has been suggested that the members of this elite would have owned chattels worth £5, for which they would have been assessed, for a fifteenth, at 6s 8d.[46] Iorwerth ab Elidyr was undoubtedly a member of this upper crust. Although by 1306 Iorwerth appears to have held twenty-five acres of arable land rather than sixteen, it is likely that between 1292 and 1306 he had enlarged his holding. There is, therefore, no need to adopt a lower threshold—of the order of 4s. 6d suggested by Iorwerth's holding of twenty-five acres—as a criterion for membership of the upper crust. Assuming a threshold of 6s. 8d, the number of members of the elite in 1292-93 would have been six at Aberffraw with its hamlets, no fewer than twelve at Trefddisteiniaid, four at Trefwastrodion, five at Dindryfwl, one at Heneglwys, one at Lledwigan Llan, and not even one at Lledwigan Llys. With this higher threshold the elite would have comprised about 9% of the taxpaying households, or possibly 7% of all households in Malltraeth Commote.

At the other extreme, taxpaying households assessed at less than 2s. 6¾d, the median for the commote as a whole, comprised nearly 67% of all taxpaying households at Lledwigan Llan, 60% at Rhosmor, 53% at Heneglwys, 50% at Lledwigan Llys, 47% at Aberffraw with its hamlets, 45% at Trefwastrodion, and only 39% at Trefddisteiniaid.

It is perhaps not surprising after the conquest of Gwynedd that the members of the elite were less numerous at Aberffraw, formerly the site of a royal court, than at the vill of Trefddisteiniaid. Nevertheless, given the particularly privileged status of one lineage in Trefddisteiniaid, it is significant that members of the upper crust were more numerous there than in Aberffraw or in any other assessment unit in the commote. Again the mean and the median assessments were higher at Trefddisteiniaid than at Aberffraw with its hamlets, where they were no doubt depressed by the presence of substantial numbers of bondmen holding reckoned land. At the other extreme was the vill of Rhosmor which was occupied solely by bondmen holding hereditary land. There the highest assessment at 4s. 6d was only slightly higher than the median of Trefddisteiniaid. At Rhosmor the two best-endowed households were in fact over-assessed, in relation to their taxable possessions, at this level of 4s. 6d. Even so, one of these households consisted of a group comprising Ieuaf ap Meilyr and an unspecified number of his sons. Yet this family group held as taxable possessions only one horse, two oxen, six cows, fifteen sheep, three crannocks of wheat, two of barley, and six of ground oats.

At Dindryfwl, despite the presence of large numbers of bondmen holding hereditary land, the mean and median assessments were higher than at Rhosmor, not least because a number of hamlets had been alienated to freemen. Among the latter were the occupants of the holding (gafael) in Grugor who performed additional military service on behalf of the prince. Hence probably the recording within the Dindryfwl assessment unit of the household inhabited in 1292-93 by Ieuaf Barth and his sons, who were assessed together for 13s. 4½d, at the highest level cited in this unit, albeit an under-assessment in relation to their taxable goods. Significantly enough they had no fewer than seven horses (equi) as distinct from mares or foals, and their other assessed possessions were seventeen affers, six oxen, thirteen cows, thirteen sheep, four crannocks of wheat, nineteen of ground oats, and utensils worth 1s.

In the vill of Lledwigan Llan, the only heir in 1352 was Hywel ap

22

Madog ap Llywelyn, who not only held it on privileged terms but was also supported by his own bondmen. It need occasion no surprise that earlier in 1292-93 there was, similarly, only one wealthy taxpayer in Lledwigan Llan, Llywelyn ab Owein, although according to the evidence of pedigrees he was not the direct ancestor of Hywel ap Madog ap Llywelyn.[47] Like many a prominent freeman, he was under- assessed at 10s. 10d; his taxable movables were no fewer than four horses (*equi*), one affer, ten oxen, fifteen cows, six crannocks of wheat, and six of ground oats. Since the majority of the inhabitants of the vill were, without doubt, bond under-tenants, it is clear from the median assessment of 2s. 4d, that not all bondmen were impoverished, and indeed the taxpayer who ranked next to Llywelyn ab Owein was assessed at 4s. 9d. One taxpayer, appropriately named for a bondman as Mab y Gwrdrwg (Son of the Evil Man), was perhaps deliberately under-assessed, in relation to his chattels, at 12½d.

Usually, however, bondmen were much more vulnerable in their dealings with the tax-gatherer than were prominent freemen. Thus in Lledwigan Llan there were two individuals, correctly assessed in relation to their taxable possessions at 11½d and 11d, respectively, who should have escaped the tax but, nevertheless, were listed as taxpayers. Significantly, however, both possessed animals as well as crops, and the poorer of the two, one Iorwerth ap Ieuan, owned one mare, two cows, and 1½ crannocks of barley. Thus, even the poorest taxpayers practiced mixed farming.

Livestock, certainly in terms of notional taxable values, were clearly the mainstay of the economy. Within the commote there was not a single taxed household without a few animals. Only in the bond vill of Rhosmor did livestock contribute less than two-thirds of the value of all assessed movables and this by the narrowest of margins. There were only ten households in the commote without taxable crops, but this may merely reflect the fact that with crops only those stocks surplus to needs were taxed. Certainly the households without taxable crops were by no means always the poorest taxpaying households.[48] Yet more than half the taxpaying households in Heneglwys, Lledwigan Llan, and Trefwastrodion were without one or more oxen, and even in the purely bond vill of Rhosmor, one out of every three taxpaying households was in this position. In fact, only in Aberffraw with its hamlets were more than three out of every four taxpaying households endowed with one or more oxen. It is clear, therefore, that in bond vills like Rhosmor where, according to some lawbooks, co-tillage had to be arranged before ploughing could begin,[49] other animals were probably included in the plough teams; otherwise there must have been a considerable amount of digging with

ASSESSMENT UNIT	TOTAL VALUE OF ASSESSED MOVABLES	LIVESTOCK VALUE %	CROP VALUE %	UTENSILS VALUE %
Heneglwys	£ 36 19s 8¼d	87.2	12.8	1.0
Lledwigan Llan	£ 59 13s 9d	81.0	18.6	0.4
Lledwigan Llys	£ 63 8s 1½d	84.6	14.8	0.6
Trefddisteiniaid	£177 9s 8¼d	72.0	27.2	0.8
Rhosmor	£ 52 2s 2¼d	66.5	33.5	-
Aberffraw	£189 8s 9d	72.6	26.7	0.7
Dindryfwl	£126 4s 0¾d	77.1	22.4	0.5
Trefwastrodion	£ 91 10s 3¾d	78.5	21.3	0.2

Table 4

Relative Importance of Assessed Livestock,
Crops, and Utensils in Malltraeth Commote, 1292-93

24

spades or forks.

Horses, affers, oxen, cattle, and sheep were present in every assessment unit; and the main cereals, oats and wheat, were recorded for each of these areas. There can be little doubt, therefore, that in Malltraeth Commote the vast majority, if not all of the inhabitants, practiced mixed farming. If these inhabitants were largely dependent on animals for sustenance, traction, or transport, then all these animals had to be fed from the varied products of the land, and this land in turn needed animal manure to restore its fertility. For the success of a largely self-contained pastoral economy it was essential to have some land under cultivation. Cereals, especially oats, were grown in order to provide filling foods for humans. The oat crop was also used to supply fodder for horses and, during the lean winter months, even for draught animals, the oxen used for ploughing and the affers used for carting and harrowing; the latter also needed additional sustenance during the busy seasons of the year. Arable and pasture were, therefore, interrelated: the one was necessary for the other to thrive. Those taxpayers with the largest numbers of animals also had the greatest reserves of crops.

Within the commote, however, there was some scope for a limited measure of specialization. Cattle were important everywhere. They were mainly cows, with followers usually specified as calves, and only the occasional heifer, young bullock, or young bull. These cattle loomed largest in the economies of the vills or hamlets in the interior of the commote, particulary in areas where there were extensive pastures on soils which, under natural conditions, were either inadequately or poorly drained. In Lledwigan Llan cattle outnumbered all other taxable animals and amounted to 55% of the number of all assessed livestock and 42% of their value. The corresponding figures for Heneglwys were 47% and 53% respectively. In Trefddisteiniaid the agrarian economy was more diversified and balanced than in any other unit. There, the only vill where young bullocks were recorded, cattle made up 24% of the number of recorded livestock and 24% of their value.

Sheep were more prominent in the economies of vills and hamlets near the coast. Their greater significance in coastal areas was probably a reflection of the effects of sea-winds, partly in inhibiting tree growth to a greater extent than in the interior, but even more, in causing the spread of blown sand. This was true especially in the area between Aberffraw proper, Tregornor, and Treberfedd, where large sandy wastes (vasta arenosa) were grazed in common by the occupants of Aberffraw and its hamlets. Within this latter assessment unit, sheep made up to nearly 54% of all assessed livestock in number, but, since each sheep was assessed at only 6d, or occasionally even at 4d, they contributed rather less than 17%

ASSESSMENT UNIT	TAX-PAYING HOUSE-HOLDS	HORSES	MARES	FOALS	TWO-YEAR AFFERS	THREE-YEAR AFFERS	OXEN	COWS	CALVES	SHEEP	OTHER ANIMALS	TOTAL ANIMALS
Heneglwys	17	20*(10)	6 (12)	8 (12)	6 (15)	11 (14)	24 (9)	79 (0)	22 (7)	42 (12)	1h (16)	219
Lledwigan Llan	30	45 (12)	13 (22)	2 (28)	5 (28)	1 (29)	27 (17)	122 (1)	42 (12)	48 (23)	2b (28) 5h (27)	314
Lledwigan Llys	30	39 (13)	20 (20)	-	-	3 (28)	59 (9)	115 (0)	31 (16)	99 (18)	2h (29)	368
Trefddisteiniaid	56	93 (27)	27 (35)	6 (53)	131 (14)	24 (46)	119 (18)	258 (2)	3 (54)	436 (17)	2x (54)	1099
Rhosmor	30	18 (18)	15 (17)	1 (29)	26 (15)	7 (24)	39 (10)	77 (0)	1 (29)	153 (9)	-	337
Aberffraw	68	74 (34)	34 (43)	-	93 (28)	38 (53)	143 (16)	258 (4)	-	747 (22)	-	1387
Dindryfwl	48	49 (28)	34 (22)	6 (43)	94 (11)	34 (35)	76 (17)	227 (0)	-	225 (27)	-	745
Trefwastrodion	34	50 (16)	15 (22)	2 (32)	72 (7)	20 (30)	61 (19)	170 (0)	-	66 (24)	-	456
TOTALS	313	388	164	25	427	138	548	1306	101	1816	12	4925

* Figures in parentheses represent the number of taxpaying households recorded as having none of the items listed.
b represents young bulls
h represents one or more heifers
x represents bullocks

Table 5

The Assessed Livestock in the taxpaying households of Malltraeth Commote, 1292-93

ASSESSMENT UNIT	TAX-PAYING HOUSE-HOLDS	WHEAT	BARLEY	GROUND OATS	OATS	PEAS	PEAS AND BARLEY	PEAS AND WHEAT	TOTAL CROPS
Heneglwys	17	3 *(14)	-	43½ (2)	-	-	-	-	46½
Lledwigan Llan	30	32⅜ (6)	17 (16)	49 (8)	4½ (27)	2½ (27)	11¾ (23)	-	117⅛
Lledwigan Llys	30	10 (19)	½ (24)	73 (5)	-	1½ (29)	3 (28)	½ (29)	88½
Trefddisteiniaid	56	127½ (3)	78 (18)	256½ (2)	-	-	10 (55)	-	472
Rhosmor	30	43 (5)	13 (21)	118 (0)	-	-	-	-	174
Aberffraw	68	117½ (3)	51 (43)	310 (8)	-	-	20 (66)	-	498½
Dindryfwl	48	49 (13)	17½ (36)	209 (4)	-	-	-	-	275½
Trefwastrodion	34	29½ (13)	12½ (23)	118 (1)	-	5 (3)	11 (30)	-	176
Totals	313	411	189½	1177	4½	9	55¾	½	1848⅛

*Figures in parentheses represent the number of taxpaying households recorded as having none of the items listed.

Table 6

The Assessed Crannocks of Crops in the Taxpaying Households of Malltraeth Commote, 1292-93 of the value of all livestock. The corresponding figures for the bond vill of Rhosmor were 46% and 7% and for Trefddisteiniaid 40% and nearly 9%.

With crops, as with livestock, there appears to have been a limited amount of specialization but always within the context of a mixed farming regime. Oats were important everywhere, especially in the interior; in Heneglwys they amounted to nearly 94% of the total number of recorded crannocks of crops and to 92% of the value of these recorded crannocks. It was in Lledwigan Llan, with its nucleus firmly centered on a small spread of well-drained brown earths of high base status, the most fertile soils in the whole of Malltraeth Commote,[50] that wheat, the most prized crop, loomed largest, making up nearly 28% of the total number of crannocks recorded there and some 36% of the value of these crops. The corresponding figures for barley were 14% and 10%, while for mixed peas and barley they were 10% and 7%. Clearly, oats were much less significant in the economy of Lledwigan Llan than in any other unit in the commote. Well- drained brown earths of high base status identical with those of Lledwigan Llan also extended into the adjoining Lledwigan Llys; here, by contrast, wheat accounted for only 11% of the number of recorded crannocks and contributed to 14% of their value. The corresponding figures for oats, on the other hand, were no less than 82% for quantity and value. This was probably the result of a particular local specialization on the part of the heirs of this free vill who were members of the privileged lineage called Gwely Einion ap Gwalchmai, so named after the Einion whose descendants (*wyrion*) also held one of the two *gwelyau* of free land in Trefddisteiniaid. In the vill of Lledwigan Llys horses made up some 16% of all the animals and contributed 27% of their value—higher figures for horses than obtained anywhere else in the commote. Nevertheless, it is puzzling that here, as in Aberffraw, only mature animals (*equi* or *jumenta*) were recorded, and no foals were listed in the taxation roll. Curious also is the fact that Lledwigan Llys is the only unit in the commote for which a mixture of peas and wheat was recorded, though the quantity involved was only half a crannock.

Lledwigan Llan apart, the only other units to attach importance to wheat—or at least recorded wheat—were Trefddisteiniaid, Rhosmor, and Aberffraw with its hamlets. At the privileged Trefddisteiniaid, wheat amounted to about 27% of the quantity of recorded crops and 34% of their value; there barley, with 16% of the quantity and 11% of the value, also was more important than in any other unit. Next in the significance of its attachment to wheat was Rhosmor, where this cereal amounted to 25% of the quantity and 30% of the value of all recorded crops. Otherwise, only oats and barley were recorded there, with the former of overwhelming importance, providing 68% of the quantity and 65% of the value of all

28

crops. At Aberffraw, because of the presence of a court before the conquest and the prominence of ground oats in renders to the king and his officials, the oat crop was quite important, contributing 62% of the quantity and 61% of the value of all recorded crops. Wheat contributed 24% of the quantity and 29% of the value of these crops, and the two remaining crops recorded were a mixture of peas and barley and barley alone, with the former less than half as important as the latter in terms of quantity and value.

The only guide to the relative prosperity of the various parts of Gwynedd in the period before the conquest is that produced by the papal levy on clerical incomes in 1254 known as the *Valuation of Norwich*.[51] This records the values of churches and, thus, parish incomes, made up as these were of tithes, oblations, and the produce of the glebe, all of which were probably a function—albeit approximate—of the size and prosperity of the parish area. Accordingly, the value attributed to any church is an approximate index of the productivity of the area it served, and this can be measured in terms of standard areal units, as in Figure 2, to give an impression of the relative prosperity of different parishes.

In the *Valuation of Norwich*, Welsh areas appear to have been undervalued. Despite this undervaluation, or perhaps because of it, the assessments recorded for the churches of Anglesey were far from being of a mere conventional kind recording only round numbers of marks or shillings. They thus give a better impression of relative prosperity than in some other parts of the country.[52] If Aberffraw church was assessed at 4 marks, and Heneglwys, in the interior, at 10s., Llanfeirian was assessed at a mere 3s., presumably because the area served by Llanfeirian had become impoverished as a result of the spreading of blown sand, which elsewhere in southwestern Anglesey is known to have occurred before 1306 and again in 1321.[53] Where blown sand has come to rest on, or has been intimately mixed into, soils such as well-drained brown earths, adequate manuring is essential in order to maintain the soil structure and prevent further soil blow.[54]

The most striking feature of the pattern of productivity of Malltraeth Commote to be inferred from an analysis of the return of the *Valuation of Norwich* is the presence of poor parishes in two distinct types of terrain. Most were in the interior, particularly in areas primarily characterized by expanses of poorly-drained soils and only small patches of well-drained brown earths. The exception was the coastal parish named in the *Valuation* as Eglwys Ail (Wattled Church) and later known as Llangadwaladr (The Church of Cadwaladr). This parish included some spreads of poorly-drained soils and some areas of blown sand, but the relatively limited areas of well-drained brown earths here also contained considerable amounts of blown sand. As a result, the more readily cultivable lands of the coastal tract appear to have experienced a reduction in productivity. Small wonder, therefore, that at Bodeon one group of four tenants holding land of the Bishop in 1306 should also have held land of the crown.

The two wealthiest parishes in 1254 were confined to the northern border of the commote. They were coterminous with the lay bond vill of Rhosmor and the Bishop's mixed vill of Tal-y-llyn. Rhosmor, which, at least in 1351, embraced one outlying carucate of Aberffraw demesne land at Trecastell, was no doubt well-managed if only to combat any soil deterioration brought about by that date as a result of sand blow; its hamlet of Treruffydd was sufficiently far inland to escape the adverse effects of sand blow, with the result that the third royal mill of Aberffraw, sited near Treruffydd, was still functioning in 1352. Tal-y-llyn, whose four hundred or so acres were made up largely of well-drained brown earths, was even further inland. As the 1306 extent records, three tenants of the Bishop held freely one carucate of land here but, in addition, a group of nineteen bond tenants held "in common" 1½ carucates.[55] If, as is likely, each carucate contained sixty acres and consisted of land in regular infield cultivation, then the territory of this vill must have been fully exploited. Appropriately, therefore, the substantial cereal component of the traditional render of the bondmen of Tal-y-llyn, as recorded in 1306, was made up of both wheat and oats in the proportion of one to two, while the relatively lighter cereal render of the bondmen of Llanfeirian, like that of the bondmen at Bodeon, was made up of oats only.[56]

In 1254 the parishes of Aberffraw and Trefddisteiniaid were at an intermediate level of productivity. Aberffraw parish embraced the vill of Dindryfwl with its large expanse of inadequately or poorly-drained soil; as a result, the average level of productivity in the parish as a whole was reduced. Trefdraeth was made up solely of the two vills of Trefwastrodion and Trefddisteiniaid save that a subsidiary vill of the latter—strictly a hamlet—was carved out of the south-western part of the parish at Bryndewin;[57] and the inclusion within the parish of Trefwastrodion, which was certainly poorer than Trefddisteiniaid in 1292-93, is likely to have reduced the average level of productivity in Trefdraeth and brought it below that which obtained in Aberffraw parish in 1254.

The results to be obtained from an areal analysis of productivity based on the subsidy roll for 1292-93 are likely to be even more impressionistic than those based on the *Valuation of Norwich*, not only because of the exemption of the poor from the subsidy but also because of the failure of medieval vill boundaries, as distinct from parish boundaries, to survive. Nevertheless, for what it is worth, a very tentative estimate of the relative prosperity of different parts of Malltraeth Commote based on the local roll for 1292-93 suggests that Trefdraeth parish was by far the most prosperous area, followed by Aberffraw and then Llangwyfan. The inversion of the order as compared with that which appears to have obtained in 1254 is probably a result of the continuation of sand blow in the coastal districts, thus adversely affecting productivity both in the Rhosmor assessment unit, which was coterminous with Llangwyfan, and in the Aberffaw assessment unit. The latter, as we have seen, is likely in 1292-93 to have included not only the south-western part of Aberffraw parish but also the whole of Llangadwaladr parish. By contrast, Trefdraeth to this day has remained immune from the adverse effects of sand blow, save in the westernmost part of the parish.

Important though the changing nature of the terrain was, however, other factors also need to be taken into account. Comparison of the 1292-93 returns for the assessment units within Aberffraw parish with the returns for the units within Trefdraeth parish provides an important pointer to these other factors. Aberffraw with its hamlets contained nearly all the royal demesne land in the commote in 1294, although Dindryfwl had earlier probably embraced the king's waste and summer pasture. Taken together, the Aberffraw and Dindryfwl assessment units may be regarded as the essentially royal component of the Iorwerth model for the subdivision of the commote (Table 2), though regalian rights of a more limited nature extending over the whole commote had existed long before 1294 and persisted long after. The area of Trefdraeth parish which embraced the two vills of Trefwastrodion and Trefddisteiniaid can be regarded as providing a very good indication of the kind of development which could take place in that component of the Iorwerth model which was ascribed to notables.

It is significant that 37% of the taxpaying households of Malltraeth Commote were recorded in 1292-93 in the Aberffraw and Dindryfwl units and that this proportion of the taxpaying population should have owned nearly 40% of the total value of assessed movables produced in the commote; and this despite the fact that the movables produced on those parts of the royal demesnes which were not leased would not have been assessed. A not dissimilar concentration of taxpaying households and of the assessed value of movables is, however, evident at Trefwastrodion and Trefddisteiniaid taken together; for nearly 29% of the taxpaying households of the commote recorded there owned about 34% of the assessed movables of the whole commote. Within the first pair of units, Aberffraw with its hamlets was by far the more important, with nearly 22% of the taxpaying households owning nearly 24% of the assessed movables of the commote. Trefddisteiniaid, the more important unit in the second pair, with a little less than 18% of the taxpayers, accounted for a little over 22% of the assessed movables of the commote (Table 4). It was only one of eight assessment units in the commote and not the unit which contained the royal court; yet, it alone supported nearly one fifth of the taxpaying households who owned more than one fifth of the total of assessed movables. Despite the importance of the royal estate near the court of Aberffraw, the estates of the heirs of the notables at Trefddis-teiniaid had clearly achieved a considerable level of development.

The multiple estate in the wider sense of a substantial territorial entity, initially a hundred and later a commote over which regalian rights were exercised, contained nearly all the resources, physical as well as human, needed to sustain its economy, including arable, pasture, meadow, woodland, water, and, not least, labor. Some of the physical resources of the multiple estate, even in this wider sense, were probably common to all its inhabitants, as was undoubtedly the case with parts of the summer pasture, apart probably from that of the king. Goods and services would have been provided from the component vills of such an estate for the maintenance of the king and his retinue. Control over these contributions and the regulation of resources would have required the services of a horse-owning aristocracy.[58] The members of this ministerial or serviential elite would have been endowed with estates, at first precariously and later permanently.

Equally important services, but of a different nature, were provided by the Church, and these were similarly supported by an even more precocious endowment of estates, resulting in that alienation of estates to the Church and to laymen which brought about the fissioning of the typical multiple estate in the wider sense into its smalller components. Fission, nevertheless, was not the only means of transformation, and there is abundant evidence that the severed components could be fused anew, either into the original wider entity or into a different combination of estates. Over the centuries, however, fission appears to have prevailed over fusion, thus giving rise to a hierarchy of lesser multiple estates, frequently a nested hierarchy, within the framework of the wider multiple estate. Not infrequently the estates of church communities and those of the most prominent laymen transcended even this framework and came to consist of the components of a plurality of wider multiple estates.

Given the distribution of natural resources within the typical wider multiple estate, there was likely to have been some degree of economic specialization between its different types of territory, as for example between arable land and summer pasture. There was also likely to have been a division of administrative and service functions between its components, a division most evident with the selection of one particu-

32

lar vill as the royal *caput*, the administrative center of the multiple estate. Near this *caput*, which contained the royal court, would be sited the mother church, which originally would have catered to the spiritual needs of the whole of the multiple estate. In the vicinity of the court there would have been an emphasis on the cultivation of the mensal land; similarly, cultivation is likely to have been encouraged in the vill containing the mother church. Nevertheless, a specialization of function in the economic sense between the component vill of the wider multiple estate should not be over-stressed, for the community of each vill would probably have engaged in mixed farming. With economic development, groups of these vills, if not single vills, are likely to have prospered enough to have been able to maintain their own churches, which became parish churches increasingly independent of the mother church.

All these features are clearly discernible in Malltraeth Commote at the close of the thirteenth century. This was an ancient multiple estate whose roots lay in a distant past.[59] Thus the court of Aberffraw was sited within the defences of what appears to have been a Roman fort[60] and was located a little over two miles from the refuge provided by the promontory fort of the Iron Age at Twyn-y-parc (Figure 1). Moreover, some two miles distant from the court of Aberffraw was the ancient church, Eglwys Ail or Llangadwaladr, probably the original mother church of the commote, a church whose royal endowment was probably enlarged by King Cadwaladr in the seventh century. Over the centuries which followed, other lands were alienated alike to the Church and to laymen. Thus, although regalian rights of extensive lordship were preserved and continued to be focused on the court of Aberffraw, Malltraeth Commote had come to be fissioned into lesser multiple estates. The economic development of these alienated estates, so well epitomized by Trefddisteiniaid, sometimes justified their proprietors in establishing their own mills, with the result that they were relieved of suit to the royal mills. This economic development had also made possible the foundation of parish churches, thus ensuring the provision of church services locally. Similarly, as is clearly revealed by the medieval extents of the commote and by the subsidy roll of 1292-93, all the vill communities of the commote were practicing a mixed farming economy with only slight local variations. Equally, the names of the taxpayers of 1292-93 provide no evidence to suggest a concentration of particular skills in any one assessment unit.[61]

As the *caput* where rents were paid to the crown and so many services were performed, Aberffraw proper was well-placed by virtue of these activities to develop into a trading center. But although it acquired a market and a fair, after the conquest, the diversion of many of its administrative functions to other royal centers outside Malltraeth Commote prevented the growth of the village into a town. If Aberffraw did not change substantially, such was not the case on the estates inherited by the descendants of notables. The continued importance, despite the English conquest, of some prominent lineages and the differential access of the more fortunate of the heirs of such lineages to key resources such as good arable land ensured the consolidation and enlargement of their landed estates.[62] Frequently, these estates were further increased in size at the expense of crown lands in bond vills, especially those held by reckoned-land tenure, which were abandoned by their grossly over-burdened bond tenants at times of hardship, plague, and strife. As a consequence, there was a decline in the significance of the wider multiple estate, and the royal components became far less important, relatively, than they had been. Nevertheless, the wider multiple estate left as a distinctive heritage the landed estates whose genesis and growth stemmed from the need to support an aristocracy whose services articulated its organization. In this way, as in so many others, the multiple estate provides a meaningful model for tracing those complex interrelationships of society, economy, and habitat involved in the evolution of settlement.

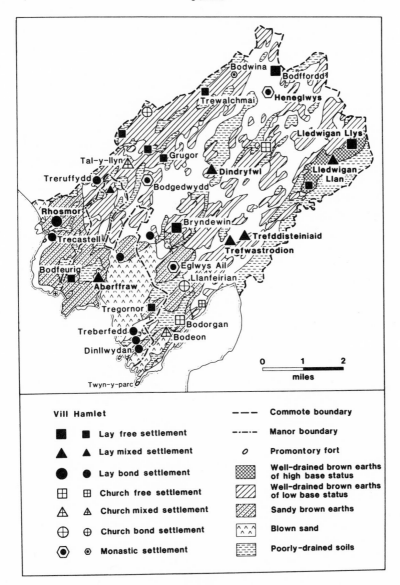

Figure 1
Distribution of Medieval Settlements
in relation to soils in Malltraeth Commote

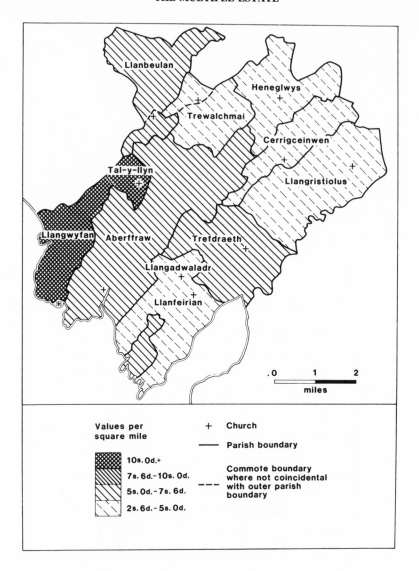

Figure 2
Areal Variations in Prosperity in Malltraeth Commote
as revealed by the *Valuation of Norwich*, 1254

NOTES

¹ Goronwy Edwards, "The Laws of Hywel Dda," in *Wales Through the Ages*, ed. Arthur J. Roderick (Llandybîe: Christopher Davis Ltd., 1959), 1, pp. 67-73.

² Goronwy Edwards, "The Historical Study of the Welsh Lawbooks," *Transactions of the Royal Historical Society*, 5th ser., 12 (1962), 141-55.

³ *The Collected Papers of Frederic William Maitland*, ed. Harold A. L. Fisher (Cambridge: Cambridge Univ. Press, 1911), 3, pp. 447-73.

⁴ Thomas Jones Pierce, *Medieval Welsh Society* (Cardiff: Univ. of Wales Press, 1972), pp. 21-38; Glanville R. J. Jones, "The Defences of Gwynedd in the Thirteenth Century," *Transactions of the Caenarvonshire Historical Society* (1969), 29-43.

⁵ *Llyfr Iorwerth*, ed. Aled R. Wiliam (Cardiff: Univ. of Wales Press, 1960), pp. 59-60; *Ancient Laws and Institutes of Wales*, ed. Aneurin Owen (London: Record Commission, 1841), 1, pp. 185-89.

⁶ Wiliam, *Llyfr Iorwerth*, p. 60; Owen, *Ancient Laws*, 1, pp. 188-89.

⁷ Wiliam, *Llyfr Iorwerth*, p. 60; Owen, *Ancient Laws*, 1, pp. 188-89.

⁸ Wiliam, *Llyfr Iorwerth*, p. 62; Owen, *Ancient Laws*, 1, pp. 194-95.

⁹ Glanville R. J. Jones, "Post-Roman Wales," in *The Agrarian History of England and Wales*, ed. Herbert P. R. Finberg (Cambridge: Cambridge Univ. Press, 1972), pp. 321-24.

¹⁰ Thomas M. Charles-Edwards, "Kinship, Status and the Origins of the Hide," *Past and Present*, 52 (1972), 3-33.

¹¹ Jones, "Post-Roman Wales," 340-49; Glanville R. J. Jones, "Hereditary Land: Its Effects on the Evolution of Field Systems and Settlement in the Vale of Clwyd," in *Man, Culture and Settlement, Festschrift to Prof. R. L. Singh*, ed. Robert C. Eidt, Kashi N. Singh, and Rana P. B. Singh (New Delhi: National Geographical Society of India, Kalyani Publishers, 1977), pp. 82-96.

¹² Underlying this model appears to have been an older one portrayed in the lawbooks of South Wales. This older model was based on the multiple estate known as a *maenor*. A complete *maenor*, ascribed to free notables and usually extending from the lowlands to the uplands, was deemed to contain thirteen vills of which one, in the uplands, was apparently supernumerary and owed no rents or services. There was also a *maenor* of seven vills in the lowlands probably belonging to the king and forming part of the group near the court known as the "vills attached to the court" (*villis curie adjacentibus*). Since the reeve who looked after these particular vills also cared for the king's cattle, it is likely that the lowland *maenor* of seven vills was matched by an area of upland pasture perhaps considered to be equivalent to seven vills. As in the Iorwerth model so in the South Welsh lawbooks vills were further sub-divided. There were said to be three sharelands in the bond vill and four sharelands in the free vill, and each shareland was deemed to contain 312 acres, of which twelve were to be for building and three hundred for arable, pasture, and fuel wood. Since these acres were small, the three hundred used for arable, pasture, and fuel wood appear, in

some localities at least, to have covered an area of very much less than a small carucate of sixty statute acres. See: *Welsh Medieval Law*, ed. Arthur W. Wade-Evans (Oxford: Clarendon Press, 1909), pp. 54-55, 204-05; *The Latin Texts of the Welsh Laws*, ed. Hywel D. Emanuel (Cardiff: Univ. of Wales Press, 1967), pp. 102, 226, 239, 349, 356; Glanville R. J. Jones, "Multiple Estates and Early Settlement," in *Medieval Settlement: Continuity and Change*, ed. Peter H. Sawyer (London: Edward Arnold, 1976), pp. 15-24; Glanville R. J. Jones, "Early Historic Settlement in Border Territory. A Case-Study of Archenfield and its Environs in Herefordshire," in *Recherches de Géographie rurale, Hommage au Professeur Frans Dussart*, ed. Charles Christians (Liège: Univ. de Liège, 1979), 1, pp. 117-32.

[13] Notably the following: Extent of Anglesey, 1294, pub. Frederic Seebohm in *The Tribal System in Wales* (London: Longmans, Green, and Co., 1895), App. A a; Extent of the lands of the Bishop and Chapter of Bangor, pub. Henry W. Ellis in *The Record of Caernarvon* (London: Record Commission, 1838), pp. 92-114 and ascribed by him to the third decade of the fourteenth century. On the basis of a detailed but as yet unpublished comparison of the many personal names recorded in this extent with those recorded in early fourteenth-century sources, this extent of the Bangor lands has been convincingly ascribed to 1306 by Dr. Anthony D. Carr. I am particularly indebted to Dr. Carr for his comments on this revised dating. An unpublished version of this extent, giving the names of many vills otherwise not identifiable from the published version, is available at the National Library of Wales, Aberystwyth (Welsh Church Commission MSS: MS 1); *Survey of the Honour of Denbigh, 1334*, ed. Paul Vinogradoff and Frank Morgan (London: British Academy, 1914); and Extent of Caernarvon and Anglesey, pub. Henry W. Ellis in *The Record of Caernarvon* (London: Record Commission, 1838), pp. 1-91.

[14] Frederic Seebohm, *The Tribal System in Wales*, pp. 1-3, App. A a, A c; *Survey of the Honour of Denbigh, 1334*, pp. 1, 53, 208; and *The Record of Caernarvon*, p. 213.

[15] Glanville R. J. Jones, "Field Systems of North Wales," in *Studies of Field Systems in the British Isles*, ed. Alan R. H. Baker and Robin A. Butlin (Cambridge: Cambridge Univ. Press, 1973), pp. 460-65.

[16] Melville Richards, *Welsh Administrative and Territorial Units* (Cardiff: Univ. of Wales Press, 1969), pp. 3, 58, 129.

[17] Ellis, *Record of Caernarvon*, pp. 48-50.

[18] Ellis, *Record of Caernarvon*, p. 50.

[19] Ellis, *Record of Caernarvon*, pp. 47-48.

[20] Glanville R. J. Jones, "The Distribution of Medieval Settlement in Anglesey," *Transactions of the Anglesey Antiquarian Society* (1955), 49-63. Cf. the upland group of reckoned-land settlements in Dinllaen Commote portrayed in Glanville R. J. Jones, "Ancient British Settlements in Their Organizational Settings," in *Paysages Ruraux Europeens*, ed. Pierre Flatrès (Rennes: Univ. de Haute Bretagne, 1979), pp. 179-93; see also note 12 above.

[21] Ellis, *Record of Caernarvon*, p. 44.

[22] Ellis, *Record of Caernarvon*, p. 44.

[23] Ellis, *Record of Caernarvon*, p. 46.

[24] Daniel A. Binchy, *Celtic and Anglo-Saxon Kingship* (Oxford: Clarendon Press, 1970), p. 23.

[25] Ellis, *Record of Caernarvon*, p. 47.

[26] Ellis, *Record of Caernarvon*, p. 44.

[27] Ellis, *Record of Caernarvon*, p. 44.

[28] Ellis, *Record of Caernarvon*, pp. 47-48.

[29] Ellis, *Record of Caernarvon*, pp. 48-49.

[30] Ellis, *Record of Caernarvon*, p. 44.

[31] Ellis, *Record of Caernarvon*, pp. 46-47; Glanville R. J. Jones, "Early Customary Tenures in Wales and Open-Field Agriculture," in *The Origins of Open-Field Agriculture*, ed. Trevor Rowley (London: Croom Helm, 1981), pp. 213-15.

[32] Colin A. Gresham, "The Aberconwy Charter," *Archaeologia Cambrensis*, 94 (1939), 142-44.

[33] Ellis, *Record of Caernarvon*, pp. 104-05.

[34] Ellis, *Record of Caernarvon*, p. 47.

[35] Public Record Office, London: E. 179/242/49; Frederic Seebohm published as Appendix A f of his *Tribal System in Wales* all those portions of this roll which were relevant to his portrayal of the Manor of Aberffraw, namely the preamble to the roll, the return for "Aberffraw with its hamlets," and the total for Malltraeth Commote but, naturally enough, not the returns for the other vills in the commote which preceded and followed Aberffraw on the roll. This particular roll was wrongly ascribed by Seebohm to the period 1320-40. The only other complete local roll for a whole commote in Gwynedd is that for the commote of Cafflogion in Lleyn (Thomas Jones Pierce, "A Lleyn Lay Subsidy Account," *Bulletin of the Board of Celtic Studies*, 5 [1929-31], 55-71). This commote, unfortunately, does not exhibit the kind of social diversity evident in Malltraeth. (Cf. Colin Thomas, "Thirteenth Century Farm Economies in North Wales," *Agricultural History Review*, 16 [1968], 1-14.)

[36] J. Ambrose Raftis and Mary P. Hogan, *Early Huntingdonshire Lay Subsidy Rolls* (Toronto: Pontifical Institute of Mediaeval Studies, 1976), pp. 111-12.

[37] On this see the excellent account in *The Merioneth Lay Subsidy Roll, 1292-93*, ed. Keith Williams-Jones (Cardiff: Univ. of Wales Press, 1976), pp. xiii-xxiv

[38] Raftis and Hogan, *Early Huntingdonshire Lay Subsidy Rolls*, p. 197; Audrey C. Chibnall, *Early Taxation Returns*, Buckinghamshire Record Society, 14 (1966), pp. 1-2.

[39] *The Taxation of 1297*, ed. A. T. Gaydon, The Publications of the Bedfordshire Historical Record Society, 39 (Streatley, 1959), pp. xvii-xxv.

[40] Williams-Jones, *Merioneth Lay Subsidy Roll*, pp. xxv-lix, cxx.

[41] Public Record Office, London: E. 179/242/49. For the sake of brevity the assessment unit recorded in the roll as "Aberffraw with its hamlets" is listed simply as "Aberffraw" in Tables 3-6.

[42] *The Valuation of Norwich*, ed. W. E. Lunt (Oxford: Clarendon Press,

1926), p. 193.

[43] Raftis and Hogan, *Early Huntingdonshire Lay Subsidy Rolls*, pp. 7-9, 105-13.

[44] It must be accepted that a few taxpayers had movables and were, therefore, liable to be taxed in more than one assessment unit, but given the nature of Welsh names it has proved impossible to determine how many. Tegwared the Red (or Redhead) assessed at 2s. 7d in Heneglwys, at 2s. 4d in Lledwigan Llan, and at 2s. 7d in Lledwigan Llys was probably one and the same person, but, since he is equally as likely to have held land in all three assessment units, one household has been attributed to him in each of these units. In the interests of consistency, the same procedure has been adopted with all other instances of the repetition of personal names. The typical taxpayer bore a name which was much less distinctive as a designation than that of Tegwared the Red.

[45] Ellis, *Record of Caernarvon*, p. 104.

[46] Williams-Jones, *Merioneth Lay Subsidy Roll*, pp. lxxxiii-xcii.

[47] *Welsh Genealogies, A.D. 300-1400*, ed. Peter C. Bartrum (Cardiff: Univ. of Wales Press, 1974), 3, pp. 445, 519-20; 4 (Cardiff, 1974), p. 893. A claim was made in a later official record that Madog ap Llywelyn, the principal leader of the major revolt of 1294-95 against the English, possessed considerable lands in Lledwigan Llan until he warred against the king (Glyn Roberts, "Biographical Notes: Madog ap Llywelyn," *Bulletin of the Board of Celtic Studies*, 17 [1956-58], 41-42). Although Madog, son of a former lord of Meirionydd and an adherent of the English cause, was privileged after the English conquest of Gwynedd, he was not recorded as a taxpayer in 1292-93 in Lledwigan Llan or elsewhere in Malltraeth Commote. Had Madog already been dispossessed before this date, and was this one of the reasons why he unfurled the flag of rebellion in 1294? If this were the case, it is curious that one Hywel ap Madog ap Llywelyn— possibly a son of the rebel leader—should have held Lledwigan Llan on privileged terms as the sole heir in 1352.

[48] Gaydon, *Taxation of 1297*, xvii-xxv; Michael M. Postan, "Village Livestock in the Thirteenth Century," *The Economic History Review*, 15 (1962), 219-49.

[49] Wade-Evans, *Welsh Medieval Law*, pp. 57, 207-08.

[50] Evan Roberts, *The County of Anglesey: Soils and Agriculture, Memoirs of the Soil Survey of Great Britain* (London: Agricultural Research Council, 1958), pp. 41-42. I am very indebted to Mr. Kenneth E. Clare, Head of the Soil Survey of England and Wales, for permission to incorporate in this paper published and unpublished data collected by the Soil Survey and to Mr. Evan Roberts for his observations about the soils of Anglesey.

[51] Lunt, *Valuation of Norwich*, pp. 76-78.

[52] Williams-Jones, *Merioneth Lay Subsidy Roll*, pp. lxxvii-lxxx.

[53] Glanville R. J. Jones, "Rural Settlement in Anglesey," in *Geography as Human Ecology*, ed. S. Robert Eyre and Glanville R. J. Jones (London: Edward Arnold, 1966), pp. 225-28; Adrian H. W. Robinson, "The Sandy Coast of South-West Anglesey," *Transactions of the Anglesey Antiquarian Society* (1980), 37-66.

[54] Roberts, *County of Anglesey*, pp. 49-50.

[55] Ellis, *Record of Caernarvon*, p. 106.

[56] Ellis, *Record of Caernarvon*, p. 105.

[57] Ellis, *Record of Caernarvon*, p. 46.

[58] Cf. Geoffrey W. A. Barrow, *The Kingdom of the Scots* (London: Edward Arnold, 1973), pp. 7-68.

[59] Jones, "Multiple Estates and Medieval Settlement," 19-24.

[60] Richard B. White, "Excavations at Aberffraw, Anglesey, 1973 and 1974," *Bulletin of the Board of Celtic Studies*, 52 (1979), 218-341.

[61] There was, it is true, one Tegwared Feddyg (Tegwared the Doctor) recorded as a taxpayer, curiously enough in the bond vill of Rhosmor in 1292-93, but, on the other hand, one cobbler (*sutor*) was recorded at Heneglwys, another at Lledwigan Llan, and two more at Dindryfwl.

[62] Thomas Jones Pierce, "Landlords in Wales: The Nobility and Gentry," in *The Agrarian History of England and Wales*, ed. Joan Thirsk (Cambridge: Cambridge Univ. Press, 1967), 4, pp. 357-81.

FIELDWORK AND DOCUMENTARY EVIDENCE FOR THE LAYOUT AND ORGANIZATION OF EARLY MEDIEVAL ESTATES IN THE ENGLISH MIDLANDS

DAVID HALL

Introduction

The research of the Harvard scholar H. L. Gray, published in his *English Field Systems* in 1915, established the English Midlands as a region of intensive pre-enclosure agriculture.[1] The system he identified there consisted of a complex array of sub-divided fields, with a given holding scattered in small parcels over a wide area. Normally, there were no hedges or permanent fences of any kind, and the arrangement was referred to as the "open-," or "common-field," system.

These sub-divided fields were not, of course, unique to the Midlands. It is possible to find evidence of them, either documentary or physical, in most areas of the United Kingdom. The form that predominated in the Midlands was called by Gray the two- or three-field system: all parcels grouped together in two or three blocks of roughly equal size, and one of them used, when fallow, for common grazing by the livestock of the community.

These field arrangements described by Gray became the model for research into medieval agriculture in this century. It is only with the synthesis of local studies, pioneered by Beresford and Hoskins in the 1950s,[2] and with landscape archaeology in the late 1960s and 70s, that a new set of questions has been asked about medieval field systems. Both local studies and landscape archaeology are used in this essay to consider regional variations of fields, early topography, and land use; the demesne and tenurial arrangements; and evidence touching on the origins of sub-divided field systems. But first, a word must be said about techniques and sources of data.

In order to study ancient landscapes, three main types of information are essential: (a) a map of the open fields; (b) a detailed description of every holding, generally called a field book or parish terrier; and (c) sources of early documents containing topographical information. This information can then be used to identify landscape features and uses.

Open-field Maps

For some parishes or townships, maps of the open fields exist; however, they are generally of eighteenth or nineteenth century date and record a landscape whose tenurial layout may deviate considerably from that of the medieval period. These maps describe the almost ubiquitous contraction of the amount of arable land in the late medieval period and rarely depict the complete physical layout of the earlier medieval landscape. Areas, often large, are marked on these open-field maps as pasture or ancient enclosure and are not shown as sub-divided holdings. Yet, examination on the ground shows that ridge-and-furrow did occur in these areas, indicating that the land there must have been part of an earlier field system.

Unfortunately, many townships did not have open-field maps prepared. Without this key document, little idea of the medieval fields can be ascertained from other historical sources available. The problem can be resolved, however, by archaeological fieldwork, for survival of medieval field boundaries in the modern landscape makes it possible to reconstruct the complete physical layout of these systems in many parts of England. Such technical procedures have been discussed in detail elsewhere, and only a summary will be offered here.[3]

Figure 1a (at end of essay) shows a schematic layout of part of a typical sub-divided field system. The basic unit of cultivation, called a *land*, was typically about eight yards wide and two-hundred yards long, which is approximately one-third of an acre. Ploughing in a clockwise direction cast soil towards the center and caused a ridge to accumulate, thus leaving a furrow to mark the outer edge of the strip. A group of strips lying together in a block was called a *furlong*, which is not to be confused with the modern unit of length. Furlongs were grouped together, usually in a compact block, to form a large, unfenced area called a *field*.

The important archaeological feature of the ploughing technique was that, in addition to ridging up the land surface, soil was moved in the direction of ploughing. Therefore, when the end of the land was reached and the plough lifted out of the ground, a small quantity of soil remained. Over the years this accumulated to form a mound which was called a *head*.

The boundaries built up by these ploughing practices consisted of two types: those where the lands ran in the same direction, called *joints*, and those where the lands of one furlong met the first land of the adjacent furlong at right angles. This first land was formed out of the ploughed-over heads of all the other neighboring lands, and for this reason was called a *headland*. It will be apparent from Figure 1a that a joint had approximately twice the amount of accumulated soil as a headland.

For completeness, Figure 1b shows some of the later modifications to furlongs that resulted from increasing the amount of grass in the arable fields. A land left to revert to grass for semi-permanent or permanent pasture was called a *ley*; a narrow strip ploughed back from a land and used as an access route was called a *balk*. Parts of several lands were sometimes partially flattened and used as *rick-places*, that is, areas where corn or hay was stored in stacks.

The visual detail of medieval ridge-and-furrow has been destroyed by modern cultivation over the greater part of lowland England. After a first deep ploughing, lands may be seen for a few years as strips of light-and-dark colored soil, but these gradually disappear. What do survive, however, are the furlong boundaries—the joints and headlands. All the original heads become smoothed over and form long, linear banks that represent the original furlong pattern. These remain as landscape features for a long time, although the smaller ones are now disappearing in some regions. A survey of such soil banks, covering every field in a given township, allows us to reconstruct the earlier medieval landscapes. It is possible to "fill in" the furlong boundaries with the detail of the orientation of the lands by collating a range of evidence, including the survival of ridge-and-furrow as an earthwork, the contrast of light-and-dark soil marks, and the details preserved in older aerial photographs, especially the verticals taken by the Royal Air Force in the late 1940s.[4]

Field work for such surveys must be undertaken in winter months when arable lands are in bare-fallow, or when pastures have been closely grazed. All that is needed is a copy of a 1:10,000 (or 1:10,560) scale map, writing material, and, of course, the appropriate permission from landowners and tenants for access. The position of a furlong boundary is recorded in relation to the modern field boundaries: it can be accurately measured, but, because of the diffuse nature of the earthworks, a sketched estimate is sufficient. The results are then transferred to a fair copy of the 1:10,000 map each day and later drawn up in a more permanent form. The orientation of the strips is represented schematically; measurement of individual land widths is not necessary. The correct number of strips is approximatly four times that marked on Figure 3 and subsequent figures, for to attempt to represent the actual number at this scale would render the plans illegible after reduction.

Field Books

Field books, sometimes called town books, terriers, surveys, or sometimes untitled, are accounts of a complete lordship in the arable fields, recorded strip by strip. The surveys usually group the information by field and furlong and give the size of the land, most commonly in an estimated form such as "one rood," or "half an acre," or, less informatively, "one land." In exceptional cases, strip widths at each end, lengths, and area are recorded, accurately measured in poles and fractions of poles. The lands and furlongs are sometimes numbered for ease in identification. Owners and tenants are named, and often the nature of the holding identified—glebe, freehold, demesne, former monastic land, and so forth. Many terriers were prepared immediately prior to enclosure or partial enclosure, which would have necessitated exchange of lands; sometimes these exchanges are recorded as marginalia in field books.

Most field books state the cardinal orientations of lands by adding after the furlong names such comments as "begin west," which implies that the land runs north and south. Abuttals relating a furlong to its neighbors or to topographical features are often mentioned. Table 1 (at end of essay) gives part of the field book of Brockhall, Northants, dated 1606, as an example.[5]

Documents Needed to Identify Furlongs and Reconstruct Early Estates

Field books do not always give enough information to permit the identification of furlongs on reconstructed maps. It is therefore necessary to study all other charters, extents, terriers, surveys, and deeds that may exist; the original source material or reliable editions should be consulted. A list of furlongs with their orientations, abuttals, and names with dated variant spellings can then be compiled. Table 2 (at end of essay) shows part of such a list for Brockhall, Northamptonshire, using the data from its field book as a framework. Additional information must then be collected on "modern" field names appearing on estate, enclosure, and tithe maps, or sale catalogues, another valuable source of these names. All this information is then transferred to a copy of the 1:10,000 ordnance survey map. The limited amount of relevant information for Brockhall, is shown in Figure 2.

Field books, used primarily to collect furlong data, also give information about the tenurial composition of a manor and particular peasant holdings. Published county histories are also useful in providing a general background. Any ecclesiastical or monastic land should also be carefully studied, for the accumulation of monastic estates will often be minutely detailed in any surviving cartulary, and glebe disputes are often informative as to the nature of the land, that is, who gave it and when.

Furlong Identification

We are now ready to identify furlongs, using the types of data compiled by the three methods just indicated. The furlong map provides the physical landscape, the collected enclosed field names give locational data, and the furlong list gives the medieval field names, their sizes, and abuttals. Simultaneous use of all three should lead to accurate and precise plotting of furlongs on the reconstructed plan.

In clear-cut cases where there is a field book, a good set of post-enclosure field names, and plenty of furlong abuttals, it is an easy matter to start from a known point on the parish boundary and plot the furlongs directly onto the 1:10,560 plan. On this scale, lands averaging eight yards in width are $\frac{1}{36}$ inch wide. In more typical areas where the data are not so good, a slightly different procedure must be adopted. A strip of thin cardboard no more than one inch wide is marked off in "furlongs" measured to scale. These are then cut up, and the name of the furlong written on the strip along with any abuttal information and the land orientation. It is then possible to arrange and rearrange these "furlongs" on the reconstructed plan until they form a reasonable interpretation of all the evidence.

The example of Brockhall is a difficult one, since few furlong names survive as modern field names. It is easy, however, to pick out the large furlongs because of the limited number of possible positions; the

47

other furlongs then fall into position fairly readily. Once the furlongs have been satisfactorily identified, it is a relatively simple matter to plot whatever information the field book or other documents impart, such as the demesne, glebe, and so forth.

Regional Variations, Land Use, and Early Topography

Throughout the Midland area proper (as defined by Gray), strips average eight yards wide and two-hundred yards long, as noted above. However, upon moving out from the region, striking differences occur. Near Peterborough, particularly on the Welland Valley gravel terraces, lands are very wide—typically about sixteen yards—and so each averages 0.6 acres.[6] On the Yorkshire Wolds, lands are approximately twelve yards wide but may be of great length; they run from dale to dale and are frequently up to one-thousand yards in length.[7] Long strips are also known at Wisbech, Cambridgeshire, on the silt fens. Here the lands are not ridged up, but marked out by ditches forming strips twelve to twenty yards wide and up to 1,700 yards long.[8]

The non-ridging of lands is a documented feature of eastern Cambridgeshire,[9] where a careful search for ridge-and-furrow proved futile. It is reported that there is no ridge-and-furrow in the whole of East Anglia. Nevertheless, the same mechanisms of headland and joint formation operate: recent work at Chippenham, Cambridgeshire, shows that although no evidence of ridging can be found, there are banks of soil that correspond exactly with boundaries marked on a 1712 map.[10] The furlong pattern of southeastern Cambridgeshire is otherwise normal; there are no long lands, just the usual "Midland" ones of about two-hundred yards length. There exist other probable examples of long lands at Middleton, near Pickering and in Holderness, both in southeastern Yorkshire, areas which have yet to be surveyed on the ground.

Reconstructed medieval field plans can be used to present and unravel various types of topographical history. The most obvious kind of landscape to re-create is that depicted by the field books themselves; the areas of arable, ley, and ancient enclosure are readily identified. The Northamptonshire landscapes of Hardingstone in 1660 and Ashby St. Ledgers in 1715 are already published elsewhere.[11] Figure 3 shows Brockhall in 1606.

Furlong names can be examined further to learn about earlier changes of land use. For instance, the central Nene valley parishes have good quality soils which have been completely opened up to arable

48

cultivation since at least the thirteenth century. The furlongs reflect such aspects of the early topography as, for example, the nature of the soil or whether it was former marsh or woodland. Farther away from these good soil regions there is a capping of heavy boulder clay that had been allowed to revert to forest in early post-Roman times. Some remnants of this woodland survive, being "crystallized" in the twelfth and thirteenth centuries by the formation of royal and private deer parks. Study of furlong names of parishes adjacent to this woodland reveals a much greater extent, where such names as *wold*, *stocking*, *stibbings*, *shaw*, and *leigh*, among others, indicate the former existence of woodland.

Figure 4 shows the land use of Little Oakley, Northants. The earliest fields would have been those on good quality soils adjacent to the village: there is here an abundance of archaeological sites of all periods and a small quantity of Middle-Saxon pottery. The furlongs betray no trace of woodland names. Several fourteenth-century charters survive, showing that much of the area to the north was under cultivation. The furlong names of the then-arable lands were *thornhawe* (1368), *stokkyng* (1373), *schakeldenesle* (1382) and *sheir hill*.[12] These indicate that wood once (appreciably before the fourteenth century) reached almost down to the settlement. The area north of the village must have always been difficult, marginal land; it was the first area allowed to revert to permanent pasture (*ley*) in the late medieval period when population levels fell, and by 1539 the reversion process was complete.

Some groups of parishes reveal a much earlier clearance of woodland. Cranford St. John, Burton Latimer, Finedon, Great Addington, Little Addington, and Woodford, Northamptonshire, share a block of boulder-clay land (see Fig. 5). All the furlongs occupying this area have *wold* names, yet many of them are recorded as arable in the thirteenth and fourteenth centuries.[13] An adjacent area of Cranford St. John has a charter of 1154-69 mentioning many furlongs, indicating that it was cultivated at this early date.[14] It seems that the woodland in this region was cleared during the late Saxon period. That the wood represented a valuable feature in the village economy is demonstrated by the parish boundary of Woodford, which has a long protruding tongue to ensure that it got its share of the resource.

The Demesne and Tenurial Arrangements

The demesne—the land held directly by the lord—is frequently described in documents, and field books usually specify it as well. The location of this land could vary in an interesting manner from village to village. In later centuries demesne was often scattered throughout the parish furlongs in small groups of three to nine or so strips, not in the usual single ones. Figure 6 shows the demesne of one of the three manors belonging to Sir Lewis Dyve at East Haddon in 1598.[15] Most of the blocks are in groups of three, scattered uniformly in the three fields of the southern part of the lordship (East Haddon had a double three-field system, each being independent of the other). Similar cases of demesne scattered in small groups of strips are known for Brockhall (1574) in nines, Great Billing (1629) in sixes, and Floore (1668) in groups of two to six.[16]

In earlier centuries some parishes had different dispositions of demesne. Ashby St. Ledgers' medieval fields were reconstructed from fieldwork surveys and a field book c. 1715.[17] Distinguished in the field book are large blocks of lands called "thirds" marked on the ground by balks. A glebe dispute of 1674 specifies these lands as paying tithes to the vicar, because they were the grant of one-third of the demesne of a previous lord of the manor, John de Cranford.[18] The original grant had been made during the term of office of Hugh de Wells, Bishop of Lincoln.[19] Thus, we are able to see the disposition of Ashby St. Ledger's demesne c. 1210 (Fig. 7).

Unlike the previous examples, the Ashby demesne was concentrated in blocks of lands comprised of half furlongs fairly close to the village. This arrangement was peculiar to the demesne at that time. It cannot be argued that all the holdings in this lordship were disposed in this way, because at the same time as the demesne grant there was a gift of 1½ yardlands by Richard de Harewedon. Figure 7 shows that this holding is scattered in the usual way, generally with one land per furlong.

Other examples suggest that originally, in Saxon times, the lord's demesne was a compact block of land adjacent to the manor and village. The Saxon demesne was called the *inland* and was almost invariably next to a manor. At Wollaston, Northamptonshire, the inland forms such a block next to a manor and includes within it an earlier Saxon settlement and a Roman villa (Fig. 8). The existence of the latter is recognized by the furlong name of *waltonacre*, meaning "town of the Welsh" (i.e., British).[20]

The village of Kislingbury, Northamptonshire, has elements of two types of demesne. The furlongs can be reconstructed using an excellent series of terriers dated 1612.[21] The Cartulary of St. Andrew's Priory, Northampton, details a terrier of Kislingbury holdings, which comprised two-thirds of the demesne of the two manors located there. The land was granted early in the twelfth century by the families of Armentier and Lovet.[22] Figure 9 shows this twelfth-century holding: next

50

to the village are complete furlongs that include the inland, and scattered around in all the furlongs are other small groups of demesne strips. The interpretation here is that there was a Saxon compact demesne, and the Norman successors of the estate added more land to it in a scattered form.

Hardingstone, Northamptonshire, also offers evidence of an ancient central core of land. A terrier of c. 1660 reveals that there was an early (probably twelfth to thirteenth century), regular tenurial cycle.[23] Most of the furlongs fell into a cycle of thirty-two lands, with a given tenant or freeholder always holding the same position. However, near the village were a few furlongs that did not form part of this regular cycle, the tenants' names being in an irregular order. One of the furlongs (penny-lands) is specified as demesne (Fig. 10). It seems that the irregular furlongs once formed a compact block of demesne, the full extent of it no longer visible in 1660, as most of the expected area had been encroached upon by enclosures. The above examples suggest the following model. First the demesne was a compact piece of land, probably containing some of the best quality soil, located next to the manor, as the lord did not intend to suffer the inconvenience of traversing the whole parish to attend to strips scattered in single units. Probably, with the passage of time, the demesne became over-exploited, and the villagers were getting better yields of corn in their scattered holdings than was the lord. There would then be a desire to disperse the demesne. Ashby St. Ledgers shows a half-way stage, with the demesne partially dispersed in half furlongs, but still reasonably accessible. The later examples, such as East Haddon, show the extreme case of complete dispersal, yet even here the demesne is distinguished by being in small parcels of land with three lands lying adjacent.

Such a model demonstrates the authority of the lord over a long period of time, for he clearly had great control over open-field holdings. Subsequent events demonstrate the same authority. At Wollaston the inland had been partially dispersed before 1430, so that the lord's demesne lay throughout the parish, and his tenants shared strips in the inlands (see Fig. 5). Yet, by 1583 matters had been reversed. The demesne had been collected back to the old inlands, and it was enclosed in severalty.[24] Similarly, at East Haddon the dispersed demesne of 1598 had been brought to compact enclosures by c. 1601, although there is no evidence that they occupied the site of an ancient compact demesne (Fig. 6).[25]

Evidence Touching Upon the Origins of Open Fields

A recent publication has outlined current research into the problem of the origin of open fields.[26] The archaeological and physical evidence suggests that in some regions there was a planned laying out of large blocks of land at some time in the Middle Saxon period. These blocks would have had strips running from one natural or man-made feature to the next, which could be as long as 1,500 yards. In the Midland region a combination of undulating topography and subsequent intensive cultivation led to a subdivision and rearrangement of these long strips into the familiar furlong patterns. On the periphery of the Midlands, long-strip fields still survive, as in Yorkshire or Cambridgeshire, mentioned above.

Further illustrations have recently given the physical evidence for the creation of furlongs by transverse sub-division of long strips to make several blocks of shorter length strips.[27] Historical evidence of this process has also been forthcoming for Hardingstone. The regular tenurial cycles described above have been plotted on a reconstructed furlong plan, revealing some remarkable features. Some of the furlong boundaries start or begin at the cycles, and cycles often coincide in adjacent furlongs. In other words, the cycles are older than the furlong pattern and demonstrate an original layout on a large scale with long lands. Even more remarkably, in some of the smaller furlongs that interrupt this long furlong pattern, the number of lands is a multiple of the cycle.

The Hardingstone cycle is thirty-two, and furlongs going in the "wrong" direction have thirty-two, sixty-four, and so on, lands in them. This is explicable if it is assumed that the smaller "cross furlongs" have been deliberately changed because of some local drainage requirement. Doing so in a whole number of cycles would insure that everyone had the same amount of land after the changeover, and it could be done piecemeal, without a reordering of strips in the whole township.[28] Thus, at Hardingstone there is historical evidence for Midland townships being originally laid out on the large scale; subsequent piecemeal changes demanded by the lay of the land account for the final complex pattern. The process of sub-division is envisaged as having occurred before the thirteenth century, if not appreciably before.

Another similar and even earlier example has been found at Muscott, Northamptonshire. This is an unusual case of a well-preserved, deserted village with a good documentary record. Originally it was part of Brockhall parish but a separate settlement with its own field system. An excellent field book survives for 1433 which seems to have been prepared for the purpose of making exchanges prior to partial enclosure.[29] Hidden in this field book is a regular tenurial cycle of nineteen holdings. It must be very ancient indeed—the compiler of 1433 cannot have been aware of its existence, for the cycle begins and ends anywhere within the furlongs being described in that year, sometimes in reverse order, sometimes with account made of whether a holding consists of one rood or half an acre, the latter having to be counted as two positions. It therefore seems reasonable to assign a date not later than the eleventh or twelfth century for this cycle (by comparison with Hardingstone, where the cycle hidden in the 1660 field book seems to be not later than the thirteenth century).

Figure 11 shows a plot of the nineteen-name cycle on part of Muscott's north field. As with Hardingstone, the cycles go through more than one furlong and correspond to the headlands of furlongs lying at right angles. Thus the two east-west furlongs numbered one and two are likely to have been created by changing through ninety degrees the strips of, respectively, one cycle of nineteen and two cycles of nineteen. The whole block of landscape would originally have been laid out in a uniform series of parallel strips eight- hundred yards long. The cases of Hardingstone and Muscott clearly suggest that medieval strip fields were laid out on a large scale well before the Norman Conquest, with a subsequent sub-division of the long strips and rearrangement to form the complex patterns that developed in the Midlands.

It is clear from the examples above that field-work surveys and field books can be used to reconstruct medieval field patterns to produce a series of plans for the many parishes which have none. Analysis of furlong names and of the tenurial arrangements described in field books have produced new evidence regarding land use and the development of demesne holdings; changes in open-field layout suggest that field patterns were once much simpler and deliberately planned. Through the combined use of such techniques we can, therefore, shed light on the organization and development of medieval estates.

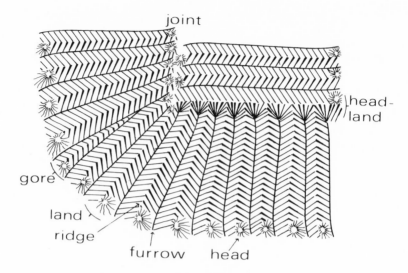

Figure 1a
Diagram of principal features of open fields.

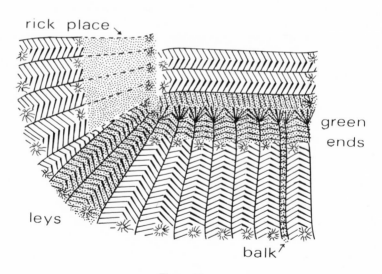

Figure 1b
Later modifications of open fields;
the stippled areas were grassed down.

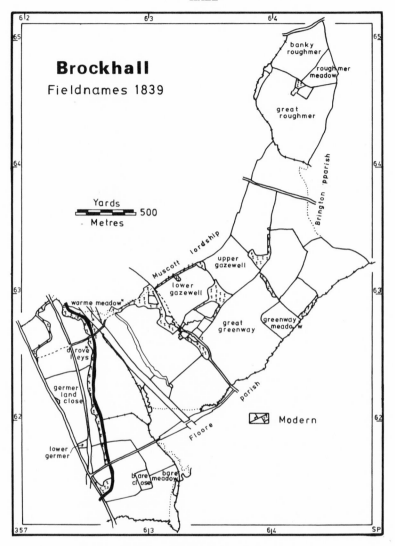

Figure 2
Brockhall, Northamptonshire; open-field names surviving as
enclosed field names. Sources: Northan Record Office MSS,
map T31 (1839) and map 1986 (1614).

55

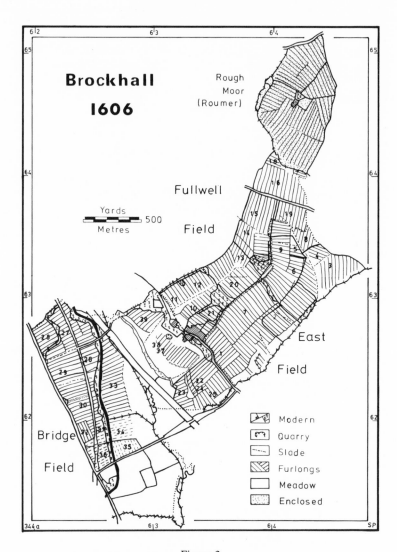

Figure 3
Brockhall, Northamptonshire; land use in 1606 (for key to
furlong names see Table 2). The Bridge Field has been
much mutilated by the transport systems of recent centuries,
and identifications here are tentative.

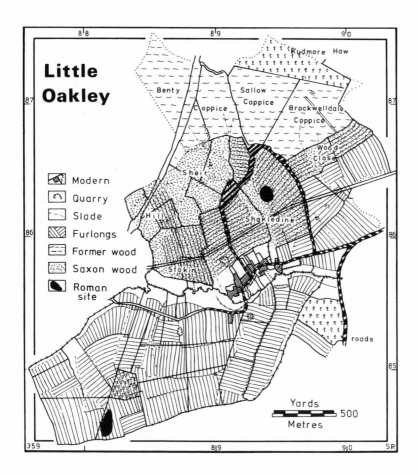

Figure 4
Little Oakley, Northamptonshire; land use at various periods.
Coppices to the north are all medieval woodland which has
been disafforested in recent centuries.

57

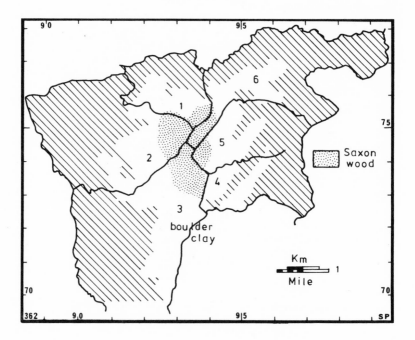

Figure 5
Wold furlongs locating positions of late Saxon woodland
shared by several parishes: 1 Cranford, 2 Burton Latimer,
3 Finedon, 4 Little Addington, 5 Great Addington, and 6 Woodford.

58

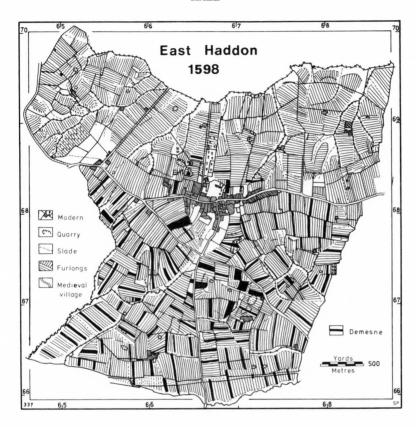

Figure 6
East Haddon, Northamptonshire;
demesne in 1598 and newly enclosed ground c. 1601.

59

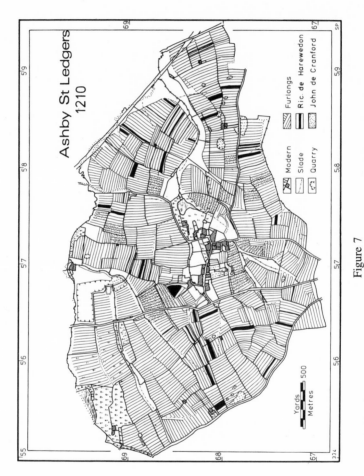

Figure 7

Ashby St. Ledgers, Northamptonshire in 1210; demesne and 1½ yardland
belonging to Richard de Harewedon.

60

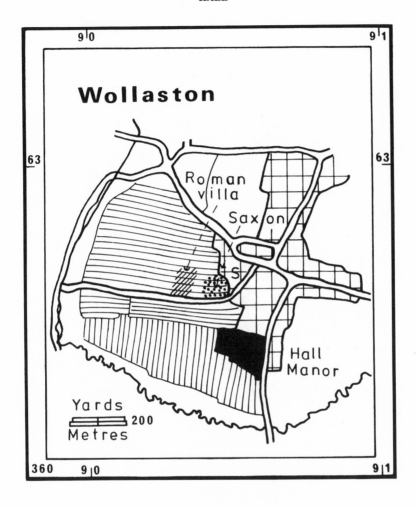

Figure 8
Wollaston, Northamptonshire; demesne of Hall Manor.
The whole was called the *inland* and had been enclosed by 1583.
Furlong 1 is *walton acre*.

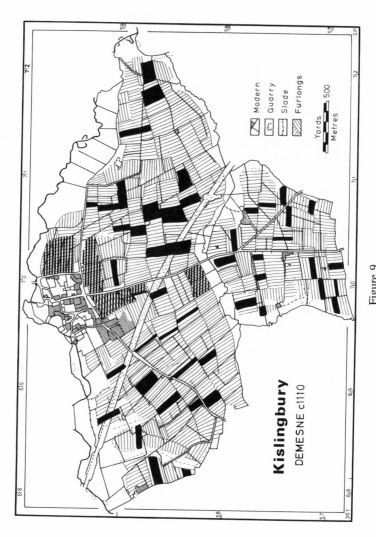

Figure 9

Kislingbury, Northamptonshire; demesne in early twelfth century.

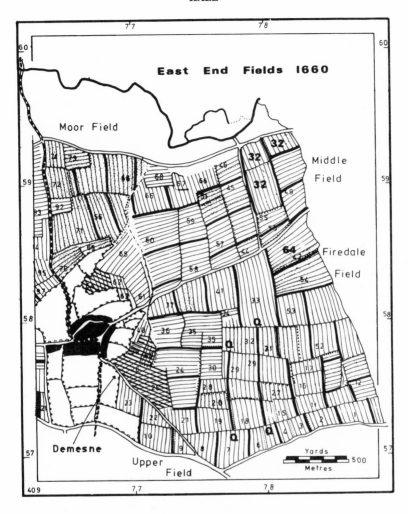

Figure 10
Hardingstone, Northamptonshire; probable demesne in
twelfth century and regular tenurial cycles.

63

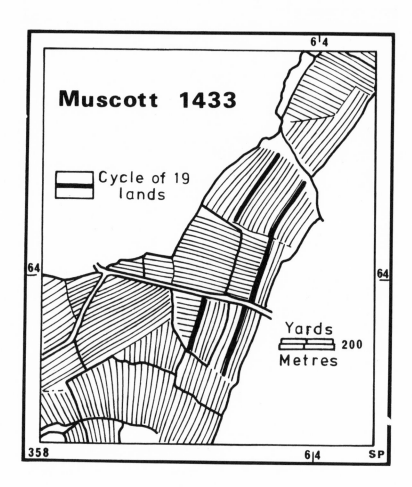

Figure 11
Muscott, Northamptonshire; regular tenurial holdings.

TABLE 1
Part of Brockhall Fieldbook, 1606

Number of land	Name of Owner	Width poles	Width feet	Length poles	Area poles	Area feet
FULLWELL FELD						
1 furlong Rushcroft goe west						
1	Godfree	1		52	52	
2			14$\frac{1}{32}$	52	47	2
3			14	51½	45	1
4-7	Whitehouse	3	6$\frac{1}{32}$	49	268	6
8-9	Lord	1	10	47½	78	3
10-11	Fulke	2	5	46	106	6
12-15	Lord	4		44	176	
16	Godfree		14½	½	39	6
17	Lord		14½	43	39	1
18-21	Smith			4	98	8
22-29	Darnell	13	½	40	540	
2 furlong, north from the last						
Gardswell furlong goe est						
Balk						
1-9	Lord	11	7	22	251	10
10-14	Smith	4	12	20	95	
15-19	Lord	4	12	19	90	4
20-21	Godfree	1	15	17	32	15
22-23	Whitehouse	3		16	48	
3 furlong, north from the last						
Muscote hill goe north						
1-2	Lord	3		28	84	
3	Smith	1		28	28	
4	Fulke		15	28	26	4
5	Darnell		15	28	26	4
6-7	Parson	3	4	28	91	
8	Lord		13½	28	23	10
9	Godfree	1	12	28	44	
10	Whitehouse	1	33$\frac{1}{32}$	28¼	34	6

TABLE 2
Brockhall Furlong Data

Number on Fig. 3	Name in 1606	Number of lands	Orienta-tion	Abuttals
EST FIELD				
1	Flexland	45		headland at end
2	Greneway	200	EW/NS	go N; shoots holmes toune; flaxland W
3	Homstonge	44	NS	go E; heads E of last
4	Pytt furlong	26	EW	go N; heads NW of last
5	Crossedalls	23	NS/EW	go W; W from last
6	Homer crossedalls	20	NS/EW	go E
7	Ridgeway furlonge	126	EW	go S
8	Crosseleis	43	NS	go E; next meer of Brockhall & Brington; shoots crossedalls
9	Hanginge leis	50	EW	ridgeway furlong W; headland at S
FULLEWELL FELD				
10	Rushcroft	29	NS/EW	go W; bellclose S
11	Gardswell furlong	33	NS/EW	go E; N from last; Muscott field N
12	Muscote hill	98	EW	go N; last a headland
13	Fulwellhedd	31	NS	go E; N from last
14	Wheatlands	23	NS	go W
15	Riehill	43	NS	go E; N of last
16	Beyond the steet	73	NS	go E; shooting Roumer hedge
17	Romer hedge	6	EW	go N; N end of last; Brington field E & S
18	Furlong in corner at romer hedge	8	EW	go N
19	Wheatland	35	EW/NS	go S; shoots hanging lees & headland; highway N
20	Ridgeway	107	EW	go S; S of last; headland W
21	Indland	36	EW	go N; town W
BRIDGE FELD				
22	Bancroft	20	NS/EW	go E; next to the manor
23	Little Flower broke	50	EW/NS	go S; heads E of last
24	Stanwell way	15	NS/EW	go W;
25	Carlese	62	NS/EW	go W; Flower field S
26	Drove leis	56	NS	go W

66

TABLE 2
Brockhall Furlong Data

Number on Fig. 3	Name in 1606	Number of lands	Orienta- tion	Abuttals
BRIDGE FELD				
27	Shooting on hay furrs	49	NS	go W
28	Rie hill	43	EW	go S; shoots to London way; beyond the brook; last headland
29	Brier furlong	54	EW	go N; beyond the brook
30	Slad furlong	41	NS	go W; beyond the brook
31	Fontstonewell	44	EW	go S; heads last S; Daventry balk near
32	Gormerland	14	EW/NS	go N; heads S of last gormerland
33	Shooting into lake gutter	80	EW/NS	go N; heads S of last
34	Bare arse furlong	18	EW	go S; heads S of last
35	Bare arse leis	38	NS	go W; S from last
36	Shooting London way	31	EW	go N
37	Lamcroft leies	14	EW	go N
38		8	NS	go W; head E of last
39	Upper lamcroft	29	EW	go N

Note: because most of the furlongs lay either northeast-southwest or northwest-southeast, there is much confusion in the manuscript sources, which conventionally only use the four simple cardinal directions. Brockhall furlong orientations are, therefore, less helpful than usual.

NOTES

[1] *English Field Systems* (Cambridge, MA: Harvard Univ. Press, 1915), pp. 17-156.

[2] M. W. Beresford, *History on the Ground*, 2nd ed. (London: Methuen and Co., 1971); and W. G. Hoskins, *The Making of the English Landscape* (London: Hodder and Stoughton, 1957).

[3] D. N. Hall, "Modern Surveys of Medieval Field Systems," *Bedfordshire Archaeological Journal*, 7 (1972), 53-66.

[4] Photographs held by the Dept. of the Environment, Prince Con-

sort House, Albert Embankment, London.

[5] Northamptonshire Record Office (N.R.O.) MSS., uncatalogued Thornton MSS. Box no. 6.

[6] Unpubl. work by author.

[7] D. N. Hall, *Medieval Fields* (Princes Risborough, Bucks: Shire Publ., 1982), fig. 32.

[8] D. N. Hall, "Elm, a Field Survey," *Proceedings of the Cambridgeshire Antiquarian Society*, 68 (1978), 21-46.

[9] An addition in 1598 in *Fitzherbert's Book of Husbandry*, reprinted by W. W. Skeat (London, 1882), p. 132.

[10] Cambridgeshire Record Office MSS., R58/16/1, map of Chippenham 1712.

[11] D. N. Hall, "Hardingstone Parish Survey 1972," *Northamptonshire Archaeology*, 15 (1980), 119-32. See also Hall, *Medieval Fields*, fig. 20.

[12] N.R.O. MSS., Little Oakley map 4321 and charters in Box X377.

[13] J. E. B. Gover, A. Mawer, and F. M. Stenton, *The Place-names of Northamptonshire* (Cambridge: Cambridge Univ. Press, 1933), p. 180; see also other MSS. sources in N.R.O..

[14] F. M. Stenton, *Facsimiles of Early Charters from Northamptonshire Collections* (Northampton: Northamptonshire Record Society, 1930), pp. 94-95.

[15] Reconstructed fields by the author, terrier of manorial lands N.R.O. MSS., IL2120.

[16] For Brockhall, see N.R.O. MSS., Th 281, terrier of 1584; for Great Billing, see N.R.O. MSS., 31/P21; and for Floore, see N.R.O. MSS., XZ 6294.

[17] N.R.O. MSS., ASL 1232.

[18] N.R.O. MSS., ASL 142.

[19] A. Gibbons, *Liber Antiquus de Ordinationibus Vicariarum tempore Hugonis Wells, Lincolniensis Episcopi, 1209-1235* (Lincoln: privately, 1888), p. 38.

[20] D. N. Hall, *Wollaston, Portrait of a Village* (Wollaston: privately, 1977), pp. 2, 140, 160.

[21] N.R.O. MSS., M(TM) 378.

[22] British Library MSS., Cotton Vesp. E XVII f. 283.

[23] D. N. Hall, "Hardingstone Parish Survey 1972," note 11.

[24] D. N. Hall, *Wollaston, Portrait of a Village*, pp. 193, 221.

[25] D. N. Hall, unpubl. work.

[26] R. T. Rowley, *The Origins of Open Field Agriculture* (London: Croom Helm, and New Jersey: Barnes and Noble Books, 1980), pp 22-38 ff.

[27] D. N. Hall, *Medieval Fields*, figs. 29 and 30.

[28] D. N. Hall, "Hardingstone Parish Survey 1972," note 11.

[29] N.R.O. MSS., Th 183.

THE FOREST: WOODLAND AND WOOD-PASTURE IN MEDIEVAL ENGLAND

OLIVER RACKHAM

The word "forest" appears here in the title as a help to the American reader, who will understand it as a place of trees. To the medieval Englishman, on the contrary, a Forest was a place of deer: a place where the king had the right to keep deer for his table. Generations of historians have confused the two meanings and have, thereby, overestimated the amount of woodland in medieval England. To avoid perpetuating this confusion, I shall spell Forest in its medieval sense with a capital "F."

This chapter covers England and is based mainly on research done in eastern England. Wales, Scotland, and Ireland have different, less conservative, forest histories and are not discussed here. While the Middle Ages are a convenient period in which to study some kinds of evidence relating to trees and their management, they are not a distinctive period for what was happening on the ground. Many practices—and many actual woods—began long before 1066 and continued long after 1536; some are still extant. Some medieval English practices were taken to New England by the early settlers.

Analogies with the eastern United States, though instructive, should not be pursued without taking due account of the differences. Medieval England was not a frontier country; its pioneering days lay back in the Neolithic, Bronze, and Iron Ages and were not remembered. There were no large areas of vacant land: the country was densely populated, and every inch of it belonged to someone. Trees were valuable property and formed part of a settled system of land-uses: a tree was usually cut down in the definite expectation that another would grow in its stead.[1] Woodlots had their own proper names, as if they were villages or hamlets.

The landscape of England has had a degree of stability which may be unfamiliar to Americans. There has not been the cycle of optimism and failure—pioneers wresting a living for a few decades from land which turns out to be unsuitable, then being put out of business as agriculture moves west—which has left such a mark on the eastern States. In the last 350 years, New England has changed from wildwood to farmland and back to old-field forest; both changes are more universal than any in England in the last thousand years. Much of the medieval English landscape, its villages, hamlets, farms, roads, woods, and hedges, has survived centuries of social and economic changes and still exists. A thirteenth-century inhabitant of Essex or Cornwall would be able to find his way about the twentieth-century landscape of his native area, whereas an early nineteenth-century inhabitant of Connecticut would not.

Systems of Land-Use Involving Trees

In medieval England, trees played a part in three separate and independent systems of land-use; woodland, wood-pasture, and hedges and non-woodland trees. A *wood* in medieval England (Medieval Latin *boscus*), like an American *woods* (singular) or *woodlot*, was a piece of land on which trees grew naturally. It was managed to yield two major products: *underwood* (ML *subboscus*), poles and rods used for fuel and for many specialized purposes; and *timber* (American *lumber*, ML *meremium*), boles of trees big enough to make beams or planks.[2] This land-use is termed *woodland*, and its management I have called *woodmanship*.

Wood-pasture involves grazing animals (cattle, sheep, deer) as well as trees. There is a conflict between the two, in that the shade of the trees spoils the pasture, and the livestock eat the regrowth of the trees. Various techniques existed for reconciling them.

Fields in most of England are divided by hedges roughly equivalent to American *fence-rows*.[3] A hedge is normally cut to a few feet in height and has bigger trees in it at intervals. Hedges and hedgerow trees, and also trees standing around houses and in fields, were sometimes an

70

important source of timber and underwood. In medieval England they were most common in the peripheral counties, for example, Essex, Dorset, and Devon, but occurred even in the predominantly open-field Midlands.[4]

A fourth tradition, that of *plantations*, differs from woodland in that the trees are established by planting and are not the natural vegetation. Plantations are the staple of modern forestry as Britain understands it; with rare exceptions they begin after the Middle Ages.

English Tree Species and Their Behavior

In England there are about forty indigenous tree species. The genera of trees are much the same as in North America, but all the species are different. There are two species of oak (which the medievals did not recognize as distinct), a large species of hazel, one ash, one maple, two limes, many elms, one hornbeam, one beech, two birches, two poplars, two hawthorns, a tree-sized holly, a tree-sized alder, and so forth. In the Middle Ages there were also two introduced wild trees, a chestnut and a third poplar. Conifers were exceedingly rare, and there was no hickory, tulip, buckeye, or locust.

Many English trees grow less easily from seed than do their American sisters. If cut down, they do not die but sprout again, either from the stump (a process called *coppicing*) or from shallow roots (*suckering*). (See Fig. 1.) Oak, hazel, ash, maple, lime, wych-elm, alder, hornbeam, and beech, among others, are coppicing trees (like American red maple). Most elms, aspen, and cherry are suckering (like American beech). When repeatedly coppiced, a tree develops a permanent base called a *stool* from which new shoots arise in perpetual succession (Fig. 2c). The young shoots (Middle English *spring*[5]) of coppice stools and suckers are very palatable to livestock; consequently, it was usual in wood-pastures to treat underwood-producing trees as *pollards*, that is, to cut them at eight to twelve feet above ground so that the spring would arise where animals could not reach it.

The history of English woodland is not interrupted by periodic fires and blowdowns as it is in much of North America. English woods will not burn, and although windfall wood is common enough to have a Medieval Latin name (*cablicium*), hurricanes uproot or break only single trees here and there. Trees can live for centuries, especially if pollarded or coppiced, and some medieval trees are still extant.

71

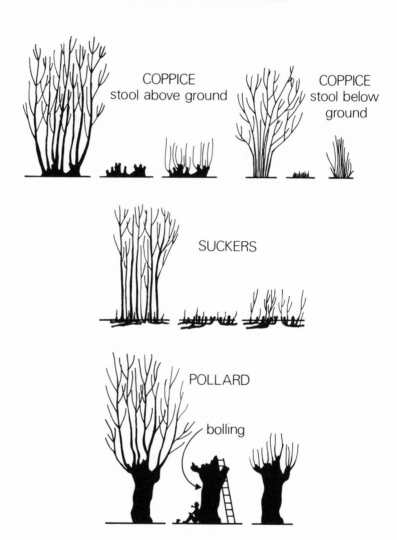

Figure 1
Different ways of managing wood producing trees. For each method the tree, or group of trees, is shown just before cutting, just after cutting, and one year after cutting. (All are drawn to the same scale.)

72

The Making of the Medieval Woods

Prehistoric Origins

After the last glacial period, England was successively colonized by different trees which, in the course of millennia, came to form prehistoric climax forests, the *wildwood*, covering the whole country. Wildwood in a natural state has long ago disappeared from Europe, but in North America, vast areas of it were known to early settlers, and smaller tracts still exist, as, for instance, in the Great Smoky Mountains of Tennessee and North Carolina.[6]

As recent interpretations of pollen deposits show, the wildwood of most of England was by 6000 B.C. a mosaic of vegetation types in which the most common tree was almost certainly lime. Other species—hazel, oak, alder, elm, and ash, for example—were abundant and could be dominant in places. In northern and western England there were different types of wildwood in which oak or hazel was commonly the dominant tree.[7] Already the woodland of England had several of the characteristics which still distinguish it from that of Continental Europe, such as lack of conifers, scarcity of beech, and abundance of hazel.

Although some kind of woodland management may well have been practiced by Mesolithic peoples, the first clear evidence of systematic human interference with wildwood comes with the arrival of Neolithic settlers in about 4000 B.C. These peoples introduced the non-woodland arts of agriculture into northwest Europe. They began the process of destroying the wildwood, a process which continued and expanded in later millennia, thereby creating the farmland and moorland which now form most of the English landscape. They also began to convert parts of the remaining wildwood into the managed woodland of the historic period.[8]

It must be emphasized (for it is often forgotten by European scholars) that wildwood was destroyed because people wanted the land, not because they wanted the trees. Trees grow again and are not done away with merely by cutting them down. Any land that is not cultivated or grazed reverts to *secondary woodland* within a few decades, differing in tree species from the original wildwood.[9] Secondary woodland does not occur in England on the same vast scale as the old-field or old-pasture woods of North America, but examples can be found from all periods, including the Middle Ages.[10]

The Anglo-Saxon Period

On present evidence, the destruction of wildwood was most active in the Iron Age and Roman period, 700 B.C. to A.D. 400. Recent research indicates that not only the farmed landscape in general but also some of its details date from these periods. For instance, in much of Essex there is a regularity in the hedges and minor roads somewhat reminiscent of the grid landscape laid out in the 1820s around the city of Kalamazoo, Michigan; this planned landscape has been shown to be older than the Roman main roads which intersect it.[11]

The discontinuity between Roman and Anglo-Saxon England seems not to have resulted in any immediate general disappearance of agriculture and consequent re-expansion of woodland. Anglo-Saxon place-name elements indicating the making of settlements in woodland— places ending in -ley or -hurst, for example—are not uniformly spread over the country but are concentrated in particular areas; this shows that the Anglo-Saxons did not colonize the whole landscape afresh but merely continued a process that the Romans had already partly completed.[12]

The Anglo-Saxon charters, covering the period A.D. 700 to 1100, are legal documents which define landed estates by listing objects along their boundaries. They are our earliest written record of the location and boundaries of woods, of hedges, non-woodland trees of named species, minor roads, footpaths, ponds, and so forth. They confirm that England was already a mainly agricultural land with islands of woodland and show that much of the landscape has changed little in the last thousand years. Indeed, anyone who walks the boundaries today can still find a suprising number of the very objects listed.[13]

I expect to publish shortly a geographical analysis of features named in the nine-hundred or so surviving charters. For instance, one of the great regional differences in the English landscape from the Middle Ages onwards, still distinctive even today, is that between areas with many and with few ancient hedges. This was already established in Anglo-Saxon times: over six percent of the objects listed in charters of the London area or northwest Dorset are hedges, but fewer than one percent of those in southwest Wiltshire or north Berkshire.

Where they mention tree species, the Anglo-Saxon charters are analogous to the eighteenth- and nineteenth-century land survey records that are an important source for the pre-settlement forests of the eastern States.[14] Less systematically, they mention coppicing, pollarding, and the distinction between woodland and wood-pasture; they show that many practices, first recorded in detail in the thirteenth century, are really much older.

74

The Woodmanship Tradition

Relatively Little Woodland in England

Domesday Book, compiled in 1086, gives particulars of some 7,800 woods; for much of England their sizes are given. These statistics do not support the popular belief that medieval England was a very wooded land. *Domesday* records 12,850 settlements, only half of which possessed woodland or wood-pasture. The areas (or their equivalent) of woodland and wood-pasture add up to only 15% of the country.[15] Woods were very unevenly distributed: the biggest concentration was in the Weald of Kent, Sussex, and Surrey, and the second biggest was in the Chilterns north of London. Large areas of the Midland, Yorkshire, and the Fens had no woodland at all.

These figures agree very well with Anglo-Saxon charters and place-name evidence and also with later medieval records. Eleventh-century England was less wooded than most countries of twentieth-century Europe. Although there had been some reduction in woodland during Anglo-Saxon times, the distribution of wooded and less-wooded areas had not changed radically and was probably a legacy from the Roman period.[16] In the subsequent centuries of land-hunger, more woodland was destroyed, especially in the Weald, Chilterns, and other well-wooded areas. The proportion probably fell to about 10% of woodland and wood-pasture by 1350 and then remained relatively stable until a further period of destruction from 1700 onwards.[17]

In England there is not a history of forests extending uninterrupted for tens of miles. No point in a wood was more than 1½ hours' walk from some habitation; but many settlements were a day's journey from substantial woodland. The story is of conservation and of making intensive use of a relatively small wooded area; it is also of trade and transport rather than of local self-sufficiency.

Medieval Woodland Management

From the thirteenth century onwards, improved documentation makes it possible to trace the histories of many individual woods. One of the earliest detailed surveys of estates, the *Ely Coucher Book* of 1251, says in its lengthy treatment of Little Gransden (Cambridgeshire):

The Wood. There is there one wood which is called Heyle which contains fourscore acres.

Item, there is there one other wood which is called Litlelund, which contains thirty-two acres.

The total of all the wood is fivescore and twelve acres....[18]

Woodland covered about 8% of the township. There were two woods which had their own names and definite boundaries and areas; they were valuable private property, were managed in specific ways, and were permanent. *Heyle* still exists as Hayley Wood, now belonging to Cambridgeshire and Isle of Ely Naturalists' Trust; the many records from intervening centuries show that it is unchanged apart from two small nineteenth-century alterations to the boundaries. *Litlelund* was grubbed out c. 1650.[19] Such continuity is by no means unusual; on another page of the *Ely Coucher Book* we find the five woods of Barking (Suffolk) ranging from five to 180 acres, all of which are still there with much the same areas.[20]

Although records of identifiable woods from earlier centuries are not common, there are many indications that the settled place of woodland was not new to the thirteenth-century landscape. Many wood-names are of pre-Conquest origin, such as those ending in -*lund* (Old Norse *lúndr*, a grove). One such is Litlelund, above. Another is Wayland Wood in Watton (Norfolk), anciently *Wanelund*, which in Anglo-Saxon times was sufficiently notable to give its name to Wayland Hundred, a unit of local government. This exceptionally historic wood—it is the "Babes in the Wood" wood—is still intact and belongs to Norfolk Naturalists' Trust.[21]

A wood normally consisted of underwood stools with a scatter of timber trees (Fig. 2). Woods might be of many different mixtures of tree species; I have described thirty types of ancient woodland from eastern England alone.[22] Which species to treat as timber and which as underwood is largely an arbitrary decision. Oak, however, was present in almost all kinds of woodland and by near-universal custom was regarded as timber. A wood, therefore, usually consisted of oak timber trees and underwood of other species; only if oak was very abundant was some of it treated as underwood.

Underwood was normally the chief product and was cut on a rotation usually of from four to nine, less often from twelve to twenty, years between successive fellings. Surveys of woods commonly state a felling cycle:

...Heylewode which contains 80 acres by estimate. Of the underwood of which there can be sold every year, without causing waste or destruction, 11 acres of underwood which are worth 55 shillings at 5s. an acre . . . A certain other Wood called Litlelond which contains 26 acres by estimate. Whose underwood can be sold as a whole every seventh year. And it is then worth in all £6. 10s. at 5s. an acre.

Hayley Wood, 1356[23]

Estate accounts also exist which show that the actual area cut fluctuated widely from year to year, presumably according to varying rates of growth, states of the market, or the labor available.[24] Underwood had many specialized uses, such as fencing and thatching wood and wattle-and-daub (see later); but its chief use was for domestic and industrial fuel. It was a valuable cash crop which involved little expenditure. In eastern England from 1270 onwards, woods were worth, in underwood alone, on the average 1½ times the value per annum of the same area of arable land.[25]

Woods also yielded nuts and edible fruits, acorns for fattening pigs, and so forth. By the Middle Ages, these had declined into useful but unimportant by-products, though some of them were more prevalent in wood-pasture. The pigs of medieval English towns and villages, like those which swarmed on nineteenth- century Broadway, New York,[26] were mainly scavengers.[27]

Woods were a scarce and renewable source of energy, and trouble was taken with their conservation. The boundaries were defined by a massive earthwork, the *woodbank* (Fig. 3), and were fenced to keep out browsing livestock. Most woodbanks were already in existence by the thirteenth century; but contractor's accounts survive for making 3.7 miles of new woodbank around the woods of Norwich Cathedral Priory at Hindolveston (Norfolk) in 1297-98, apparently as part of a scheme for converting the woods from producing mainly timber to mainly underwood.[28]

Timber and the Evidence of Buildings

By my estimate there are over 100,000 medieval houses, barns, and churches extant in England, most of which contain some original timber fabric, while many are entirely wooden. This gigantic corpus of evidence, though more studied than it used to be, is still scandalously under-used by historians.[29] (This paper, for example, was accompanied at the Sixteenth International Congress on Medieval Studies by 670 others,

77

not one of which was about timber buildings.)

Many medieval houses consist of a timber frame with panels filled with wattle-and-daub (Fig. 4). The timber gives evidence of the species, sizes, and ages of tree that were used and the circumstances in which they had grown. Wattle-and-daub gives similar information about underwood. A small house of c. 1400 which I recently examined at Hartest (Suffolk) had a frame composed of small oak trees; the wattle rods, of seven year's growth and about 1½ inches in diameter at the base, were a mixture of hazel, ash, maple, willow, and aspen, tied together with *Clematis* stems, strips of lime bark, and one-year willow rods. The most likely source is Homereshey Wood in Hartest, mentioned in the *Ely Coucher Book* and last heard of in 1605.[30] This reconstruction of a long-vanished wood agrees well (apart from the lime, which is unexpected) with written evidence for other places and also with the composition of the surviving ancient woods in the area.

Buildings, although a minor use of underwood, are an important supplement to written evidence about it. They are our main source of information about timber, of which they were the biggest single use. Oak is by far the most common timber tree both in buildings and in the records, although other species occur, especially in the timbers of small and more humble houses. Usually each member is made out of a whole log. The carpenter, where possible, chose and felled the smallest oak that would, squared up, make the beam required; he did not waste time and money in felling big trees and sawing them lengthwise. In most woods there was a rapid turnover of small oaks, felled at from thirty to seventy years of age and easily replaced. Timbers are rarely much more than twenty feet long, and when they exceed this length become crooked and knotty at the top end, where they reach into the crown of a tree that was not really big enough. This maximum length—which has an important influence on the design of buildings such as aisled barns—results from the fact that the boles of oaks grown among underwood break up into branches where they reach above the underwood canopy.

It is possible to count how many trees went into a particular building. A timber-framed farmhouse at Stanton (Suffolk), rather larger than average (an open hall and seven other rooms), was made from 333 timber trees, ranging in size from thirty-two oaks less than six inches in basal diameter used for rafters, to three oaks more than eighteen inches in diameter forming principal posts. Half the trees were less than nine inches in diameter, a small size for an oak today. These trees are typical of those that went into houses, barns, colleges, and the less grand church roofs; there was a wide range of sizes, but even the largest were little bigger than an average twentieth-century oak. Considering the probable numbers and

78

growth-rates of oaks, the average wood of, say, fifty acres could have produced one such house every six years, were there no other demands on its timber component. Local woods, which covered about 5½% of West Suffolk, could probably have produced just enough timber to keep up with the demands of rural, though not of urban, building.[31]

Most places in England had one timber which the local wood could not produce, namely the great post on which the windmill stood and turned. Mill-posts are an example of outsize timbers of unusual length or thickness, which were very expensive and were transported long distances. They were used chiefly in very grand buildings: every cathedral, for instance, had several hundred oaks of about thirty feet useful length in its roof. Outsize oaks came mainly from wood-pastures (parks and Forests) rather than from woods.[32]

Transport

Despite the incontrovertible geological evidence that stone was habitually moved around medieval and even Anglo-Saxon England, historians have traditionally believed that timber and wood were necessarily local. Large areas of England, however, did not have adequate woodland. Places with a timber-framing tradition were not necessarily wooded; the extra woodland needed to suport urban timber-framing in London, York, Norwich, Cambridge, and Lavenham, for example, rarely happened to stand immediately next to a town.[33] Occasionally an exotic tree species, such as medieval pine timbers in King's Lynn,[34] provides the same proof of transport that stone from Normandy does when found in Norfolk.

In a land with few inland waterways, most transport was by road. Underwood was seldom fetched long distances, although it was an important fuel in such towns as London and Cambridge. Substitutes could often be found, if necessary, and big users of underwood such as the Forest of Dean ironworks tended to be sited in well-wooded areas.[35]

There is abundant documentation on the transport both of outsize and of ordinary timber, which was more valuable than underwood relative to its weight. Transport follows no obvious pattern of supply and demand, and was evidently much influenced by the circumstances, habits, and whims of the individuals concerned. Timber was often used from distant rather than nearby sources, and many journeys seem to us unnecessary. Henry III repeatedly sent timber from Kingswood near Colchester, which he owned, to Dover Castle (seventy miles by sea) rather than using the many woods in Kent: the king was poor and evidently had to use his own timber rather than buying it locally.[36] But why should the twelfth-century monks of Abingdon (Berkshire) have sent twelve-ox wains 120 miles to North Wales for timber, by-passing on the way two of the four largest concentrations of woodland in England at the time?[37]

Overseas trade in timber is well documented in estate and building accounts and in port records.[38] Much of the trade was in the form of boards imported from Norway, Hamburg, and countries bordering the Baltic and used for ordinary purposes throughout England, even in places which had plenty of woodland.[39] The making of thin, accurately-cut, seasoned boards required a combination of specialized skills and equipment and special trees not available in England. Sawmills in particular appeared in France c. 1200 and rapidly spread through Europe; they transformed American carpentry from c. 1650 onwards[40] but were not adopted in England until the eighteenth century.

Later History of Woods

Woodmanship went on down the centuries with surprisingly little change. From the sixteenth century onwards, coppice rotations tended to lengthen; timber trees were allowed to grow bigger and were sawn lengthwise when felled. Coppicing, though not the boundary banks, was introduced to New England. As late as 1900, many woods differed only in detail from what they had been in 1250, and some, such as the Bradfield Woods in West Suffolk, are still so managed today.

From 1850 onwards, owing to such factors as the introduction of fossil fuels to the countryside, many woods fell into disuse or were used only for hunting. They usually remained in existence, however, until after World War II, when it became the practice to destroy woods and replace them with farmland or forestry plantations. Between 1945 and 1973, nearly half the ancient woodland area of England thus disappeared; this is the most rapid destruction in recorded history and is roughly equal to the entire losses in the previous four-hundred years.[41]

Ancient Woods as They Now Survive

Medieval woods have sharply-defined edges, bounded not by straight lines but by sinuous or zigzag perimeters. The earliest detailed maps, from c. 1580 onwards, show many wood outlines exactly the same (to within a few feet) as they are now. These stable boundaries are maintained by banks. A medieval woodbank (see Fig. 3) is typically a rounded bank with an outer ditch, some thirty to forty feet in total width. A wood with a complex history may contain many woodbanks, indicating changes of boundary or divisions of ownership (Fig. 5). Woodbanks continued to be made into the nineteenth century, but the later ones are usually straight or regularly curved and are progressively less massive than medieval banks. Woodbanks often have ancient pollard trees at intervals marking the legal boundary; occasionally there are traces of a hedge.

Medieval woods often preserve minor features of the natural land surface—ponds, natural depressions, small stream courses—that elsewhere have been destroyed or confused by cultivation. Secondary woods, in contrast, inherit many kinds of artificial earthwork remaining from the previous land-use; these range from Bronze Age barrows and Iron Age hillforts to medieval ridge- and-furrow and moats (Fig. 5).

The underwood of an ancient wood, which is the more permanent component, can be of many different trees or mixtures of trees. In parts of Essex, a twelve-acre wood may contain five different types of woodland. With few exceptions, these are not the direct result of management. Several tree communities commonly coexist within a wood under the same management history. Their boundaries are irregular and are not related to management boundaries; there is often some relation to soils.

Many tree communities are known to be of ancient origin. Lime-woods still predominate in certain very limited areas, around Sudbury (Suffolk), for example; they have a good historical record, and there can be no doubt that they are relics of the lime-dominated wildwood. Hazel-woods, now much more abundant than limewoods, can similarly be traced back to hazel-dominated wildwood. Other kinds of wildwood appear to have given rise to our surviving oakwoods, alder-woods, and some types of elmwood and ashwood. All of these have their own historical records, and some of them can be traced back at least to the Middle Ages on the very sites which they now occupy. In Essex, for instance, there is a medieval wood-name of Anglo-Saxon form, *boscus de lindris*, from *linde* = lime and *hris* = underwood; a thousand years later, this wood still contains lime as underwood.[42] Not all types of woodland can thus be explained: hornbeam-woods and maple-woods are known to be ancient, but their origin is uncertain. Woods of chestnut and beech were rare in the Middle Ages and have since greatly increased, partly through planting.[43] The post-medieval increase of birchwoods and suckering elmwoods appears to be an inadvertent effect of human activity.[44]

Woods often contain some of the actual stools which grew in the

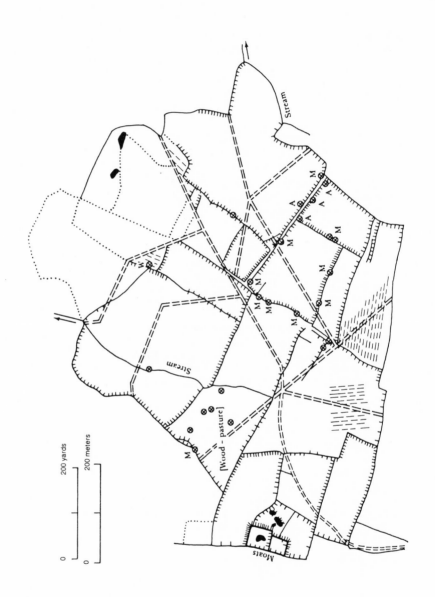

Eversden Wood, Cambridgeshire—an ancient wood with a complex history, extending into three townships and formerly in many ownerships. Several miles of massive banks and ditches mark the property boundaries, which are further defined by pollard trees on the banks. Traces of ridge-and-furrow show that at least four of the lots have been ploughed. The double moat with associated "fish-ponds" represents a deserted and undocumented settlement. Pollards not on banks indicate a small area of wood-pasture. In the early nineteenth century the ownerships were amalgamated, and a system of rides (i.e., access tracks) was set out ignoring the old boundaries, although the earthworks and pollards remain. (Pollards are marked A [ash], M [maple], W [willow]. Those unmarked are oak).

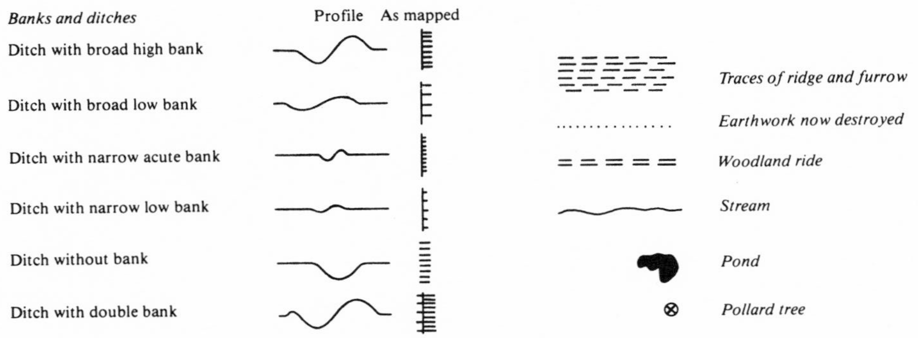

Banks and ditches

	Profile	As mapped
Ditch with broad high bank		
Ditch with broad low bank		
Ditch with narrow acute bank		
Ditch with narrow low bank		
Ditch without bank		
Ditch with double bank		

Traces of ridge and furrow

Earthwork now destroyed

Woodland ride

Stream

Pond

Pollard tree

Figure 5

83

Middle Ages (Fig. 2c). With each coppice cycle, a stool gets slightly bigger. Stools of ash occasionally reach eighteen feet in diameter and are estimated to be up to one-thousand years old.[45] Medieval stools of similar size are known in lime, maple, alder, oak, elm, and chestnut.[46]

Medieval woods contain characteristic plant species. When a secondary wood is formed, it does not suddenly acquire all the woodland plants and animals. Birch and oak appear at once; hornbeam and hazel later; and lime, though theoretically it may be the climax dominant tree, never arrives in practice.[47] Lime is one of many plants, especially herbaceous species, which rarely appear in secondary woodland even after centuries have elapsed. A list of fifty such species has been compiled for Lincolnshire alone.[48]

The Wood-Pasture Tradition

Wooded Commons

The expression *silua pastilis* first appears in Anglo-Saxon charters and is systematically recorded as a separate land-use by *Domesday Book* in some counties, as for instance, Lincolnshire. There were three kinds of wood-pasture; wooded commons, parks, and wooded Forests.

Wooded commons, which are probably of prehistoric origin, were the only wood-pasture known to the Anglo-Saxons. A *common* is a tract of unenclosed land, usually belonging to an individual landowner, on which particular local inhabitants have the right to pasture livestock.[49] Most commons are grassland or heath, but if there are trees these may be the subject of woodcutting rights. In its simplest form, wood-pasture could be little more than the turning loose of cattle or sheep to make a living on whatever grass, brambles, or low branches grew within their reach.

Parks

In Anglo-Saxon times, large native mammals were already much reduced, owing to millennia of dense settlement; but in some areas there were red deer, roe deer, and, rarely, wild swine. These creatures were hunted for meat or for sport but seem not to have been the object of special land management. The Normans introduced the systematic keeping of deer in parks and Forests.

A park is a private wood-pasture on which the owner keeps deer (and often sheep or cattle as well). An essential feature is the *pale*, a special and expensive deer-proof fence which retains the livestock. A park was usually formed, at least in part, out of an existing wood, although treeless parks are known. Although the earliest example, Ongar Great Park (Essex), is just pre-Conquest, parks, like rabbit-warrens,[50] reflect the enterprise of the Normans in seeking alternatives to conventional agriculture on poor-quality land. In 1086 there were about thirty-five parks, presumably for native deer. Shortly after, the wood-pastures of England were transformed by the introduction from the Near East— possibly via the Normans in Sicily—of the fallow deer, *Dama dama*. Fallow proved particularly suitable for parks and Forests and soon became the most common deer in England, as they still are. By 1300, England had roughly 3,200 parks,[51] most of which belonged to the nobility, gentry, bishops, and religious houses; anyone could have a park who could afford it.

Wooded Forests

A Forest is a common on which, in addition to the usual landowner's and commoners' rights, the king or some other magnate has the further right to keep deer. The deer are retained by force of habit and not by a perimeter pale. Forests had their own system of laws, administered by special officials and courts, for the ostensible purpose of protecting the deer. Forest boundaries as defined in medieval documents are those of the jurisdiction, not of the physical Forest, and are of little practical significance. Many historians, unaware that the jurisdiction usually included a much wider area than the Forest itself, have been misled into supposing that Forests covered up to a third of England instead of the roughly 3% which they actually occupied.[52]

Forests appear soon after the Conquest. By 1086 there were about twenty-five Forests; after the introduction of fallow deer more were declared, and by 1200, the zenith of the system, there were about 140. A Forest was much more complex in organization than a park and was the supreme status symbol of the king—who had more than half the Forests but only a few parks—and the greatest nobles.

Forests were not correlated with woodland. Of the two largest concentrations of woodland in England, the Weald had few Forests and the Chilterns had none. There were wooded Forests (e.g., Epping Forest), moorland Forests (e.g., Dartmoor), fenland Forests (e.g., Kesteven, Lincolnshire), and heathland Forests (e.g., most of Sherwood).

Forests were usually adapted from pre-existing commons. The king's deer were added to, but did not replace, the existing grazing and woodcutting rights; nor did declaring a Forest give the king the ownership of the land. In Hatfield Forest (Essex), the king happened to own the land on which he kept his deer; in Epping Forest, he kept deer on other people's land and had no right to graze other animals or to cut trees. Forests, although much less efficient at producing venison than parks, were not merely a hobby of the king and the nobility; they produced a small but much-needed income from fines for violations of Forest Law, and their elaborate bureaucracy with its opportunities for bestowing honorific sinecures, as in the case of Chaucer, was an important part of the royal prestige.

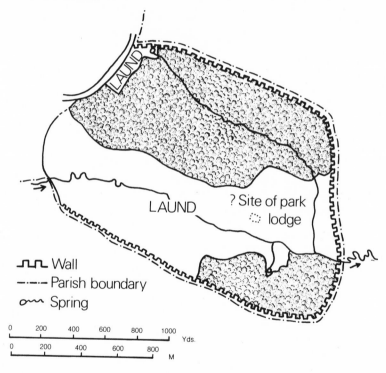

Figure 6
Barnsdale Park (Rutland) as it survived in 1850. A large, early deer-park—first heard of in 1269—surrounded by a wall instead of the more usual pale and compartmented into two coppice-woods and two launds.

86

Wood-Pasture Management

Parks, being very expensive to fence, tended to be more compact in shape than woods. The earlier parks were often rectangular with rounded corners for economy in fencing (Fig. 6).

Many early parks had a boundary with an *internal* ditch, designed to make it easier to keep animals in, the inverse of a woodbank designed to keep animals out. Commons and Forests had no perimeter fence or woodbank and, in consequence, were typically less compact in shape than woods, with concave outlines funnelling out into roads (Fig. 7) and often with enclaves of private land in the interior.

Arrangements for reducing the conflict between grazing and trees were of two kinds: uncompartmented and compartmented. In *uncompartmented* commons, parks, and Forests, the whole area was accessible to livestock at all times. Underwood was produced by pollarding in order to protect the regrowth (see Figs. 1 and 9). Timber trees were usually allowed to grow larger than in woods to reduce the problem of replacement. New trees were usually of distasteful species like oak and arose in the protection of spiny thickets of hawthorn or holly. This practice is still in partial operation in Epping Forest and the New Forest (Hampshire). In *compartmented* commons, parks, and Forests, each wood-pasture was divided into a number of *coppices*, enclosed by woodbanks, which were felled like ordinary woods and were then fenced to keep out livestock until the underwood had grown up sufficiently not to be harmed. Usually there were also permanent grassy areas (*plains*, *launds*) accessible to animals at all times and often containing pollard trees (Fig. 6). Examples are Hatfield and Writtle Forests in Essex (Fig. 7).

A minor use of shoots from pollarded trees was to provide *browse-wood*, iron rations for cattle, sheep, and deer in hard winters. Browse-wood, which is still occasionally cut, is the last survivor in England of the important prehistoric practice of feeding livestock on the leaves and branches of trees.[53]

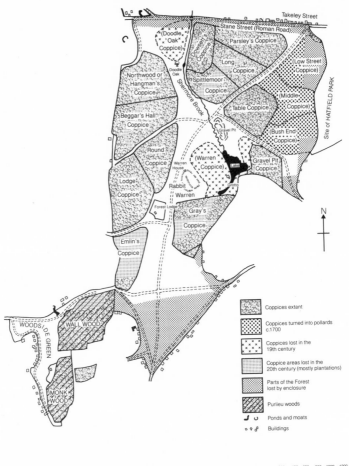

Figure 7

Hatfield Forest (Essex): this is a small Forest compartmented into coppices—of which eleven of the original seventeen survive—and plains. The coppices are surrounded by banks and ditches. Not being a park, the Forest did not have a perimeter fence and, therefore, is not compact in shape. The pillow mounds are earthworks of an artificial rabbit warren. Wall and Monk Woods were *purlieu woods*—outside the legal Forest but subject to some Forest regulations. Woodside Green is a wood-pasture common resembling the Forest plains but not part of the Forest.

88

Later History of Wood-Pastures

Wood-pastures are more stable than might be expected from their apparently conflicting land uses. Commons and Forests have slowly declined since 1350, but losses have usually been due to interference from outside rather than to imbalance between woodcutting and grazing. Epping Forest, for instance, was heavily grazed for more than seven-hundred years, yet the distribution of trees and treeless plains was much the same in 1880 as it had been in 1180. Only in the last hundred years, owing to the suppression of the woodcutting rights—in the mistaken belief that they were a malpractice—and the decline of grazing, has the Forest lost much of its historical character.[54]

The destruction of Forests and commons was most rapid between 1770 and 1860. Influential writers on agriculture and forestry took a narrow view of land ownership and despised the multiple land-uses of wood-pasture, which they failed to understand. In Forest after Forest the common-rights were abolished by Enclosure Acts, and this usually resulted in the destruction of the wood-pasture, as, for example, at Enfield Chase (Middlesex) in 1777 and Hainault Forest (Essex) in 1851.[55]

Parks were a more troublesome and precarious enterprise, and some of them were short-lived, either reverting to ordinary woods or becoming farmland. However, the tradition of deer-parks continued and in later centuries merged with that of landscape parks surrounding country mansions; for instance, the medieval royal park of Woodstock (Oxfordshire) was incorporated into the vast eighteenth-century park of Blenheim Palace.

Wood-Pastures as They are Now

A few wood-pastures have escaped some of these changes and still exist. Rarely do they survive in working order: the supreme example is the small Forest of Hatfield, which still has almost all the complex structures and land-uses of the coppices and plains (Figs. 7 and 8). More often they survive in partial disuse, like Epping Forest, or, as with Woodstock Park, have been put to a different use without destroying their original character. Wooded compartments survive better than plains which, if not destroyed altogether, become overgrown with trees.

Wood-pastures do not preserve the wildwood tree composition to the same extent as do woods. If there is no compartmentation, the more palatable trees—elm, ash, hazel, lime—are often replaced by oak, beech, and hornbeam which are less easily destroyed by browsing.

89

Maple, a tree intermediate in edibility, has a long history of prevalence in compartmented Forests.[56] Uncompartmented wood-pastures do not preserve the herbaceous plants characteristic of ancient woods.

The distinctive feature of wood-pastures, better represented in England than almost anywhere in Europe, is their ancient trees, especially pollards. Examples are the many 500-year-old oaks of Sherwood Forest (Nottinghamshire); the oak pollards of Windsor Forest (Berkshire), up to nine-hundred years old; the four-thousand ancient pollard oaks of Staverton (Suffolk), a miraculous survival of a disused but little-altered medieval park; and the ancient beeches of Burnham and Frithsden (Buckinghamshire) and Felbrigg (Norfolk). Ancient trees have a distinctive beauty, and each of these places, different from the others in its history, has its own special character. They are also the specific habitat of many lichens and of beetles and other animals, some of which are believed to be relics of the wildwood, analogous to the flowering plants specific to ancient woods.[57]

Medieval Woods and Wood-Pastures in the Future

Ancient woods are of value for many scientific, historical, and aesthetic reasons. They are not isolated relics of antiquity but belong to an unbroken tradition extending through the Middle Ages back to the beginnings of civilization (Fig. 2). They have accumulated many diverse meanings through their vicissitudes in different ages. Their value resides in the patchwork of tree communities, the herbaceous plants (including those species that appear after felling), some of the animal life, and archaeological features including ancient stools and pollards. Some features depend on continued coppicing, but many survive, or can be restored after, a period of neglect. Any more drastic change, such as the replanting which has lately become fashionable in England, destroys irreversibly the natural composition and historic structure of a wood.

The value of wood-pastures lies especially in their old trees. The English have long appreciated the beauty of pollards and other ancient trees and of the strange and glamorous landscapes which they form (Fig. 9). Sherwood Forest, Burnham Beeches, and many other wood-pastures are popular places of public resort. We now appreciate the value of old and decaying trees as the specific habitat of particular plants and animals.

Since 1973 the destruction of ancient woods has lessened, partly because of lack of funds but also because of increasing knowledge of and respect for ancient woods. It is widely thought that foresters and farmers

90

have had their fair share of native woodland and ought not to have any more. Legal protection for woods is now more effective, and many woods have been acquired by public or semi-public bodies as nature reserves or places of public recreation. As fuel increases in price, the chief reason for neglecting woods disappears, and more woods are being restored to their medieval management and uses.

Figures 2a - 2d

Medieval woodmanship as still practiced in the Bradfield Woods (West Suffolk). These scenes have been repeated on the same spot at intervals of nine to fifteen years for at least seven centuries. Before the Dissolution, the woods belonged to Bury St. Edmund's Abbey. They are now owned by the Royal Society for Nature Conservation. (Photographs by W. H. Palmer)

Fig. 2a

Newly-felled underwood. Cut poles, which in this part of the wood are chiefly of ash, have been stacked awaiting transport. Scattered timber trees of oak. In background is uncut underwood of two different ages of regrowth. (March, 1971)

Fig. 2b

Same scene as in Fig. 2.a, two years later (March, 1973), showing regrowth of underwood. This part of the wood was felled again in 1981 after ten years' regrowth.

Fig. 2c

Coppice stool of ash, repeatedly cut over several centuries and now some seven feet in diameter (March, 1971).

Fig. 2d
Similar ancient stool of ash, showing poles of some fifteen years' growth since
last felling (March, 1971).

Figure 3

Medieval—or earlier—boundary bank, with external ditch, separating wood from field. Note pollard tree on edge of ditch; underwood on bank just felled; one years' growth in left foreground; old underwood in left background (Bradfield Woods, February, 1973).

Figure 4

Medieval timber-frame house at Kersey (Suffolk). The panels between the timbers are filled with wattle-and-daub. The whole of the frame was originally visible; the plaster which now hides parts of it is a later addition.

Figure 8

The central plain of Hatfield Forest, still in its medieval state with grassland, pollard oak and ash trees, and tracts of hawthorn scrub. Behind the scrub, and clearly demarcated from it, is one of the coppices (February, 1977).

Figure 9

Staverton Park (East Suffolk): this early deer-park of the uncompartmented type still has its medieval trees. There are some four thousand of these ancient pollard oaks which were last cut in the eighteenth century (May, 1982).

NOTES

The American parallels in this paper result from a tour financed by the Royal Society of London. It is a pleasure to acknowledge the generous help given me by many American friends, including Dr. Susan P. Bratton, Professor Abbott L. Cummings, Dr. David R. Houston, Dr. Hugh Raup, Dr. David Smith, Dr. Peter S. White, and Dr. Gordon G. Whitney.

[1] This tradition of conservation survived into the seventeenth century and was carried over for a short time by the settlers of New England. See Abbott L. Cummings, *The Framed Houses of Massachusetts Bay, 1625-1725* (Cambridge, MA: Belknap, 1979), p. 50.

[2] To be a timber, a stem usually has to be at least six in. in diameter at the base.

[3] In England most of the later hedges are known, and the earlier assumed, to have been deliberately planted. Americans generally suppose that their fence-rows have arisen by accident.

[4] Hedges and non-woodland trees are largely outside the scope of this paper. See Oliver Rackham, "Hedgerow Trees: Their History, Conservation, and Renewal," *Arboricultural Journal*, 3 (1977), 169-77.

[5] Oliver Rackham, *Ancient Woodland: Its History, Vegetation and Uses in England* (London: Edward Arnold, 1980), pp. 159-60.

[6] E. Lucy Braun, *Deciduous Forests of Eastern North America* (Philadelphia: Blakiston, 1950).

[7] Rackham, *Ancient Woodland*, pp. 99-103.

[8] Oliver Rackham, *Trees and Woodland in the British Landscape* (London: Dent, 1976), p. 48.

[9] Attention is drawn to two errors prevalent among scholars: First, the notion that "scrub"—an early phase in the establishment of secondary woodland—was the permanent vegetation of much of Anglo-Saxon and medieval England; second, the confusion of "regeneration"—the growth of a new generation of trees within an existing wood—with the appearance of secondary woodland on previously unwooded land.

[10] Rackham, *Ancient Woodland*, pp. 51-52, 130, passim.

[11] Paul J. Drury and Warwick Rodwell, "Settlement in the Later Iron Age and Roman Periods," in *Archaeology in Essex to A.D. 1500*, ed. D. G. Buckley, Council for British Archaeology Research Report, 34 (London, 1980), pp. 59-75.

[12] Rackham, *Ancient Woodland*, pp. 127-33.

[13] W. G. Hoskins, *Fieldwork in Local History* (London: Faber, 1967), pp. 34-40; Christopher C. Taylor, *Dorset* (London: Hodder & Stoughton, 1970), pp. 47-72.

[14] For example, see John C. Goodlett, *Vegetation Adjacent to the Border of the Wisconsin Drift in Potter County, Pennsylvania*, Harvard Forest Bulletin, 25 (Peterham, MA, 1954), pp. 48-56.

[15] Detailed analysis may be found in Rackham, *Ancient Woodland*, pp. 112-27.

[16] See note 12.

[17] Rackham, *Ancient Woodland*, pp. 133-34.

[18] Oliver Rackham, *Hayley Wood: Its History and Ecology* (Cambridge: Cambridgeshire & Isle of Ely Naturalists' Trust, 1975), pp. 9-48.

[19] Rackham, *Hayley Wood*, pp. 9-48.

[20] Rackham, *Trees and Woodland*, pp. 66-68.

[21] Rackham, *Trees and Woodland*, pp. 63-64.

[22] Rackham, *Ancient Woodland*, pp. 63-65.

[23] See note 18.

[24] Rackham, *Hayley Wood*, p. 29; *Trees and Woodland*, pp. 70-71.

[25] Rackham, *Ancient Woodland*, p. 170.

[26] Charles Dickens, *American Notes* (1842).

[27] Rackham, *Ancient Woodland*, pp. 155-56.

[28] Rackham, *Ancient Woodland*, pp. 157-58.

[29] Cecil A. Hewett, *English Historic Carpentry* (Chichester: Phillimore, 1980).

[30] Public Record Office, MS. E178/4548.

[31] Oliver Rackham, "Grundle House: On the Quantities of Timber in Certain East Anglian Buildings in Relation to Local Supplies," *Vernacular Architecture*, 3 (1972), 3-10.

[32] Rackham, *Ancient Woodland*, pp. 152-53.

[33] Rackham, *Ancient Woodland*, pp. 163-64.

[34] Vanessa Parker, *The Making of Kings Lynn* (London, Phillimore, 1971).

[35] Cyril E. Hart, *Royal Forest: A History of Dean's Woods as Producers of Timber* (Oxford: Clarendon, 1966).

[36] Rackham, *Ancient Woodland*, pp. 151-52.

[37] L. F. Salzman, *Building in England down to 1540* (Oxford: Clarendon, 1952), pp. 244-45.

[38] Bryan Latham, *Timber: Its Development and Distribution* (London: Harrap, 1957), pp. 23-31.

[39] Oliver Rackham, "The Growing and Transport of Timber and Underwood," in *Woodworking Techniques Before 1500 A.D.*, ed. Sean McGrail, BAR International Series 129 (Oxford: British Archaeological Repts., 1982), pp. 199-218.

[40] Cummings, *The Framed Houses of Massachusetts Bay*, pp. 46-47.

[41] Rackham, *Trees and Woodland*, p. 174; *Ancient Woodland*, p. ix.

[42] Rackham, *Ancient Woodland*, p. 241.

[43] Rackham, *Ancient Woodland*, chaps. 20, 21.

[44] Rackham, *Ancient Woodland*, chaps. 16, 19.

[45] Rackham, *Trees and Woodland*, p. 29.

[46] Rackham, *Ancient Woodland*, p. 15. In New England, coppicing has left surprisingly little evidence in the present structure of the woods, but I have occasionally found stools of a size appropriate to 250 years' coppicing (as red

maple up to 5 ft. 5 in. diameter in Harvard Forest, Petersham, MA). Stools of American chestnut, now dead, may be found bigger than this, but their significance is uncertain, because American chestnut, like American basswood, is "self-coppicing" and can form giant stools even in wildwood (as in the Great Smoky Mountains).

⁴⁷ Rackham, *Ancient Woodland*, pp. 51-56.

⁴⁸ George F. Peterken, "A Method of Assessing Woodland Flora for Conservation Using Indicator Species," *Biological Conservation*, 6 (1974), 239-45.

⁴⁹ In New England the word "common" is used in the more restricted sense of an area of public land in the middle of a town. Such village commons are known in England as *greens* or *tyes*.

⁵⁰ John Sheail, *Rabbits and Their History* (Newton Abbot, Devon: David & Charles, 1971).

⁵¹ Rackham, *Ancient Woodland*, pp. 190-91.

⁵² Rackham, *Ancient Woodland*, pp. 190-91.

⁵³ Wood-pasture was in decline at the time of the colonization of North America, and as far as I am aware was never formally introduced there. Although the United States lacks any direct descendant of the English wood-pasture tradition, there are a number of analogies. Parts of the city of Kalamazoo (in and around Pioneer Cemetery and on the campus of Western Michigan University) look curiously like an uncompartmented park or Forest, with great oaks (*Quercus macrocarpa*) widely spaced. The oaks, which date from before any white man saw the area, are relics of what has been interpreted as a system of wood-pasture managed by Indians in favor of the native game animals: see Bernard C. Peters, "Michigan's Oak Openings: Pioneer Perceptions of a Vegetative Landscape," *Journal of Forest History*, (Jan. 1978), 19-23. The famous grassy balds of the Great Smoky Mountains are surrounded by scattered ancient trees of buckeye and yellow birch, now embedded in young secondary woodland; they appear to be the equivalent of launds in a wood-pasture system begun by white men in the nineteenth century: Mary M. Lindsay and Susan P. Bratton, "Grassy Balds of the Great Smoky Mountains: Their History and Flora in Relation to Potential Management," *Environmental Management*, 3 (1979), 417-30. In Kalamazoo and the Smokies, as in Epping Forest and other English wood-pastures, cessation of grazing causes the grassland to turn rapidly into secondary woodland.

⁵⁴ Oliver Rackham, "Archaeology and Land-Use History," in *Epping Forest—The Natural Aspect?*, ed. D. Corke, *Essex Naturalist*, n.s. 2 (1978), pp. 16-57.

⁵⁵ Rackham, *Ancient Woodland*, p. 185.

⁵⁶ Rackham, *Ancient Woodland*, pp. 207, 241-42.

⁵⁷ Francis Rose and P. W. James, "The Corticolous and Lignicolous [Lichen] Species of the New Forest, Hampshire," *Lichenologist*, 6 (1974), 1-72.

101

PART II:
FORMING AND TRANSFORMING AGRICULTURAL
SYSTEMS
IN TEMPERATE EUROPE

FIELD EDGE, FOREST EDGE:
EARLY MEDIEVAL SOCIAL CHANGE
AND RESOURCE ALLOCATION

KATHLEEN BIDDICK

Thus behind the classic seigneurie our
inquiry reveals long and obscure beginnings.[1]

Recent archaeological research demonstrates increasingly that traditional society in northwestern Europe passed a watershed in the seventh and eighth centuries.[2] During this period political, economic, and social relations shifted dramatically, marking a major episode in the history of Europe as a developing area in the first millennium after Christ. Transformation of such magnitude is of interest to students of social and ecological change and provides fertile ground for exploring the links between social structure and resource organization in traditional agricultural systems.

Traditionally, historians and archaeologists have explained change in resource organization by environmental and population pressure models. An unexplored question, however, is whether the reorganization of resource allocation was a cause or consequence of social change. My own research on animal husbandry and pastoral land use in a local area over two millennia has convinced me that social change requires exploration as a significant variable in our models.[3] Admittedly, the study of the ecological impact of social change is an exceedingly

105

difficult and complex puzzle, only a few pieces of which we can position accurately. The hypothesis and model presented here, therefore, are offered in the spirit of posing a problem and suggesting some guidelines for future research.

As a working hypothesis, I propose that the political transformation and social change of the seventh and eighth centuries broke up systems of territorial organization of great antiquity. These territorial structures were firmly based on an extensive rather than intensive form of pastoral resource utilization. Since the evidence for this is still sparse, I will use both prehistoric and historical illustrations in discussion.

The core areas of northwestern Europe in the last centuries of the first millennium B.C. provide good comparative material for the early medieval period.[4] Both periods share a similar history—complex, chiefdom-like societies evolved into more sophisticated, simple-state social systems.[5] In fact, a comparative study tells much about social change in each period.

Archaeology has made an enormous contribution to understanding the structure of these societies, and our current concepts depart radically from the traditional textbook model of the "tribe." The societies of the late first millennium B.C. and the mid first millennium after Christ were actually chiefdom-like societies. As a type of social organization, chiefdoms were structured quite differently from tribes. They were stratified by rank and grouped hierarchically. Tribes, in contrast, were egalitarian, kin-based societies that were organized segmentally.[6] Chiefdom societies had an office of chief open only by rank ascription to recognized aristocratic lineages, and kinship ethic operated only within this upper stratum.[7]

Relative status and dominance among the lineages were determined by competition in material wealth. This inherent rank-status competition produced expansive and outward-looking communities that maintained long-distance exchange with neighboring chiefdoms and fought for control over rights to surplus production and tribute. The ruling elite maintained itself by the regular flow of agricultural goods and services from peasant communities.[8] The more complex the chiefdom, the more elaborately this flow was organized; the types of "soke" that Professor Jones has reconstructed in his multiple estate model describe a model for the flow of goods and services in a complex chiefdom.[9] Chiefdoms not only included peasants—that is, farmers who supported their own household economies as well as a political economy structured by a non-local elite—they also employed slave labor to exploit specialized resources which further aggrandized the elite, or extended long-distance exchange contacts.[10]

We know from ethno-historical material that the competitive, expansionistic, and political side of chiefdoms was counterpoised by an extremely rationalized organization of subsistence that ensured the smooth flow of goods and services to the elite. The organization of resources was carried out by structuring the landscape into basic resource units.[11] The unit was a repetitive module that contained the full range of resources used in the subsistence economy and varied in size, though not in its basic resource composition. Depending on the executive complexity of the chiefdom, the basic unit could be combined with others of its kind into intermediate administrative districts for the collection of goods and services. These districts were in turn organized into regional territories. The hierarchical regional territories reconstructed from historical documents by Professor Jones are possible models for chiefdom-like territories.[12]

In Britain, evidence for the existence of such territories is growing. The first widespread divisions of the landscape and definition of resource areas occurred around the second millennium B.C.[13] The elaborate division of the landscape on Dartmoor in southwestern England defined arable, river-valley grazing areas and an intercommoning area for a possible six to seven territorial units.[14] Fragments of analogous landscapes have also been located in Sussex, the Midlands, and along the fen-edge in eastern England. Portions of a large-scale system of pasture allotment along the Peterborough fen-edge have been excavated at the Fengate sites.[15]

These territorial systems did not remain fixed through time; shifts in power and wealth and the advance and decline of regional areas are as much a part of prehistory as history. A certain land-use element—a large tract of rough pasture or woodland incorporated within regional units— does stand out, however, in the prehistoric and historic landscapes, reconstructions of which have been attempted using various methodologies and different kinds of evidence.[16] How were these tracts of pastoral resources used? Were they seasonal transhumance areas? What types of woodland management regimes were practiced? Answers to such questions will allow us to evaluate the potential of woodland areas as pastoral resources.[17]

What social role did these areas serve, if they were used as intercommoning areas for several communities? They could have served as political buffer zones between adjoining social groups. This is suggested in Caesar's familiar description of the Suevi: "It was their greatest glory to lay waste the frontiers of their neighbors for as wide a distance as possible, considering this real evidence of their prowess."[18] These rough grazing areas could also have served as ecological buffers for the cereal sector of agricultural production. They could be used for temporary, emergency cultivation—a common feature of later shieling use in trans-humance areas of Scotland.[19] In social systems that do not have a redis-tributive mechanism for agricultural products, the existence of these buffer zones is critical for readjusting shortages in times of local agri-cultural crisis.

The evolution from chiefdom social organization to more central-ized, simple-state systems with ideological and material access to the coercive use of force allows greater territorial integration. The integra-tion, in turn, releases political frontiers for enclosure and development. The development of market systems capable of redistributing agricultural produce can promote greater agricultural specialization, since the ex-change of produce may be used to restore balances. The release of pastoral resource areas and the enlarged scope for economic specializa-tion can stimulate technological innovation.

The palaeobotanical record for the latter part of the first millen-nium B.C. in England may bear out such social interpretation[20] (see Fig. 1). The record suggests that major and widespread woodland clearance episodes of the mid-first millennium B.C. were followed by further encroachment, and that by the second century B.C. pastoral areas were being turned over to arable land use.

During the last centuries of the first millennium B.C., other indications of resource reorganization appeared. Fields were either reorganized in the later Iron Age—as at Ashville, Oxfordshire, or Little Waltham, Sussex—or laid out in new areas—such as on the heavier clay soils of the West Riding, Yorkshire.[21] The economic relations to pastoral resources also seem to have shifted. The ubiquitous smaller hillforts which garrisoned pastoral resources across the landscape were aban-doned as territorial central places came to predominate.[22] At the same time there was a proliferation of specialist stock enclosures, the most famous but under-investigated type being the banjo enclosure.[23] The various types of enclosure suggest a more intensive rather than extensive approach to livestock husbandry. Livestock managers in the later Iron Age were able to breed selectively for true fine wool, short wools, and the common hairy wools—a range of wool types and selective developments usually attributed to the medieval period.[24]

Change in resource use was accompanied by a settlement shuffle. A growing body of evidence suggests the existence of discontinuity between mid Iron Age and later Iron Age settlement.[25] Patterns in other aspects of the material culture also shift. The distribution networks of pottery change;[26] a genuine market system evolved in southeastern England;[27] and technical innovations such as the improved iron shares of

108

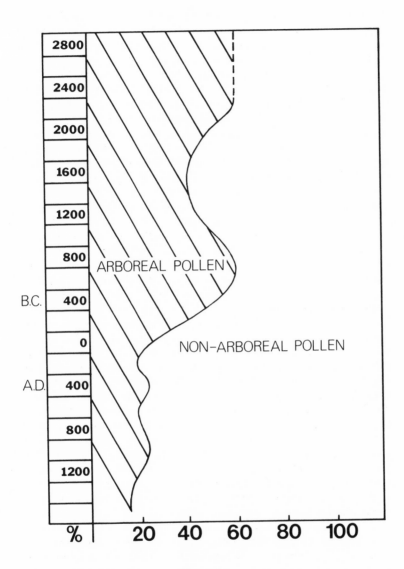

Figure 1
Composite graph of forest clearance episodes in Britain

the later Iron Age eased the cultivation of heavier soils.[28] These strands of evidence suggest that in southern Britain changes in the configuration of territory and resource accompanied the transformation of social structure in the last two centuries of the first millennium B.C.

We can now turn to a consideration of seventh and eighth century England. It is probable that here we are dealing once again with competing chiefdom-like social groups that contract and expand in their competitive struggles for hegemony.[29] A shaft of light falls on these social groups in a document, the *Tribal Hidage*, dated by Wendy Davies to the period A.D. 670-90.[30] The archaeologist Haio Vierck has argued persuasively, on the grounds of material culture and environmental setting, for placing the social aggregates enumerated in the document into regional areas. The location of rough grazing or woodland zones in these areas is an aspect of his argument that I would like to develop here.

The question must be raised again for the historical context: were these areas used for the seasonal feeding of livestock? In the end, this question must be settled by archaeological techniques; however, the inference has already been made that these rough grazing/woodland zones were transhumance areas. In a very interesting study of the detached portions of hundreds in the Warwickshire-Avon area of the Midlands, W. J. Forde has traced a pattern between mother hundreds and their links with detached pieces in the "intercommoning area."[31] Forde has interpreted the mutually exclusive patterns that these detached portions describe as political areas of the *Tomsetna, Feppingas* and *Stoppingas* of the *Tribal Hidage*. A similar study based on historical reconstruction from thirteenth century documents isolates analogous, discrete, intercommoning areas in the silt and peat fens.[32] The Weald of Kent and Sussex is another area with comparable patterns as reconstructed from historical documents.[33] The reconstructions suggest that the pastoral resource areas and intercommoning patterns within these areas were formative in structuring territorial units. The patterns are preserved as archaeological layers in later historical documentation, by which time the system had already functionally disintegrated. How these coherent patterns grew incoherent may have to do, once again, with the consequences of the transformation of traditional chiefly power.

For Anglo-Saxon dynastic chiefs in the seventh century, granting land—or, rather, the chiefly rights over goods and services from this land—to the Church in perpetuity was a radical catalyst in promoting social change. The very act of granting something in perpetuity in return for a non-material reward was a radical step, for chiefly power does not know proprietary rights over land. Through interaction with and support of the bishops of the Roman mission to England, a radical change in the configuration of power, property, and social organization was effected.

In granting perpetual rights to land, the chiefs accrued a new source of symbolic and material power over the base of the economy, which reinforced their overlordship. The connection between the act of granting and power was maintained as chiefly kingdoms moved toward simple-state systems under Mercian hegemony in the later part of the eighth century. Mercians monopolized the right to make perpetual grants, taking this authority away from client chiefs who were undergoing a sharp decline in their own power.[34] By assuming the right to make grants of land outside their own Mercian territories, Aethelbald and Offa underscored their radical, complex lordship.[35] Offa was then able to extend the perpetual grant to non-ecclesiastical personages. This act both broadened the scope of his power and lined his pocket. The extension of granting marked a critical turning point. As Anglo-Saxon social systems shifted from chiefly hegemonies to simple-state systems, and the non-ecclesiastical elite gained access to tenure, the structure of the estates themselves, as can be traced through documents and archaeology, changed.

The restructuring of estate territories in the Dark Ages is a new area of investigation in which much research remains to be done. Fortunately, Dr. Wendy Davies has explored a case study in her work on the early charter material in the *Liber Landavensis*.[36] The earliest grants of land made to the church in the sixth and seventh centuries are described as large territorial units, or *agri*. As grants proliferated in the eighth century and were extended to members of the lay elite, this pattern changed sharply. After A.D. 780, only small estates of less than 250 acres were granted, and these were defined in terms of specific settlements. A new topography of estates emerged as tenurial structure became disengaged from territorial structure.[37]

Social and ecological implications are built into this disengagement. As cohesive territorial units broke down, it became more pressing to link local units with the central authority by new administrative means. The hundred (of whose territorial antiquity I am convinced) became the administrative vehicle for distributing fiscal and military requirements evenly across the landscape and for promoting the new distribution network based on markets.[38] Future research, I believe, will illumine how in the ninth century a formal administrative grid was laid over districts which previously had functioned in the collection of goods and services and the definition of access to resources under chiefdoms.

During the period that estate structure was changing, other patterns in the material record also shifted. The poly-focal settlement pattern of the earlier Anglo-Saxon period shuffled during the eighth century.[39]

111

The early Anglo-Saxon settlements of Bishopstone (Sussex), Chalton (Hampshire), New Wintles (Oxfordshire), and West Stow (Suffolk) were all abandoned during the eighth century.[40] The older exchange network serviced by ports of trade also fell out of use. Hamwih, for instance, declined after the mid eighth century, although fresh activity after this hiatus is recorded for a short period in the early ninth century.[41] A new network of intermediary lordship was also promoted by social change, as may be seen in the growing importance of ealdorman and the manorial complex at the local level.[42]

The ecological implications of this transformation can be suggested by using the Weald as an example. The charter of Eadwulf of Kent granting Wealden swine pasture to St. Andrew's, Rochester (A.D. 746) is a good starting point.[43] In his parcelling-out activities, Eadwulf was subtracting from the ancient commons and allotting parcels to emerging ecclesiastical estate systems. Within about a hundred years, the memory of an integral commons faded from the written record. By the ninth century the commons had been transformed into a maze of dens appendant to a specific manor. By the time of *Domesday Book*, the old pannage system was largely artifactual; the breakdown of the ancient commons opened them up for tenurial and economic development. By the thirteenth century a new regionalism had already taken shape, with specialized cattle husbandry being practiced in the Western Weald and with the exploitation of timber in the Eastern Weald.[44]

The model sketched in this paper is intended to stimulate discussion about the politics and ecology of the breakup and reform of landscape units. The evolution of increasingly complex social organization seems to have a marked impact on the management and organization of territorial structures and on the patterning of subsistence resources.[45] As sophisticated modes of social integration open political and ecological buffer zones for development, resources are made available and permit intensive exploitation. This encourages specialization, and markets help to adjust the imbalances that specialization produces.

The more sophisticated social organization that developed in the eighth century in southern England and in France multiplied the positions of power at intermediate levels. The new layer of lordship had a long-term effect on the local organization of resources. We can look for technical innovation in this reorganization; it is not surprising that in the time of Offa we begin to find new agricultural installations, such as the water mill.[46] On the basis of this model, it can be predicted that some of the traditional earmarks of medieval agricultural intensification, such as open-field systems, use of heavy ploughs, and more intensive (but not necessarily better) animal management, would be adopted after this political transformation. The ninth century, then, marks an agricultural watershed. In England, improvements in the technology of estate management in the next two centuries prepared the way for productivity in the late twelfth and early thirteenth centuries. The question—whether or not the elite managers of this later period exhausted resources in short-term efforts to aggrandize themselves—is an area of research that carries our investigation into later periods.

NOTES

[1] Marc Bloch, "The Rise of Dependent Cultivation and Seignorial Institutions," in *The Cambridge Economic History of Europe*, ed. M. M. Postan, 2nd ed. (Cambridge, 1966), 1, p. 290.

[2] Over the past decade, archaeologists have moved beyond constructing typologies for metalwork, pottery, and glass to uncover how the communities of Dark Age Europe were internally articulated, linked on regional levels, and how they structured communications, exchange, and agricultural and craft production. Examples of change and transformation appear in this volume; see Richard Hodges, David Hall, Walter E. Berry, and Pamela Crabtree. More examples will be cited in the course of this essay.

[3] Kathleen Biddick, "Animal Husbandry and Pastoral Land Use on the Fen-Edge, Peterborough, England: An Archaeological and Historical Reconstruction (2500 B.C. - A.D. 1350)." Diss. University of Toronto 1982. See also Elizabeth Brumfiel, "Regional Growth in the Eastern Valley of Mexico: A Test of the 'Population Pressure' Hypothesis," in *The Early Meso American Village*, ed. Kent Flannery (New York, 1976), pp. 234-49 for a study of how population pressure can be induced in developing social systems without real change in the population itself. For a broader consideration of social complexity and change, see Kent Flannery, "The Cultural Evolution of Civilizations," *Annual Review of Ecology and Systematics*, 3 (1972), 398-426.

[4] Social competition intensified in the last quarter of the first millennium across much of northwestern Europe. Reorientation of settlement around central places *(oppida)* is a primary marker of changing complexity in these core areas. Through these central places, Mediterranean luxury goods were redistributed, and craft manufacture, ritual, and power were regulated. An overview of this development in respective regional areas appeared in *Oppida in Barbarian Europe*, ed. B. Cunliffe and T. Rowley, British Archaeological Reports, supp. ser., no. 2 (Oxford, 1976). The regional approach of this collection of papers is critical, since it helps to establish the range of variability of timing, rhythm, and intensity that this change could take on. For some recent thoughts on the radical nature of social reorganization in this period in southern England, see Richard Reece, "Bagendon," *Current Archaeology*, no. 75 (1981), 103-04. Further references appear in n. 22.

[5] Labels such as "complex chiefdom" and "tribe" are for perceptual convenience and do not constitute rigid compartments of social organization. A

comprehensive reappraisal of the archaeology and anthropology of complex chiefdoms is contained in Timothy Earle, "Economic and Social Organization of a Complex Chiefdom," *Anthropology Papers, Museum of Anthropology, University of Michigan*, no. 63 (1978).

[6] For a clear discussion of a complicated topic, see Marshall D. Sahlins, *Tribesmen* (Englewood Cliffs, NJ, 1968), pp. 10-13, 20-21. See also his discussion of the relations between household economies and political structures in "Poor Man, Rich Man, Big-Man, Chief: Political Types in Melanesia and Polynesia," *Comparative Studies in Society and History*, 5 (1962-63), 285-303, esp. p. 300: "the sources of any primitive political organization is decided here, in the control that can be developed over household economies."

[7] For examples of this: "Complex Chiefdoms," passim.

[8] It is useful to consider peasants and their relations to closed or open elite systems. This is a point that may be developed in the future in considering the changing role of the peasant in pre-feudal and feudal systems in northwestern Europe. For a standard, comprehensive introduction to peasants, see Eric R. Wolf, *Peasants* (Englewood Cliffs, NJ, 1966).

[9] See his article in this volume and G. R. J. Jones, "Multiple Estates and Early Settlement," in *Medieval Settlement*, ed. P. H. Sawyer (London, 1976), pp. 15-40.

[10] For an ethno-historical illustration of the role of slavery and exchange, see Emmanuel Terray, "Long-Distance Exchange and the Formation of the State: The Case of the Abron Kingdom of Gyaman," in *Economy and Society*, 3 (1974), 34-45.

[11] Earle, in "Complex Chiefdoms," offers a good ecological discussion of this territory-as-resource-module in complex chiefdoms.

[12] See n. 7 for reference to the research of G. R. J. Jones. See also G. W. S. Barrow, "Pre-feudal Scotland: Shires and Thanes," in *The Kingdom of the Scots: Government, Church and Society from the Eleventh to the Fourteenth Centuries*, ed. G. W. S. Barrow (London, 1973), pp. 7-68.

[13] Here I exclude earlier land-use divisions defined by Neolithic burial areas. For this, see G. J. Wainwright, "Religion and Settlement in Wessex, c. 3000 - 1700 B.C.," in *Recent Work in Rural Archaeology*, ed. P. J. Fowler (Bradford-on-Avon, 1975), pp. 57-71.

[14] For the Dartmoor studies, see A. Fleming, "The Prehistoric Landscape of Dartmoor - Part I: South Dartmoor," *Proceedings of the Prehistoric Society*, 44 (1978), 97-123 and "The Dartmoor Reeve Project," *Current Archaeology*, no. 67 (1979), 234-37.

[15] The report on the excavations of a fragment of a large-scale ditch system also includes an overview of other landscape divisions so far observed in Britain: Francis Pryor, *Excavation at Fengate, Peterborough, England: The Third Report*. Royal Ontario Museum Archaeological Monograph no. 3 and Northamptonshire Archaeological Society Monograph no. 1 (Toronto, 1980), esp. pp. 180-86.

[16] This is suggested by archaeological reconstruction at Dartmoor: see Fleming, "The Prehistoric Landscape"; by botanical investigation for Angeln: reported by Wendy Davies and Haio Vierck in "The Contexts of the Tribal

Hidage: Social Aggregates and Settlement Patterns," *Frühmittelalterliche Studien*, 8 (1974), 241-87; in documentary reconstruction: Jones, "Multiple Estates and Early Settlements"; and in comparative studies: Christopher Peebles and Susan M. Kush, "Some Archaeological Correlates of Ranked Societies," *American Antiquity*, 42 (1977), p. 444, where the authors suggest that warfare among chiefdoms in the southeastern United States was engaged in for "maintenance of boundaries and the perpetuation of large areas of forest as buffer zones to deer hunting."

[17] For the use of woodland as pasture area, see Rackham in this volume.

[18] Cited by Vierck, "Tribal Hidage," p. 246 from Caesar, *De Bello Gallico*, 4.3.

[19] Ronald Miller, "Land Use by Summer Shielings," *Scottish Studies*, 11 (1967), p. 200.

[20] The prehistoric graph of dated clearance horizons published by Richard Bradley in *The Prehistoric Settlement of Britain* (London, 1978), figs. 2 and 3, p. 14, has been extended into the historic period. The radio-carbondated pollen profiles used in constructing this graph are cited at length in Biddick, "Animal Husbandry," p. 197. A range of other types of evidence corroborates expansive clearance toward the end of the first millennium B.C.: see P. J. Osborne, "Insect Evidence for the Effect of Man on the Lowland Landscape," in *The Effect of Man on the Landscape: The Lowland Zone*, ed. S. Limbrey and J. G. Evans, Council for British Archaeology Research Report no. 21 (London, 1978), pp. 32-34; and Christopher Smith, "The Landscape and Natural History of Iron Age Settlement on the Trent Gravels," in *Lowland Iron Age Communities*, ed. B. Cunliffe and T. Rowley, British Archaeological Reports, supp. ser., no. 48 (Oxford, 1978), pp. 91-102.

[21] For the Ashville evidence see: *The Excavation of an Iron Age Settlement, Bronze Age Ring-Ditches and Roman Features at Ashville Trading Estate, Abingdon, Oxfordshire*, ed. Michael Parrington, Council for British Archaeology Research Report, no. 28 (London, 1978), p. 109. For Little Waltham, Sussex see: Paul Drury, "Little Waltham and Pre-Belgic Iron Age Settlement in Essex," in *Lowland Iron Age Communities*, pp. 43-76, esp. p. 65. For more controversial evidence for field systems detected by aerial photography on the limestone and sandstone of South and West Yorkshire and on the Bunter Sandstone formations between Doncaster and Nottingham, see Derrick Riley, "Air Photography Based on Sheffield," *Current Archaeology*, no. 66 (1979), 219-22.

[22] There is an enormous literature on hillforts. Only one basic reference guide will be cited here: *Hillforts: Later Prehistoric Earthworks in Britain and Ireland*, ed. D. W. Harding (London, 1976). For the study of hierarchization of hillforts, see Ian Hodder, "Simulating the Growth of Hierarchies," in *Transformations: Mathematical Approaches to Cultural Change*, ed. C. Renfrew and K. L. Cooke (New York, 1978), pp. 29-55. Oppida are currently under critical reappraisal by archaeologists: see *Oppida in Barbarian Europe*, ed. B. Cunliffe and T. Rowley, esp. the essay by W. Rodwell, "Oppida and the Rise of Belgic Power in Southeastern England," pp. 181-366.

[23] See Bradley, *The Prehistoric Settlement of Britain*, p. 48.

[24] J. P. Wild, *The Textiles from Vindolanda 1973-75* (Vindolanda Trust, Bardon Mill, Hexham, 1977), p. 30, summarizes the specialist analysis of textile fibers made by M. L. Ryder: "there is evidence in the Vindolanda wools for selective breeding of flocks to improve the quality of the fleece. Iron Age farmers, however, were already adept at selective breeding. The wool-types represented at Vindolanda range from short-wool and true fine wool to hairy wool; they appear together in the same textiles."

[25] Iron Age settlement in the later first millennium B.C. could range from isolated farms to agglomeration of houses of village proportions, located in a variety of subsoils including heavy clays. The actual distribution of lower level rural settlement in the Mid-Later Iron age bears an interesting analogy to Early Saxon rural settlement. This settlement pattern has been identified as poly-focal. For a loose definition of this word see C. C. Taylor, "The Anglo-Saxon Country-side," in *Anglo-Saxon Settlement and the Landscape*, ed. T. Rowley, British Archaeological Reports, no. 6 (Oxford, 1974), p. 9: "there are indications that many of the apparently nucleated villages in the country were, at an early period, not nucleated at all, but were composed of two, three, or more distinct small units or groups of farmsteads, sometimes up to 1 km (just over half a mile) apart." The shifts in settlement in the second century B.C. include: movement toward enclosing unenclosed settlement with ditches and palisades; incorporation of new economic components into the settlement in the form of pastoral enclosures; proliferation of droveways; planned settlements, even at the lower levels of rural settlement (see *The Excavaction of an Iron Age Settlement* [n. 21 above], p. 39); and abandonment of settlement—phenomena no longer attributed simply to the political disturbances of the Roman invasion. See Biddick, "Animal Husbandry," pp. 202-04.

[26] For Ashville and Farmoor, Iron Age rural sites in Oxfordshire, for example, see: in *Lowland Iron Age Communities*, G. Lambrick, "Iron Age Settlements in the Upper Thames Valley," p. 111 and fig. 2; and Drury, "Little Waltham," pp. 59-73. For Bishopstone, Sussex, see: Sue Hamilton, "The Iron Age Pottery," in *Excavations at Bishopstone*, ed. M. Bell, Sussex Archaeological Collections, 115 (1977), pp. 83-117. The Bishopstone report is a good source of new methodology for the examination of residual coarse wares frequently excavated from unsealed deposits on Iron Age rural sites.

[27] The development of a marketing system at the end of the first millennium B.C. is in need of further study. For two representative overviews, see: W. Rodwell, "Trinovantian Towns and Their Setting," in *Small Towns in Roman Britain*, ed. W. Rodwell and T. Rowley, British Archaeological Reports, no. 15 (Oxford, 1975), pp. 85-102; and Ian Hodder, "The Human Geography of Roman Britain," in *An Historical Geography of England and Wales*, ed. R. A. Dodgshon and R. A. Butlin (New York, 1978), pp. 29-55. In this essay, Hodder emphasizes the degree to which pre-existing Iron Age settlement patterned the Roman distribution.

[28] As more attention is given to social and economic change in southeastern Britain before the Roman occupation, it will be easier to appraise technological innovation. In this respect, the development of interchangeable shares for ards

should be examined.

[29] See Biddick, "Animal Husbandry," ch. 3.

[30] Davies and Vierck, "Tribal Hidage," p. 227.

[31] W. J. Forde, "Some Settlement Patterns in the Central Region of the Warwickshire Avon," in *Medieval Settlement*, pp. 274-94.

[32] Nellie Neilson, "A Terrier of Fleet, Lincolnshire," in *Records of Social and Economic History of England and Wales*, 4 (Oxford, 1920): "the Cambridgeshire hundred of Wisbeach, west of the marshland, within the liberty of Ely, offers interesting evidence of intercommoning of all the vills included within the hundred and of the rating of the hundred as a unit in common rights and duties," p. xxi.

[33] K. P. Witney, *The Jutish Forest* (London, 1976).

[34] Cyril Hart, "The Kingdom of Mercia," in *Mercian Studies*, ed. A. Dornier (Leicester, 1977), pp. 43-61, esp. p. 43: "there is no evidence that any of these small princely houses survived later than the end of the seventh century, and most of the larger provincial dynasties became extinct during the reign of Offa."

[35] Eric John, "'Orbis Britanniae' and the Anglo-Saxon Kings," in *Orbis Britanniae*, ed. Eric John (Leicester, 1966), p. 26.

[36] Wendy Davies, *An Early Welsh Microcosm: Studies in the LLandaff Charters* (London, 1978).

[37] By the time of *Domesday Book*, tenurial estates were physically very dispersed, as Reginald Lennard emphasized in *Rural England 1086-1135: A Study of Social and Agrarian Conditions* (Oxford, 1959).

[38] Eric John, "Liberty of Oswaldslow," in *Land Tenure in Early England* (Leicester, 1964), p. 115: "the military nature of the English hundred has not usually been recognized. . . ." See also Nicholas Brooks, "The Development of Military Obligations in Eighth and Ninth Century England," in *England Before the Conquest: Studies in Primary Sources Presented to Dorothy Whitelock*, ed. P. Clemoes and K. Hughes (Cambridge, 1971), pp. 75-88. For the economic aspect of the hundred, see R. H. Britnell, "English Markets and Royal Administration Before 1200," *Economic History Review*, 2nd ser., 31 (1978), 183-96, esp. p. 183: "a regular relationship between early markets and hundredal organization has sometimes been suggested, but has never been explored."

[39] See n. 2 and further articles by C. Taylor: "Polyfocal Settlement and the English Medieval Village," *Medieval Archaeology*, 21 (1977), 189-93.

[40] See, for Bishopstone: "Bishopstone," pp. 192-242; for Chalton: B. Cunliffe, "Saxon and Medieval Settlement Pattern in the Region of Chalton, Hampshire," *Medieval Archaeology*, 16 (1972), 1-12; and T. Champion, "Chalton," *Current Archaeology*, no. 59 (1977), 364-69; for New Wintles: S. C. Hawkes and I. M. Grey, "Preliminary Note on the Early Anglo-Saxon Settlement at New Wintles Farm, Eynsham," *Oxoniensia*, 24 (1969), 1-4; and for West Stow: S. E. West, "The Anglo-Saxon Village of West Stow: An Interim Report of the Excavations," *Medieval Archaeology*, 13 (1969), 1-20.

[41] See Richard Hodges in this volume.

[42] For archaeological evidence of an early manorial complex, see "Goltho: A Deserted Medieval Village and its Manor House," *Current Archaeology*, no.

117

56 (1977), 262-70. From an administrative point of view, consider the development of the position of ealdorman: "this development of the office of ealdorman must be regarded as one of the most important features of royal administration in the period of Mercian supremacy," in Hart, "Kingdom of Mercia," p. 46.

[43] For the charter, see *Charters of Rochester: Anglo-Saxon Charters I*, ed. A. Campbell, The British Acad. (Oxford, 1973): charter no. 4; = Birch, no. 175 = Kemble, no. 96. For a discussion of the implications of this charter, see Witney, *Jutish Forest*, p. 83.

[44] Eleanor Searle, *Lordship and Community: Battle Abbey and its Banlieu, 1066 - 1538* (Toronto, 1974), pp. 49-50.

[45] The work of Immanuel Wallerstein traces this complexity for the early modern period: *The Modern World System: Capitalist Agriculture and the Origins of the European World Economy in the Sixteenth Century* (New York, 1974).

[46] For a reconstruction of a water mill excavated at Tamworth, the royal Mercian center, and for further discussion of the Old Windsor water mill, see Philip Rahtz, "Buildings and Rural Settlement," in *The Archaeology of Anglo-Saxon England*, ed. D. Wilson (London, 1976), p. 68 and figs. 2.18 and 2.19. See also the archaeological evidence for furlong organization of field systems and additional citations by David Hall in this volume. For metallurgy, see J. Haslam, "A Middle Saxon Iron Smelting Site at Ramsbury, Wiltshire," *Medieval Archaeology*, 24 (1980), 1-68.

SOME ECOLOGICAL DIMENSIONS OF MEDIEVAL FIELD SYSTEMS

H. S. A. FOX

The continuing vitality of studies of English field systems owes much to the variety of viewpoints from which the subject may be examined. H. L. Gray conceived his fundamental monograph as "a contribution to our knowledge of the settlement of England and to the history of English agriculture."[1] He related regional types of field system to regional differences in settlement history, a viewpoint which, though often discredited, has much to commend it so long as we do not carry our ethnic determinism too far. He rightly regarded transformation of field systems through time as a central element in agricultural progress, the cause and consequence of other types of technical change in farming. The chapters of his work which deal with this theme must be regarded as pioneering essays in English agricultural history. Gray gave the impression of an inevitable, though slow and at times episodic, development of agricultural technique and, thus, of field systems. More recently, variations and changes in field systems have been studied from a demographic viewpoint, not as independent variables in agrarian development but as dependent on the size of populations and on episodes in their growth or decline.[2] "A model of the evolution of field systems in the British Isles," Baker and Butlin suggest, "might well be based upon the assumption that population growth is the main force by which agrarian change is brought about."[3] Then again,

119

other studies have viewed medieval field systems, or important aspects of them, as the products of *mentalités*,[4] or of the complexities of land-holding.[5]

More recently still, William Cooter, in his essay "Ecological Dimensions of Medieval Agrarian Systems,"[6] has examined the characteristics of certain types of medieval European agrarian arrangements in terms of the properties of ecosystems—that is, functioning systems composed of living organisms and their effective environment—and has attempted to give an ecological perspective to some well-known trends in their evolution. To view a medieval field system as an ecosystem may seem highly anachronistic, so divorced is the concept from the age to which it is applied. Yet, the main visible living components of a cultivated ecosystem—its crops, its weeds, and the livestock which fed from them—could be minutely managed and accounted for by an ordinary medieval husbandman, as any reeve's account will show. It is clear from a reading of these documents, or of Walter de Henley and other medieval treatises on farming, that the properties of the environment, varying from season to season and from place to place, were understood with some sophistication, and its productivity would clearly have been the subject of endless comment and speculation. The essential facts of the ecosystem, though by no means all of the relationships between them, were duly appreciated in the Middle Ages and were the fundamental facts of the husbandman's year. To discuss medieval field systems from this viewpoint may well cast a little light upon some curious features of their distribution, operation, and development.

For my title, I have borrowed from that of Cooter's paper, though I do not intend to take up in purely ecological terms the many interesting issues which he raises. Solutions to such problems as the time lag between intensification of cultivation (without intensification of fertilization) and an eventual decline in output must be left to those competent to apply the quantities revealed by experimental analysis of ecosystems to data presented to them by agricultural historians.[7] Rather, my intention here is to examine one particular type of English medieval field system in more detail than Cooter was able to do in his broad survey of European practices, to see how much information historical evidence from the Middle Ages can provide about the gross aspects of its functioning as an ecosystem, and to speculate briefly about some aspects of its relationship to the populations it supported—the point at which the study of ecosystems becomes human ecology. That system is the Midland system, based upon the cultivation, in turn, of one out of two (or two out of three) large, expansive fields divided into open strips. From a core area in the Midland shires, which have given the system its name, its distribution spread discontinuously outwards toward the borderlands of the Highland Zone in the West and North and toward the Fens and East Anglia in the East. The "Midland" zone was extensive, taking in parts of over twenty counties, and the performance of the system cannot have failed to exert considerable influence on the population of medieval England.

The Midland System: Ecological Setting and Function

The ecological setting of the Midland system at the end of the High Middle Ages may be illustrated by the example of Leicestershire, a county largely given to three-field arrangements. Figures from extents in Inquisitions Post Mortem provide our best widely and easily available evidence on land-use and, for Leicestershire, have been conveniently summarized by J. A. Raftis.[8] To be sure, the figures in many extents of this kind are rounded approximations rather than the results of measurement; but I have become convinced, from the way in which they consistently reflect known local contrasts in physical setting, that they provide a good generalized picture of medieval land-use. In approximately 120 Leicestershire extents drawn up between 1254 and 1350, covering manors in all parts of the county, arable land occupied 87.9% of the combined demesne acreage, meadow 8.7%, and pasture 3.4%. The figure for meadow may, perhaps, be a little low, for it has been demonstrated that extents in some Inquisitions Post Mortem tend to underestimate meadow acreages. This tendency may not have been the result of a deliberate concealment of a valuable resource[9] but, rather, arose because the acreage returned was what existed over and above the amount of meadow needed to sustain ox-teams. Provision of hay for oxen was, of course, the prime function of meadowland, a fact which is occasionally stated in surveys from *Domesday Book* onwards, though more usually taken for granted.[10] The figure for pasture may also be on the low side. Several pastures were, in many places, so limited in area that, although valued in extents, they were not measured and thus do not find their way into these summary acreage figures.[11] Although we must concede that the nature of the source gives it a certain bias toward the recording of arable acreages, we cannot escape the conclusion that Leicestershire was a county in which the frontier between plough-land and pasture had been pushed almost to its furthest limits by the thirteenth century. Those limits were never again to be reached in the county's subsequent agrarian history.

It is the same strong impression of a predominantly arable landscape which confronts us in thirteenth-century sources from places throughout the lowlands of central England where the Midland system predominated. In a typical township the arable had already been extended to touch the vill's boundary in all directions. Such was the Leicestershire vill of Wigston Magna where, by the thirteenth century, "the fields were being tilled as far as the boundaries of the township" and of Cuxham in Oxfordshire where the outer limits of the three fields were also the outer limits of the vill.[12] Within the boundaries of a typical township, the only continuous stretches of grassland were wetlands along streams, usually reserved for meadow. Their vital function as a source of feed for the oxen whose traction was indispensable in a predominantly arable system is revealed by their values: in Leicestershire, meadow was often valued at 12d. or 24d. per acre, compared to 4d. or 6d., which were the values most frequently given to arable land. Within a township's boundaries there might, too, be some small acreages of permanent pasture in closes separate from the common fields. Their scarcity is again revealed by values which were almost always greater than those of arable, though not as great as those assigned to meadows, with their prized two crops of grass—one for grazing, the other for hay.[13] By no means did all townships enjoy these small acreages of enclosed permanent pasture; many Leicestershire extents make no mention of this type of land-use; occasionally an extent will contain the laconic statement, "There is no pasture."[14]

Many Midland townships would have looked in vain for supplementary pastoral resources outside their boundaries, for the possibility of inter-manorial movements of stock among the members of an estate was presumably a luxury enjoyed only by lords. In Leicestershire, the only significant upland area was Charnwood, a tract of wood and rough grazing on thin, poor, sandy soils and rising in places to over nine-hundred feet. The name of one of its bordering townships is Markfield, which means "the open land of the Mercians," suggesting that at one time the upland may have been intercommoned by the people of a wide area. By the thirteenth century, however, its resources were shared by only a small number of vills forming a ring around its borders. Again, if communities in the Avon lowlands of Warwickshire had once enjoyed access to the wood-pastures of Arden, as the evidence of tenurial and ecclesiastical ties indicates, such links had probably ceased to have much functional significance by the thirteenth century.[15]

As with pasture, so with woodland. The importance of woodland pasture in the rural economy of some parts of medieval England has recently been stressed by Oliver Rackham, who has discussed for the first time in detail the ecology of tracts of land which were managed so as to yield both non-edible woodland products and pasture, acorns, and browse for livestock.[16] Few of his examples, from survivals and documentary evidence, come from the Midland lowlands, however, where, one suspects, wood was already very scarce by the thirteenth century. In Leicestershire, for example, *Domesday Book* shows only two concentrations of woodland, although it should be mentioned that some other small acreages may have gone unrecorded in 1086.[17] One of these concentrations was in the very east of the county, adjoining Rutland. Here, what were probably relatively small, discontinuous patches of woodland in 1086 were subsequently drawn within the ambit of the Forest of Leicestershire[18] and Rutland in the reign of Henry I.[19] In all probability, they had already been much reduced in area by the first decade of the thirteenth century, perhaps leaving stands no larger than those shown on the present day map. Only thus, by supposing that reclamation had proceeded almost to the limits of each township, can we explain the miserably small acreages of assarts recorded here in the regard made in the tenth year of John's reign (1208-09), shortly before the area was disafforested; significantly, the assarts were said to have been the responsibility of "the men" of Horninghold, of Cranoe, of Skeffington, and of Stonton, suggesting that they were incorporated into the common fields of those vills.[20] The other concentration of woodland revealed by the Domesday folios for Leicestershire was around the upland of Charnwood. In the following centuries many of these woods, by no means on prime agricultural land, came to be emparked as preserves for deer.[21] This did not necessarily result in the conservation of pasture for farm stock, for there was conflict here between agricultural needs and the needs of the chase: medieval extents often emphasize that parks were not prolific sources of pasture "beyond the sustenance of the deer" or "because of the shade of the trees."[22]

The crisis in provision of pasture experienced by the thirteenth century in lowland countrysides within the territory of the Midland system becomes even clearer if we turn briefly, by way of contrast, to *pays* of a different kind. From the manor of Knapp Fee, located close to the great wet moorlands of the Somerset Levels, a reeve reported that he was unable to find lessees for one of the lord's woodland pastures because of a "great abundance of pasture in the moors" (*magna copia pasture in moris*).[23] At Baltonsborough, another Somerset manor bordering on the Levels, those who made an extent in the middle of the thirteenth century reported that the moors "could not be measured" (*mensuari non poterunt*), presumably because they were too extensive.[24] A more precise picture may be gained from figures on land-use from extents in Inquisitions Post Mortem relating to manors in east Devon, a tract of country lying between the Devon-Dorset border, along which Gray drew the western boundary of the Midland system, and the River Exe twenty-five miles to the west.[25] This countryside is typical of the western borderlands just beyond the territory of the Midland system in that it combines both fertile lowlands and extensive tracts of upland, unsuitable for cultivation, in close proximity to one another. What is said here of medieval land-use in this variegated countryside could also apply, therefore, to other borderland *pays*, in Herefordshire and Shropshire, for example. Extents of east Devon manors drawn up between 1244 and 1347 reveal the following figures (equivalents for Leicestershire are given in parentheses): arable 68.6% (87.9%), meadow 8.8% (8.7%), pasture 22.6% (3.4%).[26] The most notable figures are those for pasture. Some manors in east Devon had small acreages of permanent pasture attached to their demesnes, in two extents said to be reserved "for oxen" or "for working oxen."[27] But by far the greatest part was rough, unstinted grazing on the summits of the Greensand hill ranges, running between the east Devon valleys and used largely as pastures for sheep.[28] At Uplyme, for example, extensive rough grazings were reckoned in 1266 to support seven-hundred sheep; at Blackborough in 1336 the *mora* was described as "pasture for one-hundred sheep;" both figures refer to demesne flocks, to which we must add the stock of tenants.[29] Later evidence likewise indicates the importance of the hill ranges as sheepwalks: the grazings of Northleigh were described in the reign of Elizabeth as "verye good sheepe pasture mixed with ffearnes," and those of Southleigh supported two sheep for each of their three-hundred acres.[30] The abundance of these rough grazings meant that values of even the best quality permanent pasture were relatively low in the Middle Ages, a mean of 1.8d. per acre compared to 12d. per acre in Leicestershire.[31] In addition to the rough pastures within their own boundaries, townships in east Devon's largest hundred could send stock to Kentis Moor, which was common to all the men of the hundred. Furthermore, the whole region, along with the rest of Devon, enjoyed rights of pasture on some 160 thousand acres of thin *Molinia* and *Nardus* grasslands, heather moors and wet moors on Dartmoor at the center of the shire.[32]

By such arrangements and provisions the borderland *pays* beyond the western boundary of Midland England were spared the need to take up an agricultural system founded upon a shortage of pasture. For that is how we should see the Midland system itself. In seeking to explain how it functioned in its deprived ecological setting, we must turn from generalized figures on land-use provided by extents to details of the management of field systems furnished by *compoti* and court rolls, and we must turn from the regional to the manorial scale. The place selected for examination is the manor of Podimore, lying at the center of one of the most westerly of the lowlands within the Midland zone, the rolling Lias claylands of mid-Somerset. Podimore belonged to Glastonbury, and the findings which follow form part of a wider survey of medieval agricultural practice on the Abbey's Somerset estate.[33]

Figures from an extent of 1332 introduce the manor's setting. Of a total demesne area of approximately 300 acres, 75.5% was arable, divided neatly and symmetrically into two fields; 16.9% was meadow; only 6.6% was permanent pasture; and there was no rough grazing. The permanent several pasture was to be found in "La Greve" (six acres, presumably once a grove of wood), "Colvacre" (five acres, perhaps once reserved for calving cows), "La Somerlese" (ten acres, each worth twice as much as an acre of the most valuable arable land on account of their use for summer pasture), and two other patches of an acre each. The extent and other sources reveal a few other minute pieces of pasture which might be pressed into service for the value of their herbage: the manorial garden next to the *curia* at Podimore, a debilitated rabbit warren, and two *vie pasture*, greenways running through the open fields.

Surviving *compoti* from the late thirteenth century and early fourteenth allow a reconstruction of the movements or flows of demesne livestock within the manor. This must be a rather generalized reconstruction, because reeves were not charged with accounting for the detailed day-to-day management of stock whose whereabouts and movements may, in many cases, only be known through elimination or through incidental or oblique references in the accounts. At Podimore, the system was a closed one: that is to say, the manor—locked away in the center of the Lias lowlands of mid-Somerset—was not one of those places which, in the thirteenth century, retained access to common rights on the great summer pastures of the Levels which had given the county its name. Although the demesne flock at Podimore was, on occasion, replenished with or used to supply flocks elsewhere on the Glastonbury estate, the manor was not used as one of the hubs in a system of regular intermanorial movements of sheep of the kind made famous by Miss Page's study of *Bidentes Hoylandie*.[34]

To begin with, consider the system at Podimore as it was in early May. By this time the demesne's working oxen would be out of the stalls of the new oxhouse constructed for them in about 1300. By this time, too, the meadows were strictly out of bounds for livestock, having been "in defence" since February 2nd[35] for production of the hay which was so vital for feeding oxen during the following winter. Only occasionally did a desperate reeve allow livestock onto an acre or two of meadow before mowing time. In early May, then, the oxen—the most essential and most valuable of all farm stock—would have found themselves on the best available grazing, the small amounts of permanent pasture attached to the demesne. The demesne was run with three teams, each of eight oxen. Permanent pastures available to them totalled twenty-three acres, but these were encumbered by grazing rights for twenty-one oxen belonging to privileged free tenants and by four more animals allowed to the reeve. In all, then, twenty-three acres of pasture had to support forty-nine oxen during the summer months, twice the maximum stocking rate recommended at the end of the eighteenth century by the *General View of the Agriculture of the County of Somerset*.[36] During these months, grains were growing in the sown field, which was therefore clearly unavailable for grazing, except to oxen and horses tethered on greenways and headlands, a practice which is observable in the accounts and which, to a small degree, must have relieved pressure on the several pastures. The demesne sheep flock, however, which averaged about two-hundred animals in the early fourteenth century, could not have been managed in this way. Its only place was the fallow field in which the demesne holding amounted at this time to about one-hundred acres. Podimore's reeves seem to have considered that an acre of fallow would support two sheep during the summer months.

Let us move forward now through the summer months to Michaelmas, the onset of the winter season. Pressures within the system would appear, at this time, to be somewhat relaxed. Oxen would soon be back in the stalls of the oxhouse, relying on the previous summer's hay harvest, and meadows would be free for grazing. However, the growth of grasses and weeds would soon slacken, at a time when, in some years, Podimore's sheep flock reached its maximum size. The new fallow field, recently emptied of grain, would therefore be needed to sustain the flock during the winter months. This critical juncture in the annual cycle of the Midland system—the time when the two fields exchanged functions— gave rise to more by-laws than any other point in the farming year.[37] It was on the new fallow field that demesne sheep at Podimore spent the winter months. We can be sure of their presence there through a process of elimination of other possible sources of feed. Meadows and permanent pasture, now free from the demands of oxen, might have given some relief, but their acreage was not great enough to sustain the whole flock. The flock at Podimore was certainly not folded, nor housed and fed with hay over the winter, as appears to have been the practice on some demesnes in medieval England;[38] no *bercaria* is mentioned in a comprehensive list of farm buildings there in 1332, and no surviving *compotus* mentions the expenses of folding or any disbursements of forage for the winter feeding of sheep. And, indeed, we have glimpses through the accounts of the flock roaming at large on the fallow field when the reeve explains that winter herbage on greenways and stubbles yielded little cash profit "because the sheep of the lord and of the commoners pasture there."

Winter and summer alike, the fallows at Podimore, first one field and then the other, were essential for sustaining the demesne flock. The system was a finely balanced one, close to crisis in years such as 1314-15, when the reeve explained that meadows yielded little hay "because they were inundated" (thus straining the manor's other meagre supplies of herbage) or 1304-05, when the grass in the fallow field was poor "because of the dryness of the season."[39] Such crises must have come all the closer and occurred more frequently on peasant holdings. The evidence, such as it is, seems to indicate that Podimore conformed to the general picture which Postan has given us of village livestock in the thirteenth century.[40] Some holdings were seriously understocked: when one cottager died in 1346, the "best beast" that the lord could exact from his heirs was a poor fowl. On the other hand, it was expected that a thirty-acre holding would maintain a full ox-team of eight beasts,[41] while individual tenant flocks of forty or more sheep are mentioned in the manor's court rolls. Neither large nor small holdings could have been relatively better supplied than the demesne with meadow and permanent pasture. For the animals of tenants, the onus of providing pasture fell, even more heavily than for the demesne stock, on the fallows of Podimore's two-field system.

To judge by what more generalized sources tell us, Podimore's ecological setting was typical of countless other manors on the Midland plains in the thirteenth century. Examination of livestock management there brings us straight to the fundamental features of the functioning of the Midland system which was, in essence, a system for integrating, on the same soil, both grazing and crop production in settings poorly endowed with permanent pasture. In the terms of our own age, it was a man-made ecosystem designed to manage the output of plant and animal products in settings where "natural" habitats, whose resources might have been used to replenish the system, had been reduced almost to nothing. Where good grasslands were in short supply, meadows and those small pieces of permanent pasture which had escaped the attacks of the plough were both reserved largely for oxen. Flocks, therefore, found themselves displaced to the fallows. Sheep are excellent foragers; I have been told by one Leicestershire farmer that, until very recently, he still maintained the now old-fashioned practice of letting his flock onto the fallows immediately after harvest, where they spread out and found ample sustenance around hedgerows, on plants growing among the stubble, and in other places not touched by reaping machines. These scavengers would have found far more to feed on in the fallow fields of the Middle Ages than in those of today, for medieval croplands were notoriously weed-infested, and the sickle at harvest time left standing a far greater bulk of weeds, including grasses, than do modern machines.[42] Then too, there were grasses and other weeds growing on unploughed headlands, on damp, uncultivated patches within the open fields, and around the hedges at the field edge. Such sources of forage were no doubt in the minds of those who drew up the "Rules" (c. 1240) for the better management of the Countess of Lincoln's estate, when they estimated that "each acre of fallow land can support at least two sheep for one year."[43] The evidence of stints suggests that this estimate of the carrying capacity of fallows in the Middle Ages was close to the mark;[44] the same rate of stocking, it will be remembered, was used at Podimore in the early Middle Ages.

Present-day specialists in livestock management, accustomed to systems in which grasslands are made to yield their maximum feed (by control of the timing of the onset of grazing as related to plant growth), may well wonder at the ability of medieval fallows to support village flocks. That they did so is clear from the historical evidence, although it will be equally clear that fallow grazing could not have been capable of maintaining animals in the peak of condition and weight. Today, throughout most of the area once occupied by the Midland system, the growing season for grass (using soil temperature as the critical factor) lasts for about 250 days.[45] It may have been marginally longer in the slightly warmer climatic era between approximately A.D. 800 and 1300, the hey-day of the system.[46] In late summer and early autumn, just after harvest, when the aftermath was still virtually untouched and plant growth was still active, the resources of the fallows were most prolific, "fresh and full of grass."[47] Thereafter, as winter progressed and as growth began to slow, the available food mass diminished, perhaps forcing farmers occasionally to provide hay and other feed for their sheep, although this was by no means a universal practice. By early spring, the growing season for grass and other weeds had begun again. The first ploughing of the fallows, carried out in April according to Walter de Henley,[48] must have temporarily diminished the supply of feed, although it did not, of course, touch headlands and other uncultivated patches among the arable strips. Summer saw continued growth of weeds upon which sheep could graze—apparently with relish, according to John de Brie who wrote a treatise on flock management for Charles V in 1379, "for they find the feed of thistles good" (*car la pature des chardons leur est bonne*).[49] Walter de Henley recommended a second ploughing of fallows, or *rebinatio*, at the end of June,[50] but here there was a degree of conflict stemming directly from the alternate use of the land for arable and pasture. The *rebinatio* would certainly improve grain yields by further cleansing the soil, but at the same time it reduced feed for livestock on the fallows. The practice, for which to my knowledge the earliest English reference comes from about 1190,[51] has been described as an important early medieval innovation; important, that is, from the standpoint of arable husbandry.[52] However, as with so many unspectacular agricultural improvements of the Middle Ages, as yet we know little about its incidence. When historians come to examine it in more detail, they could well find that the progress of its adoption was slowed because of its effect on the supply of pasture at a crucial time in the year.

By the means outlined above, fallows maintained the flock. Up to a point, the reverse also applied: flocks were important in the recuperation of the land during the fallow year. In his discussion of the ecology of medieval farming systems, Cooter argued that "in most cases, medieval open-field systems were sustained only through a process of robbing arable hinterlands of their fertility."[53] In other words, nutrients whose ultimate sources were rough grazings and other pastures (the hinterland) were moved towards and served to replenish arable land, drained yearly as it was by removal of crops for human consumption. Nutrient flows certainly took place between meadows and the arable, as dung from the ox-stalls, where beasts were fed with hay, was carted onto the fallows.[54] In some medieval field systems, like those of the borderland countrysides beyond the western boundary of the Midlands previously discussed, movements of the animals themselves played a role; here, arable fields were set amid extensive wastes, and flocks moved between hill ranges and lowlands. But where extensive wastes were absent, where hinterlands beyond the arable had been virtually reduced to nothing, as in the classic settings of the Midland system, we must envisage a rather different role for the flock as an instrument for the replenishment of cropland. A flock pasturing day and night in a smooth field of uninterrupted stubble—like one of those large enclosures produced by restructuring of field layout in the eighteenth and nineteenth centuries, "so smooth that you could whip a mouse across it"—does little to enrich the soil; the system is virtually closed. But a medieval common field would not have looked like this. No large field divided into strips could be operated without numerous unploughed headlands at the furlongs' ends; in some parts of medieval England, unploughed grassy balks separated one strip from another.[55] Many access ways also provided grassy patches amid the arable and were valued for doing so: at Podimore the two widest greenways (*vie pasture*) in the open fields were important enough as sources of pasture to be separately listed as assets in an extent of 1332,[56] while on another Somerset manor (Winscombe) in 1306-07 the reeve accounted for profits from sale of herbage in a number of "ways" and pieces of pasture "around furlongs."[57] In addition, and especially on heavy land, the gently undulating surface of the Midland lowlands made for the survival within the arable fields of many wide strips of pasture which were too damp to be ploughed under conditions of drainage technology known to the Middle Ages. Mark Pierce's well-known map of the environs of Laxton in 1635 shows just how much of the area of the open fields could be occupied by these damp grassy hollows, locally known as "sikes" after the Old Norse *sik*, meaning a wet, low-lying place.[58] Sheep, roaming over fallow strips and grassy patches alike, must have acted as agents moving nutrients from pasture to cropland *within* the open fields. Contemporaries seem to have realized the value, however limited it may have been, of this function of the flock. At Podimore, for example, in years when no demesne flock was present on the manor, the lord was concerned to maintain stocking levels on the fallow field by ensuring that his grazing rights there were taken up by others;[59] at Hallaton in Leicestershire there was a complaint in 1665 against graziers who made use of the common fields only by day or after harvest when they were "fresh and full of grass," removing stock at night or later in the year and thereby depriving the soil of the benefit of their manure.[60] The Midland system, in which nutrients were cycled towards the arable only through movement of sheep within the fallow field and through the spreading on cropland of farmyard dung (the ultimate source of which was meadowland), must have functioned at a lower level of productivity than did systems where there were additional flows from a hinterland of rough grazing grounds.[61] But function it did: moreover, its very origins may well have been closely connected with the need to develop a type of land management which worked as well as possible in settings where rough grazing grounds had become scarce.

By the thirteenth century, there was a general coincidence between farming regions which were short of rough or several pastures and the Midland system with its two or three great continuous tracts of arable and obligatory common grazing on fallows. In upland areas within the "Midland" zone (such as Charnwood in Leicestershire) and beyond the limits of that zone (as in the western borderland countrysides) pasture was more plentiful. Field systems less "regular" than the classic two- or three-field system were to be found in such areas. That is to say, the lands of a township were not divided into only two or three great continuous tracts of arable; rather, there were usually many arable units haphazardly arranged within the territory of the township, in places separated from one another by pastures and wastes, and not brought within a single scheme for the communal organization of grazing practices.[62] It is reasonable to suggest that such field systems were akin to those which, in the lowlands of the Midlands, had been the immediate prototypes for the two-

or three-field system. It is easy, also, to envisage some of the pressures which, in lowland *pays*, had encouraged their transformation into fully-fledged Midland systems: ploughlands expand; wastes and pastures diminish in area; it becomes increasingly difficult to find spaces on which animals may be left to graze; and as wastes diminish, it becomes necessary to adopt practices for the better re-cycling of nutrients within the arable fields.

The Midland system, through well-organized common grazing by the whole village flock on each of its two or three prairie-like fields in turn, offered a viable solution to these pressures. We should consider in detail the particular benefits which came from the great size of these fields, for their size, as well as their symmetry, was a characteristic and diagnostic feature of the Midland system. Some of these benefits were operational:[63] livestock did not need to be moved frequently from one field to another; the single flock in a single field was by no means a labor-intensive method of managing animals; a single fallow field simplified the risky boundary between grazing ground and growing crops, thereby reducing damage from trespass. Other benefits of the large fallow field are more closely connected to the theme of this paper. The question of whether livestock feed from and manure the land more efficiently in confined or in extensive spaces has long been debated. This point was discussed in one of the earliest Tudor agricultural treatises; the seventeenth-century pamphlet literature on enclosure argued about it; and the question naturally entered into the very large body of nineteenth-century writings promoting enlargement of field size.[64] The answer clearly depends upon the goal of the type of livestock farming which is being practiced. Dairy cattle need to be moved frequently from one lush pasture to the next, a system of management favoring small fields. John Hooker, writing in late sixteenth-century Devon, which was by then already in parts an enclosed dairy county, observed that the cattle "by theire often chaunges...feede styll as it were upon a new springnynge grasse."[65] However, if the coverage of herbage is relatively thin, as it was on the fallows of the Midland system, and if one of the purposes of stock management is to manure the land without undue costs, then large spaces are desirable. Observation will show that a flock of sheep turned onto a large field will at once naturally spread out in search of forage; in the past, their roaming was further encouraged by the placing of posts here and there in the field.[66] Sheep, if managed in this way, do not trample and render unpalatable the grasses on which eventually they will have to feed, nor do they run the risk of poaching heavy soils. Moreover, their constant movement makes them efficient agents in the process of cycling nutrients within the fallow field. Large fallow fields were thus ideal for extensive

131

flock management, facilitating both the feeding of livestock and their manuring of the land. It was for these reasons, among others, that we sometimes find two adjacent medieval communities, already with fully-fledged field systems, coming together to arrange their rotational sequences in such a way that, every second or third year, their two fallow fields interlocked, creating a vast intercommonable tract of land between the two villages.[67] It was for these reasons, too, that although there was a general coincidence in medieval England between the Midland system and areas which were short of pasture, examples may be found of communities which practiced a two- or three-field system despite access to relatively plentiful rough grazing.[68] In such cases, adoption of a system of two or three great fields may have been more a response to the advantages of the system for particular types of flock management than an absolute necessity imposed by the need to find spaces on which animals could graze.

The open expanses of the fields of the Midland system have been described here as ideal for an extensive form of grazing, altogether different from the close and careful folding of sheep on acre after acre in turn which some modern writers have assumed was normal and well-nigh ubiquitous in medieval England.[69] The texts usually cited in this context are Walter de Henley's clear reference to the sheep-fold and Kerridge's description of complex and highly-developed folding practices in seventeenth-century Wiltshire. But Walter de Henley may well have implied "ideal" or advanced practices which were not everywhere common or feasible; in any case, he refers only to folding for a limited period before the commencement of sowing.[70] Likewise, Kerridge's description cannot be taken as representative of general practice in medieval England. He makes it clear that continuous, year-round folding of huge village flocks on the fallows was entirely dependent upon the presence of downland: Wiltshire sheep were "bred for folding, that is, bred to walk" their twice-daily journey between downs and fields. At its most productive, the system also depended upon flooded water-meadows (yielding a very early bite on which sheep were fed during the day before being moved to the fold at night), and these were a post-medieval innovation.[71] Like the double ploughing of fallows previously discussed, systematic folding of sheep on arable is one of those elements of agricultural practice which is often assumed to have been a widespread norm in the Middle Ages, yet whose distribution requires a good deal of further investigation. Some references to it, from outside East Anglia where it was a deeply-rooted and well-recorded practice, can certainly be found in medieval sources, particularly in custumals which sometimes state the obligation of tenants to move folds.[72] But medieval by-laws from Midland England seem seldom to touch upon folding, which is surprising in view of the complex and cooperative nature of the operation.[73] It may well be that systematic year-round folding was restricted to those types of environments where the effort was worthwhile, where the practice drew nutrients from downs or other pastures towards the fallow, and where the large flocks which it demanded could be built up.[74] Elsewhere, in settings where rough pastures were scarce and flocks relatively small, the practice may have been absent or restricted to the sowing season, when it had the additional purpose of consolidating the soil. From an operational viewpoint, close folding with a common flock was most easily accomplished on wide, hedgeless expanses; but it was probably a less intensive type of flock management which lay behind the original division of many a township's land into two or three great fields or sectors.

The Midland System in an Age of Crisis: The Thirteenth Century

Having examined some aspects of the functioning of the Midland system in its typical medieval settings, I wish now to turn to the question of how well it responded to the pressures of the thirteenth century. Few historians would doubt that many English rural communities approached a crisis in the relationship between people and resources in the hundred years before the Black Death. Population densities, already great in some places at the end of the eleventh century, became greater in the following two-hundred years; small holders and the landless increased. Yet the land appears to have been yielding less well. On some manors, evidence of crisis and its interrelated elements is incontrovertible: high and rising land values, declining yields, reports of debilitated land, signs of poverty, and high mortalities which correlate with years of poor harvests. The severity of such conditions throughout the whole of England has, quite rightly, been questioned; it will be a long time before we are able to produce a geography of poverty in the thirteenth century, although the materials are available in the form of levels of rates, and changes in rates, at which lords fined manorial populations for petty misdemeanors.[75] The extent to which technical progress in agriculture alleviated, postponed, or even—in the view of a minority of historians—reduced to a minimum the elements of crisis in the thirteenth-century countryside has also been questioned. Field systems need to be examined in this context as fundamental assemblages of interrelated techniques for the production of foodstuffs and, in addition, as delicate ecosystems which, while capable of regulation by man, also embody self-regulating mechanisms which may limit their productivity.

133

In the minds of many historians today, adoption of the two- and three-field system itself offered one solution (for a time at least) to Midland communities faced with pressures from mounting populations in the post-Conquest period. R. C. Hoffmann, for example, writing on the "Maturation and Diffusion of Common Field Agriculture" in western Europe at large, links the arrival of mature field systems in England with trends in which "the demographic curve approached its medieval peak."[76] However attractive this model may seem, in the precise chronological context of the twelfth and thirteenth centuries it must be rejected. I have discussed in detail elsewhere the chronology of English documentation relating to field systems and—a rather different matter—the bearing that the documents have upon the chronology of the Midland system, particularly in Gloucestershire and Lincolnshire. The sources reveal not a system which was still undergoing a major extension around the end of the twelfth century and the beginning of the thirteenth, but one which, in the settings which most demanded it, had already taken root very widely by the time that relatively large numbers of detailed charters conveying open-field holdings begin to become available in the reign of Henry II.[77]

This is, indeed, as we should expect, for in many of the lowlands of Midland England that state of an almost fully reclaimed arable landscape, described in the previous section and conducive to development of the Midland system, was achieved at a very early date. When it is viewed through *Domesday Book*, it is the landscape of the Midland lowlands, above all others, which has that appearance, in Lennard's words, of an "old country" which had "passed well beyond the colonial stage" before it ever came under the scrutiny of King William's men.[78] From the point of view of their history of settlement (and thus of their field systems), these countrysides cannot be accommodated within a chronological model dominated by the idea of "*L'âge des grands défrichements*" lasting from about 1050 to about 1300[79] and witnessing development of mature field systems as landscapes rapidly became replete with settlements and clearings. That model, without doubt, finds much support in some localities within continental Europe. In the heartland of a newly vigorous Capetian France, for example, where woodland still occupied large tracts between Seine and Loire, there was space for many new settlements on both royal land and land belonging to ecclesiastics: it was here in the twelfth century that *villeneuves* were established near the "royal road" between Paris and Orleans; here too, that Abbot Suger of Saint- Denis carried out those schemes for development which he made much of in his treatise about the administration of the abbey's estate.[80] And, to a degree and for certain places, a model which stresses extensions of cultivation during the twelfth and thirteenth centuries accords with some of the English evi-

134

dence. As for large-scale schemes of development involving the planting of scores of new vills, like the schemes of regional development carried out by a *Lokator* class east of the Elbe, we hear little of them in England, unless the regular villages which seem to have re-emerged on northern estates devastated by William I come into this category.[81] Yet despite the fact that the progress of medieval settlement is so often hidden from us, occasionally there are glimpses of seigneurial projects less ambitious than these. When we find the officials of the Earldom of Cornwall accounting for new rents in 1301-02 from arable land at Dunnabridge high up in the Forest of Dartmoor, certain features of the new settlement (its sudden appearance in the record, the regularity of its land holding, the duties of its tenants, its location next to one of the points from which the moor was "drifted") suggest a deliberate seigneurial foundation, in this case of settlers who were to assist in forest administration.[82] Again, we catch a glimpse of the establishment of the same kind of settlement through a plea made before the King's justices in 1228: in the high Pennines within the Forest of Wensleydale, members of a family which had held the forest from the Crown are accused of having "made" a vill which began as a collection of lodges for foresters and was then expanded by reclamation and the construction of "stone houses".[83] This appears to have been the origin of one of the settlements near present-day Bainbridge. And on the marshlands of coastal Somerset, Henry de Blois enthusiastically contemplated a holding brought under cultivation between the beginning and the third quarter of the twelfth century: formerly it had been worthless, but now, he wrote, it was "a field full of standing corn, glowing gold, murmuring in the breeze, yielding handfuls rather than ears."[84]

These examples of relatively small-scale seigneurial ventures belong to the Highland Zone of England, however, and to her marshland frontiers, beyond the limits of the Midlands—inhospitable countrysides where rough grazing was so plentiful that mature common field systems never developed.[85] Within the Midlands there were, to be sure, some upland countrysides which boasted enough unreclaimed land for them to be classed as minor frontiers for colonization in the post-Conquest period. Here again we occasionally come across records of a kind to bring to life the foundation of new settlements and expansion of the arable, processes for the most part hidden behind the terse wording of charters, behind swelling rentals and the records of forest regards.[86] Just four illustrations may be given. So enflamed with the theme of reclamation was the member of the Ridware family who compiled a cartulary concerning his lands near the minor uplands of Cannock and Needwood in Staffordshire that he decorated the manuscript with drawings of woodland and felled trees.[87] These early fourteenth-century sketches are perhaps the first English pictorial representations of assarts. From Northamptonshire, chronicles of Peterborough Abbey record the creation in Rockingham Forest of a grange which they grandly style *Novum Locum*, although the name which endured was the more prosaic Middle English *biggin*, which simply means "building". To a nucleus of assarts already existing at the end of the twelfth century, sixty-six acres of meadow were added in order to provide a base for the oxen which would be essential for the economic development of the grange, and over the following decades many new clearings were made to produce what became "the abbey's largest manor, comprising at least a thousand acres by the late thirteenth century."[88] In Leicestershire, two places called Newtown are to be found in the vicinity of Charnwood. One, Newtown Linford, in a hollow within the upland, is first recorded by name in 1293, although it is almost certain that the beginnings of the settlement are represented by the "new assarts" said to belong to its parent vill of Groby in an Inquisition Post Mortem on the estate of William de Ferrers in 1288. The other, later dubbed Newtown Unthank from the unpromising nature of its setting, was a daughter settlement of the de Ferrers vill of Ratby.[89] There is good reason to suppose that these two new hamlets represent a policy of the family, or of its predecessors, to initiate, encourage, or channel the conversion of rough pasture and wood to arable. Further towards the southern limits of the Midland zone, on the Winchester manor of Downton near the borders of Melchet Forest, the bishopric's exceptionally early and detailed account rolls record year by year the creation of a new farm complex and its surrounding arable fields. In 1251-52, 254 stumps are dug up "to make way for the ploughs"; the ground is levelled and rid of thorns; hedges are raised and planted with quick-sets; and a barn and ox-stalls constructed.[90] No later age was to furnish us with documents giving such a vivid picture of conversion of woodland to arable.

These examples make it clear that in select parts of the Midlands, Marc Bloch's phrase *"L'âge des grands défrichements"* captures the spirit of the twelfth and thirteenth centuries. Most Midland counties possessed one or more of these minor frontiers on which, given the relatively unattractive physical endowments of Cannock, or Charnwood, or Rockingham Forest, colonization never totally eliminated woodlands and rough pastures. For this reason such areas tended to adopt neither the Midland system nor the regularly spaced, tightly-knit villages to be found in the adjacent lowlands, anciently settled and anciently reclaimed.

It is on the lower flanks of these minor Midland uplands, in countrysides intermediate in pace of settlement between them and the lower lands, that we might expect to find two- and three-field systems developing late enough for their arrival to figure in the documentary record. In fact, the only two cases known to me, both from the third quarter of the twelfth century, come from countrysides of this type, neither true "felden" nor true "woodland."[91] I have discussed the evidence in another publication, but it is worth commenting here on the settings of each place, which have some significance in the context of this essay. The first is Dry Drayton in Cambridgeshire, from which a charter, later confirmed by Henry II, recounts how a "new partition of the vill, both field land and meadow" was undertaken in the 1150s.[92] There can be little doubt that this complex operation saw the creation of the three-field system which was practiced there in later times. Dry Drayton, or Wold Drayton as it was called in one of the documents relating to the remodelling of its field system, lies on the flank of a minor upland forming the southwest boundary of the shire, a plateau overlain by Boulder Clay at about two-hundred feet. Whereas lowland Cambridgeshire appears to have been largely devoid of wood in 1086, and the bolder uplands rising to over four-hundred feet in the southeastern part of the shire were still well-wooded, the Wolds around Wold Drayton retained only a little woodland at the time of Domesday, just enough for "making fences" or "for the houses."[93] In short, it was an intermediate type of countryside. We still have much to learn about subtle differences in the date and pace of colonization from region to region within the Midland shires, but it is significant that Segenhoe in Bedfordshire, the other place for which documentary evidence has been found for adoption of the Midland system, also lies amid intermediate countryside of the same type. To the north of this gentle Greensand upland is the vale of the Ouse, to its south the high scarp of the Chiltern Hills. From Domesday, from a narrative which touches on the place in the early twelfth century, and from field names, we catch glimpses of a semi-wooded setting in which wood-pastures fed not only pigs but also sheep; we catch glimpses, too, of the progress of settlement, already quite well-advanced at the time of the Conquest—of "stockings" (land cleared of stumps) and of *rustici* settling on and pushing back the woodland edge.[94] Then, towards the end of the century, the haphazard field arrangements which had evolved over a long period of assarting became re-organized and welded together and, "under supervision of the old men" of the vill, with the assent of its lords, "knights, free men and others," a system of two fields was created.[95]

These two examples[96] are instructive for the details they give of a stage when fully-fledged Midland systems were still emerging, but they add nothing to the case for a widespread movement in this direction during the twelfth and thirteenth centuries. The two examples are specific to a particular type of locality intermediate in chronology of settlement and agrarian development between the upland *pays* of Midland England

and the lowlands which comprise the largest part of the Midland shires. The lowlands themselves passed through the same stages far earlier, arriving sooner at that condition of shortage of pasture suitable for the emergence of mature field systems, which has been described in the first section of this paper. They were largely untouched by the developments of the classic "age of large-scale clearances" because, by the eleventh century, relatively little wood or pasture remained to be reclaimed. The lowlands on either side of the Avon, for example, taking in parts of Felden Warwickshire and parts of Worcestershire, formed the heartland of the kingdom of the Hwicce, which was already a populous province in the late seventh century, to judge from the number of hides ascribed to it by the *Tribal Hidage*, and which was later absorbed into Mercia; by the time of the Norman Conquest they could look back to half a millennium of relatively stable and settled conditions under folk of Anglo-Saxon origin.[97] It is not surprising, therefore, to find that this part of the West Midlands furnishes some of the best evidence we have of elements of mature common field systems already in existence by the tenth century.[98] To take another example, the central lowlands of Leicestershire on either side of the Soar valley in the East Midlands yield not only abundant traces of Romano-British occupation, to be expected in the vicinity of a tribal capital, and of early Anglo-Saxon settlement,[99] but also considerable evidence of further Scandinavian land-taking in the late ninth century—if that is how the testimony of numerous Old Norse place-names is to be construed.[100] By the time of the Conquest, after this series of occupations, the vicinity of Leicester was the most densely populated area in all of Midland England.[101] These anciently settled lowland regions of England may have seen the emergence of two-or three-field systems at a date no later than that at which similar developments took place in the most favored parts of continental Europe.[102] They cannot be accommodated within diffusionist models, outdated now even among prehistorians,[103] which place the British Isles as detached, remote outliers, receiving agricultural innovations only rather late in the day.

If little evidence can be found for further extension of the Midland system during a period of mounting population pressure at the end of the High Middle Ages, is there any evidence for a second possible solution, a change from two-field to three-field plans? Again, the idea of such a transformation is frequently encountered in general accounts of medieval agrarian development. It appears first to have entered the literature in 1888 with the publication of *The Pioneers and Progress of English Farming* by R. E. Prothero.[104] At a time when the study of English agricultural history was in its infancy, Prothero could produce no evidence to support his contention, which was little more than an extension, applied to field systems, of the Victorian conception of an inevitable, though slow, progress of institutions and modes of production. Cunningham, too, and Maitland, toyed with the idea that three-field systems were for the most part derived from two-field prototypes, although they did not allow themselves to state when they thought the development occurred.[105] H. L. Gray, in 1915, was the first formally to test the hypothesis against some of the surviving evidence. He concluded that three-field systems represented "derived" agricultural practice, having been transformed from an earlier two-field system in the period between 1250 and 1350. He wrote of an "important movement from two-field to three-field tillage. . . brought about in many parts of the eastern and northern midlands during the thirteenth and fourteenth centuries."[106] His conclusion has been accepted with enthusiasm in subsequent writings on English medieval agriculture, so that we find M. M. Postan, for example, stating that "the period between the end of the twelfth century and beginning of the fourteenth. . . saw further improvements in. . . field plans and, above all, the substitution of three-course rotation for two-course."[107] Thence, it was taken up in writings on agricultural trends in medieval Europe as a whole where, again, an "isolated" England can easily be represented as having "received" the innovation at a relatively late date.[108]

More recently, a re-examination has been made of the rather small number of cases which Gray mentioned of transformation from two- or three-field systems and of examples to which attention has been drawn since 1915. A search has been made for further evidence. The full conclusions will be presented elsewhere;[109] suffice it to say here that the evidence hardly allows us to speak of an "important movement" in medieval England from two to three fields in the sense of an agricultural transformation affecting large numbers of townships and akin to the "movement" towards enclosure and conversion to grassland which swept over vill after vill in some parts of the Midlands during the later fifteenth century. Midland field systems were certainly flexible during the Middle Ages, but the permutations and changes which were allowed touched the sown rather than the fallow field;[110] they displayed then, as in later times, a "combination of inflexibility of field course with maximum freedom in cropping."[111] A very small number of townships did change from one system to the other during the thirteenth century and the early fourteenth. But in general, the coexistence of the two variants of the Midland system which we find in later sources was already present at the start of the thirteenth century. Before then we cannot speak with certainty, but there is much to be said for the notion that the choice of the more or the less intensive variant was made at the time of, or soon after, the adoption of the Midland system itself.

The most probable reason for lack of "progress" from two- to three-field systems lies close to the theme of this essay. Gray was the first to point to a general coincidence between areas which adhered to the less intensive variant and the more "bleak, chalky, unfertile" parts of Midland England. More recently his view has been endorsed by Miller and Hatcher who state that "the correlation noted by Gray between field systems and fertility is still not entirely without foundation."[112] The note of caution in these last words is entirely proper, for it is surprising that, in view of the importance of the subject, we still have no accurate and detailed maps of the distributions of the two systems in the Middle Ages. Despite this imperfection in our present knowledge, it is difficult to escape the general truth of Gray's observation. Deep, intrinsically fertile claylands on the whole tended to support three-field systems; lighter, thinner, more easily leached soils, especially where combined with steep slopes which encouraged removal of nutrients, tended to support two-field systems. Thus, Finberg found that the less intensive two-field variant "prevailed over the greater part of the Cotswolds"; Joan Thirsk, while rightly stressing that factors other than soil type could sometimes be critical in influencing degree of intensity of land-use, nevertheless found that in the east Midlands there was a general coincidence between two-field systems and "the most barren land" in the post-medieval period.[113] The fact that some clayland soils supported two-field systems does little to undermine the general applicability of Gray's observation, for in places, and especially where problems of drainage were perhaps more than usually severe, clays as well as lighter lands could render relatively poor yields. The influences were basic ones, and there is every reason to suppose that they were appreciated at an early date.

In ecological terms, transformation from two to three fields would have had several important consequences. First, assuming that yields remained constant, output of crops was increased by one-third. In a two-field system of six-hundred acres, three-hundred acres (one half) was sown, compared with four-hundred (two-thirds) in a three-field system. Second, the land's carrying capacity for livestock was reduced, and inputs of manure, made after the fashion described in the previous section, were consequently diminished. The reduction was not as great as has sometimes been supposed; it was less than one-third if we assume one field of three-hundred acres available for grazing throughout the year under a two-field system, but one field of two-hundred acres for a whole year and another of two-hundred acres (the spring-sown field) for half of the year under a three-field system.[114] But some reduction in available grazing was inevitable; in one of the relatively few known instances of the transformation in medieval England (at South Stoke in Oxfordshire) we find that the instigator was brought before the assize to answer a complaint that he had deprived others of sources of pasture.[115] Third, occasions when the land was given over to a whole-year fallow were less frequent; under the three-field system it was once every three years rather than once every two that the soil was "rested" by being given over to weedy growths, whose uptake of nutrients was less than that of cereals, and by being "cleansed," as far as the numbers and techniques of medieval ploughings permitted, of pathogens harmful to ensuing crops. This also meant that soils would have the benefit of the flock less frequently.

Transformation from a two-field to a three-field system would have increased outputs from the land, decreased inputs, and accelerated the cycle of crops and fallow. It could not be achieved with profit except where permitted by the natural fertility of the land or where inputs from outside the system could be channelled towards it, but this, as we have seen, was not normally possible in the classic settings of the Midland system. Where such conditions did not apply, change from one system to the other might eventually result in smaller yields. That the margins were narrow indeed is shown by the following two models, one for a two-field system of six-hundred acres in which the yield ratio is four, the other for a three-field system of similar size in which the yield ratio has fallen to 3.25.

	Acres Sown	Sowing Rate*	Bushels Sown	Yield Ratio	Gross Output (bus)	Seed Corn (bus)	Net Output (bus)
Two-field system	300 x 2		= 600	x 4	= 2400	− 600	= 1800
Three-field system	400 x 2		= 800	x 3.25	= 2600	− 800	= 1800

*bushels per acre

Here a small decline in yield ratio has entirely eliminated the benefits, in terms of increased output, which should have stemmed from the sowing of the greater number of acres which the three field system permitted.

It would be quite wrong to suppose that medieval husbandmen did not appreciate considerations such as these, which would have made them reluctant to change from one system to the other unless yields could be sustained. Naturally, there is little direct evidence relating to their opinions in the matter. From Sweden, where there was greater codification of agricultural practice and land division than in England, Oestergoetland Law declared that in cases of disagreement, "the party in the village shall prevail that wants to let half the land lie fallow." An English extent of 1361 refers to the possibility of sowing two-thirds of the land "if they are well cultivated" (*si bene coluntur*), perhaps implying that it was well-recognized that more intensive rotations required careful management of the soil; in 1626 some of the inhabitants of Caistor in Lincolnshire, justifying the taking of two successive crops from part of one of the township's two fields, claimed that the practice was feasible "where the strength and nature of the land will bear it."[116] Husbandmen and reeves (on behalf of their lords) would certainly have had the opportunity to observe yields on *inhoks*,[117] small acreages occasionally sown in the fallow field; and although to write of medieval "experimental plots"[118] is perhaps to anticipate a little, they could observe the effects on yields of the variations in cropping which were permitted in common field systems and of subtle differences in soil types between one part of a field and another. Walter de Henley did not in fact "advocate" the "more progressive" three-field system.[119] When he wrote of arable land "parted into three parts, one for winter corn, another for spring corn, and the third fallow," and of lands "parted into two—as they are in many *pays*" he passed no judgement on which was the superior system. Of the different needs and capabilities of different soils he was deeply aware,[120] and they may have been considerations which were in his mind when he described what he clearly regarded as a natural coexistence of the two systems. In view of the fact that the evidence does not support the idea of a transformation from one system to another in thirteenth-century England, it is probable that a coexistence of this kind, based upon the differing capacities of the land from place to place, had existed for some time, perhaps for several centuries, before Walter de Henley wrote of it in the 1280s.[121]

A change from two-field to three-field management was not, then, for reasons discussed, a widely adopted response to population pressures before the Black Death. What of other strategies involving a more radical break with traditional practices? Some strategies, taken up later, were not appropriate to the thirteenth century. Conversion of whole townships to extensively managed grass sheep-walks—a course experienced by no small number of Midland village lands in the late fifteenth century—was clearly inappropriate at a time when demand for basic foodstuffs dictated agricultural trends and labor was freely available. The advanced rotations which reached their full development in some parts of the Midlands in the final phase of open-field farming—rotations which relied much on carefully sown rather than "accidental" leys—had to await perfection in the management of clover, sainfoin, and other "artificial grasses" in the seventeenth century; they too belong to a time when it was not the high price of grain which dictated agricultural trends.[122] But one alternative solution to the obligatory whole-year fallow of the Midland system was available earlier; this was the field cultivation of peas or beans which, when combined with intensive management of the soil, allowed the fallow area to be much reduced without diminishing either the acreage or yields of grain crops. This system has received detailed study in the meticulous work of B. M. S. Campbell on the coastlands of northeast Norfolk.[123] Here there took place, in the thirteenth century, the full flowering of a system of cultivation correctly described by Campbell as anticipating many of the technical advances normally attributed to the "new husbandry" of the seventeenth century. Much of Campbell's quantitative data comes from demesne accounts, but there is every indication to show that the same practices were followed on peasant holdings.

At the heart of this agricultural system was the field cultivation of legumes, especially peas. The proportion of the sown area devoted to legumes could be as much as 33% (as on the Earl of Norfolk's marsh-edge manor of Halvergate); more normally it was between 15% and 25%,[124] figures which were nevertheless very high by thirteenth-century standards.[125] Another essential feature of the system was the careful attention given to a variety of labor-intensive manuring practices. Stall feeding of oxen and other large beasts produced quantities of dung which were carefully applied to the arable; where transport by boat and cart was feasible, night soil from the provincial capital of Norwich was also spread on the fields. Dung from sheep was far more carefully managed than in the rather random and extensive methods which appear to have been the norm under the Midland system. In some places, dung gathered from sheep pens in the neighboring marshes was laboriously carted inland and spread systematically upon the arable; in others, sheep were fed on marshlands and heathlands by day and led in the evenings to folds on the arable, which they dunged beautifully without damage to the prevailing loamy soils of the region. A further essential feature of the system, as labor-intensive as the management of manure, was the very careful treatment of the seed-bed, which was given repeated ploughings before sowing time and was weeded meticulously during the growing season.

All of these devices allowed fallows to be reduced, a course which could be achieved without difficulty in a region where rigid common field systems had never developed. Normally, only about 10% of the arable was fallow in any one year, as compared with 33% or 50% under the Midland system. On some demesnes, fallows were dispensed with altogether: manors on the Earl of Norfolk's estate again provide examples, but there are others from different lordships, small lay estates, and the marsh-side manor of Flegg belonging to St. Benet's at Holm.[126] Yet, cereal yields did not suffer. Campbell calculates a mean yield ratio of 5.6 for wheat on demesnes for which data are available before 1350, yields which compare very favorably with a mean of 3.85 on the Winchester estate over the same period.[127] High yields per acre, combined with high proportions of the arable under crops, made these the most productive of all medieval farming systems. Their productivity was founded, in part, on labor-intensive methods of cleansing the soil and of replenishing it with nutrients and, in part, on incorporation of legumes into the system. The use of legumes had the triple function of fixing reserves of nitrogen required for subsequent high yields of cereals, of giving a rich feed for livestock, to some degree recycled as farmyard manure, and of providing one of the system's outputs in the form of saleable foodstuffs. Also very important were inputs into the system from a wider hinterland, of Norwich night soil, and of the dung of sheep whose ultimate origins were heathland and, particularly, rich marshland pastures. The variegated countryside of northeast Norfolk, with good loams everywhere in close proximity to small patches of marsh and of heath developed on Glacial sands and gravels, allowed for a system of flows and movements of nutrients which must, to a degree, have compensated for the heavy transfers away from the arable fields that characterize all market-oriented systems of cereal production.

Thirteenth-century England boasted several other pockets of intensive husbandry. P. F. Brandon was the first to describe many elements of the system as it operated on the coastands of Sussex, where it seems to have been already developed by the middle of the century.[128] Campbell points to further examples in Holderness and in coastal Kent. Details of other localities have yet to be described in print. On some of the Abbey of Glastonbury's "island" manors in Somerset, surrounded by partially reclaimed marshes, legumes formed the dominant field crop in the early fourteenth century, occupying 33% of the acreage sown at Zoy in 1312-13 and 29% at Brent in 1311-12.[129] Indeed, in 1189—and this may be our earliest precise reference to the existence of intensive husbandry in England—Abbot Henry de Sully's survey reported ricks of beans harvested from demesnes on the members of the manor of Brent.[130]

Intensive husbandry never spread far beyond these favored localities in the thirteenth century; the debate about whether or not legumes "loomed as large as the cereals"[131] in medieval England is easily resolved once it is realized that in a few areas they were field crops crucial to local agricultural systems, while elsewhere they were of relatively minor importance, at least until the late fourteenth century.[132] In seeking to explain why the system flourished in particular coastal settings and did not spread more widely during the early Middle Ages, particularly within the Midlands, it would be too simplistic to suppose a primitive state in the mechanisms by which ideas and techniques were diffused. Many large medieval estates had numerous outliers, so that the Earls of Norfolk, to take just one example, possessed manors in Hertfordshire, Berkshire, Sussex, on the Welsh borders, and in Ireland, as well as their considerable East Anglian properties.[133] To a degree, such scattered lands would have been linked by the itineraries of their lords. Far more important in this context were the constant comings and goings between manors of bailiffs and stewards, often professional men who served several lordships in turn; Geoffrey Russel, for example, was successively steward to Peterborough Abbey, Isabella de Fortibus, the Palatinate of Durham, and the Honour of Wallingford, offices which put him in close touch with almost half the counties of England.[134] Stewards may not have concerned themselves with the minutiae of husbandry on individual manors (where reeves were perhaps responsible for setting the pace), but being highly mobile and much concerned with profits from the land by virtue of their profession and sometimes of their birth, they made for a great deal of mobility of ideas touching agricultural practice. It would not be wholly wrong to place some emphasis on institutional factors as brakes on the widespread diffusion of the "new" husbandry in thirteenth-century England. These practices developed and flourished in parts of the country which never took up strict, fully-fledged common field institutions. Despite the fact, rightly stressed in recent writings, that cropping practices were flexible even in the most rigorously managed and binding of common field systems, it cannot be denied that where common rights on the arable and where farming rhythms centered on the fallow year were most strongly developed, it would have been difficult to implement a departure from tradition as radical as the virtual elimination of fallow grazing. Particularly at a time of population pressure, small holders and others without access to extensive wastes or woods relied much on grazing rights over the arable. Here we have touched upon another, perhaps crucial, factor. The high productivity of medieval systems of intensive husbandry was dependent upon imports of nutrients from a wider hinterland. Where no large cities were present to provide night soil, where no waterways existed to make its carriage cheap and, above all, where no rich marshland or other pastures remained from which nutrients could be drawn towards the arable—in settings such as these, the classic settings for the Midland system, intensification of agricultural practice was rendered difficult indeed.

Conclusion

The discussions in the previous section leave many loose ends, particularly from the centuries before the thirteenth, centuries for which information on the development of field systems is vague and data on crops, livestock, and population vaguer still. I shall conclude by suggesting only three of the many questions which must still be answered. First is the question of the mechanisms which, in a few localities, initiated developments towards an intensive type of husbandry far more productive than the Midland system. According to figures in *Domesday Book*, northeast Norfolk was the most densely populated part of England in the late eleventh century; coastal Sussex, another area where an intensive system was adopted, was almost as well-populated.[135] These figures might suggest that elements of the system were already present by the time of the Conquest; alternatively, these high densities of population, whatever their ultimate cause, may have initiated cycles of intensification in cropping and in the application of labor, which in turn may have encouraged further population growth, culminating in the high state of cultivation which we see in the thirteenth century. Whichever is the answer, one fact does seem clear: what permitted such developments to take place was the ecological diversity of their settings, with easily worked soils everywhere in close proximity to small patches of marsh and heath. These patches were "negative" lands in terms of the expansion of cultivation, but their existence was crucial in steering the development of field systems away from communal practices and in providing rich adjuncts to arable fields. By contrast, a typical township in the Midland lowlands possessed very little negative land of this kind, perhaps only a tract of stream-side meadow reserved for plough-beasts. Such settings encouraged development along a different course; a township's ploughlands would expand until little "natural" grazing remained, so that it became necessary to evolve a system for closely integrating and alternating crop production and grazing on the same land. That system, the Midland system, was neither as productive nor as labor-intensive as the advanced husbandry found in northeast Norfolk and a few other favored localities. It was appropriate to relatively low levels of population, which perhaps lends support to evidence suggesting that it evolved at an early date. Its persistence in not radically altered form throughout the twelfth and thirteenth centuries raises a second question, the supposed inevitability of intensification of agriculture under population pressure, an assumption of some more optimistic models of agrarian development. The Midland system seems to have been doomed to remain at a modest level of productivity in the early Middle Ages. It embodied strong institutional restraints upon any radical alteration and was founded upon the virtual elimination of "natural" grazings, a trend difficult to reverse under conditions of population pressure. In such a delicately balanced ecosystem, intensification of cultivation, particularly by reduction of fallows, presented stubborn problems, and this fact, in turn, raises a third question: what part did the Midland system, widespread as it was, play in the crisis of the late thirteenth century?

146

Cooter has suggested that difficulties may have arisen from a short "burst of increased productivity" around the beginning of the thirteenth century, soon resulting in a long-term fall in yields, while the more well-established interpretations of the crisis stress the role played by inferior, newly reclaimed land which yielded well for a time, but then rapidly deteriorated.[136] These interpretations are not applicable to the Midland lowlands if, as the evidence suggests, their field systems remained relatively inert during the thirteenth century while their history of active colonization had been terminated even earlier. The combination of a relatively inflexible cultivated ecosystem and a mounting population can easily account for evidence of poverty and landlessness, when the numbers of people grow and the size of effective holdings diminishes while the sytem expands neither in area nor in output per acre. But it is more difficult to account for evidence of deterioration of the land and of yields under these circumstances; such trends might, in fact, seem to contradict the finding that the Midland system underwent no major developments leading to reduction of the fallow area during the thirteenth century.[137] To judge from experimental data which suggest relatively quick stabilization of yields under a constant method of management, a thirteenth-century decline in productivity can hardly be attributed to the intensification of cultivation which occurred at the inception of the system several centuries earlier. Nor can it be attributed to a tendency of the system to repel certain advanced practices in soil management: it has been suggested here that the logic of the system made it incompatible with multiple ploughings of fallows and, in places, with the systematic folding of sheep. Although their absence may have contributed to a prevailing low level of yields, however, it is unlikely to have resulted in a decline. We shall have to examine other changes in the minutiae of the system's operation which, under thirteenth-century conditions, may have disturbed its delicate balance. Perhaps, for example, there was a tendency for demesne and peasant holdings alike to react to the inflationary trends of the century by concentrating upon production of the more highly priced yet in ecological terms more demanding among bread grains; perhaps there was a tendency toward under-investment in the livestock so essential to the functioning of the system. Perhaps, too, as crises deepened, there occurred generally that shortage or *caristia* of labor of which we hear for certain on some demesnes. In short, much remains to be learned about the finer details of the operation of Midland fields, their ecological rationale, and the ways in which even relatively small changes in routine could adversely affect a finely balanced ecosystem.

147

NOTES

[1] H. L. Gray, *English Field Systems* (Cambridge: Harvard Univ. Press, 1915), p. 3.

[2] For example, B. M. S. Campbell, "Population Change and the Genesis of Commonfields on a Norfolk Manor," *Economic History Review*, 2nd ser., 33 (1980), 174-92.

[3] A. R. H. Baker and R. A. Butlin, "Conclusion: Problems and Perspectives," in *Studies of Field Systems in the British Isles*, ed. A. R. H. Baker and R. A. Butlin (Cambridge: Cambridge Univ. Press, 1973), p. 653.

[4] Thus, to R. C. Hoffmann, "those characteristic experiences and priorities that produce the mentality of peasants" were responsible for the emergence and persistence of communal control of field systems, while to D. N. McCloskey the scattering of strips may be traced ultimately to "self-interest as well as fellow-feeling and conservativism" among medieval peasants. See R. C. Hoffmann, "Medieval Origins of the Common Fields," in *European Peasants and their Markets: Essays in Agrarian Economic History*, ed. W. N. Parker and E. L. Jones (Princeton: Princeton Univ. Press, 1975), p. 61; and D. N. McCloskey, "English Open Fields as Behavior towards Risk," *Research in Economic History*, 1 (1976), 165.

[5] R. A. Dodgshon, "The Landholding Foundations of the Open-field System," *Past and Present*, 67 (1975), 3-29.

[6] W. S. Cooter, "Ecological Dimensions of Medieval Agrarian Systems," *Agricultural History*, 52 (1978), 458-77.

[7] For comments from this viewpoint, see R. S. Loomis, "Ecological Dimensions of Medieval Agrarian Systems: An Ecologist Responds," *Agricultural History*, 52 (1978), 478-83.

[8] J. A. Raftis, *Assart Data and Land Values: Two Studies in the East Midlands 1200-1350*, Subsidia Mediaevalia, 3 (Toronto: Pontifical Institute of Mediaeval Studies, 1974), pp. 19, 50, 74.

[9] R. H. Hilton, "Medieval Agrarian History," in *Victoria County History* (hereafter *VCH*), *Leicestershire*, II, ed. W. G. Hoskins (London: Oxford Univ. Press, 1954), p. 162.

[10] For example: *The Domesday Geography of Midland England*, ed. H. C. Darby, 2nd ed. (Cambridge: Cambridge Univ. Press, 1971), pp. 32, 89, 249, 408; and Public Record Office (hereafter PRO), C. 145/20/15 where it is stated that some of the arable lands of Deerhurst Priory in Gloucestershire could not be stocked because meadow was insufficient.

[11] Thus an extent of Ashby Folville in 1310 mentions "separate pasture in divers plots" worth two shillings, which, at prevailing prices, cannot have amounted to much more than two or three acres; an extent of Broughton Astley in 1301 mentions "divers separate pastures" worth five shillings, that is about five to eight acres: G. F. Farnham, *Leicestershire Medieval Village Notes*, 1 (Leicester: the author, 1929), pp. 56, 203.

[12] W. G. Hoskins, "The Fields of Wigston Magna," *Transactions of the Leicestershire Archaeological Society*, 19 pt. 2 (1937), 171; P. D. A. Harvey, *A*

Medieval Oxfordshire Village: Cuxham 1240 to 1400 (Oxford: Oxford Univ. Press, 1965), map 2.

[13] Raftis, *Assart Data*, pp. 53, 77.

[14] For example: PRO C. 134/51 and 133/71/13, extents of Salwarpe on the Plain of Worcester and Lydeard Puncherton, a small manor in the Vale of Taunton Deane, Somersetshire; *The Domesday of St. Paul's*, ed. W. H. Hale, Camden Society, 69 (London, 1858), pp. 59, 69, extents of Tillingham and Runwell in Essex.

[15] W. J. Ford, "Some Settlement Patterns in the Central Region of the Warwickshire Avon," in *Medieval Settlement: Continuity and Change*, ed. P. H. Sawyer (London: Edward Arnold, 1976), p. 294.

[16] O. Rackham, *Ancient Woodland: Its History, Vegetation and Uses in England* (London: Edward Arnold, 1980), pp. 173-202.

[17] *Midland England*, ed. Darby, p. 343; Hilton, "Medieval Agrarian History," *VCH Leicestershire*, II, p. 149.

[18] That is, east Leicestershire.

[19] R. A. McKinley, "The Forests of Leicestershire," *VCH Leicestershire*, II, pp. 265-66.

[20] Raftis, *Assart Data*, pp. 154-55.

[21] L. M. Cantor, "The Medieval Parks of Leicestershire," *Transactions of the Leicestershire Archaeological and Historical Society*, 46 (1970-71), 11.

[22] For example: PRO C. 135/32/28, 135/51/12, 135/76/19, 135/70/7, and E. 149/9/24, extents of Sapperton, Tewkesbury, and Chipping Sodbury (in Gloucester shire) East Luccombe, Dundon, and Yarlington (in Somersetshire).

[23] Somerset Record Office, D.D. C.C. 112968/4. There is a similar reference to the only extensive upland pasture in Leicestershire, from one of whose bordering manors a bailiff reported (in 1324) a "plenitude of pasture in Charnwood Forest." See Hilton, "Medieval Agrarian History," *VCH Leicestershire*, II, p. 165.

[24] *Rentalia et Custumaria Michaelis de Ambresbury, 1235-1252, et Rogeri de Ford, 1252-1261*, Somerset Record Society Publications, 5 (Taunton, 1891), p. 196.

[25] Gray, *Field Systems*, front.

[26] Data principally from escheators' extents in Inquisitions Post Mortem, Miscellaneous Inquisitions, and Alien Priory files: PRO C. 132-5, C. 145, and E. 106. To figures from these have been added data from a few extents drawn up in the course of estate administration.

[27] PRO C. 132/3/10 and British Library (hereafter BL), Add. MS. 17450, fol. 218, extents of Honiton and Uplyme.

[28] For this practice and for other aspects of the liberal management of the region's rough pastures in the Middle Ages, see H. S. A. Fox, "Field Systems of East and South Devon. Part I: East Devon," *Transactions of the Devonshire Association*, 104 (1972), 97-100.

[29] BL Add. MS. 17450, fol. 218; PRO C. 135/45/19.

[30] Devon Record Office, 123M/E/31.

[31] N. 26 above and Raftis, *Assart Data*, p. 84.

[32] T. W. Whale, "Principles of Domesday Survey and Feudal Aids," *Transactions of the Devonshire Association*, 32 (1900), 546; E. G. Fogwill, "Pastoralism on Dartmoor," *Transactions of the Devonshire Association*, 86 (1954), 112. For similar arrangements in another of the western borderlands lying just beyond the limits of the zone of Midland field system, see R. T. Rowley, "The Clee Forest: A Study in Common Rights," *Transactions of the Shropshire Archaeological Society*, 58 (1965-68), 48-67.

[33] Unless otherwise indicated, sources for the following paragraphs are BL Eg. MS. 3321, fols. 233-36 (an extent of 1332); Longleat House MSS., 11273, 11272, 11246, 11215, 11216, 10655, 10656, 10766, 10761, 10632 (*compoti* from the late thirteenth century and the early fourteenth), 11250, 10778, 11252, 10770, 10711, 10773, 10774, 11251, 11179 (court rolls). I am grateful to the Marquis of Bath for access to these documents.

[34] F. M. Page, "Bidentes Hoylandie," *Economic History*, 1 (1926-29), 602-13.

[35] Date from Longleat House MS. 11273 (for Podimore) and confirmed by extents for other Somerset manors, e.g., PRO E. 149/9/19, 21, 24.

[36] J. Billingsley (Bath, 1797), p. 239.

[37] W. O. Ault, "Open-field Husbandry and the Village Community: A Study of Agrarian By-laws in Medieval England," *Transactions of the American Philosophical Society*, N.S. 55 pt. 7 (1965), 40.

[38] R. Trow-Smith, *A History of British Livestock Husbandry to 1700* (London: Routledge and Kegan Paul, 1957), pp. 158-60.

[39] These two years, one excessively dry, the other wet, were years of adverse weather in southern England at large: J. Z. Titow, "Evidence of Weather in the Account Rolls of the Bishopric of Winchester, 1209-1350," *Economic History Review*, 2nd ser., 12 (1959-60), 382, 384-86.

[40] "Village Livestock in the Thirteenth Century," *Economic History Review*, 2nd ser., 15 (1962-63), 219-49.

[41] *The Great Chartulary of Glastonbury*, ed. A. Watkin, 3 vols., Somerset Record Society Publications 59, 63, 64 (Taunton, 1947-56), II, p. 478.

[42] W. Harwood Long, "The Low Yields of Corn in Medieval England," *Economic History Review*, 2nd ser., 32 (1979), 469.

[43] D. Oschinsky, *Walter of Henley and Other Treatises on Estate Management and Accounting* (Oxford: Clarendon Press, 1971), p. 397.

[44] The evidence collected by Ault, although rather late, suggests that stints of one or two sheep per acre were normal, but the figure might in some places be 1½ or even three: Ault, "Open-field Husbandry," 26-27. A few other examples of comparable figures are: J. Thirsk, "Field Systems of the East Midlands," in *Studies of Field Systems*, ed. Baker and Butlin, pp. 248-49; R. C. Chibnall, *Sherington: Fiefs and Fields of a Buckinghamshire Village* (Cambridge: Cambridge Univ. Press, 1965), p. 284; and Somerset Record Office, D.D. F.S. box 52, court roll of Podimore, 1658.

[45] C. R. W. Spedding and E. C. Diekmahns, *Grasses and Legumes in British Agriculture* (Farnham Royal: Commonwealth Agricultural Bureau, 1972), p. 19.

[46] H. H. Lamb, *Climate, Present, Past and Future*, vol. 2, *Climatic History and the Future* (London: Methuen and Co., 1977), p. 374.

[47] A description of Hallaton in Leicestershire in 1665: J. Nichols, *The History and Antiquities of the County of Leicester* (London, 1795-1811), vol. 2, p. 599.

[48] Oschinsky, *Walter of Henley*, p. 321.

[49] *Le Bon Berger ou le vray régime et gouvernement des bergers et bergères*, ed. P. Lacroix (Paris: I. Liseux, 1879), p. 109.

[50] Oschinsky, *Walter of Henley*, p. 321.

[51] *The Kalendar of Abbot Sampson of Bury St. Edmunds and Related Documents*, ed. R. H. C. Davis, Camden Society, 3rd. ser., 84 (London, 1954), pp. 127-28.

[52] C. Parain, "The Evolution of Agricultural Technique," in *The Cambridge Economic History of Europe*, vol. 2, *The Agrarian Life of the Middle Ages*, ed. M. M. Postan (Cambridge: Cambridge Univ. Press, 1966), p. 151.

[53] Cooter, "Ecological Dimensions," 468.

[54] It should be noted here that an interesting recent study of the historical ecology of English meadows has suggested that the caloric value of most natural meadowland was in fact relatively low before the improvements of post-medieval times: C. Lane, "The Development of Pastures and Meadows during the Sixteenth and Seventeenth Centuries," *Agricultural History Review*, 28 (1980), 18-30.

[55] For the distribution of balks and their uses for grazing, see E. Kerridge, "A Reconsideration of Some Former Husbandry Practices," *Agricultural History Review*, 3 (1955), 36-39. For a description of the grassy balks which still survive at Braunton, see H. P. R. Finberg, "The Open Field in Devon," in W. G. Hoskins and H. P. R. Finberg, *Devonshire Studies* (London: Jonathan Cape, 1952), p. 266.

[56] BL Eg. MS. 3321, fol., 234.

[57] Somerset Record Office, D.D. C.C. 131911a/10.

[58] C. S. and C. S. Orwin, *The Open Fields* (Oxford: Clarendon Press, 1938), end maps.

[59] Longleat House MS. 11273.

[60] Nichols, *The History and Antiquities of the County of Leicester*, vol. 2, p. 599.

[61] The high yields which were a feature of some Devonshire demesnes in the later Middle Ages may owe something to movements of this kind, although other influences were also at work there, notably convertible husbandry. For the yields, see H. P. R. Finberg, *Tavistock Abbey: A Study in the Social and Economic History of Devon* (Cambridge: Cambridge Univ. Press, 1951), pp. 110-15.

[62] For examples of this type of field system from the borderlands beyond the western boundary of the zone of Midland systems, see A. J. Roderick, "Open-field Agriculture in Herefordshire in the Later Middle Ages," *Transactions of the Woolhope Naturalists' Field Club*, 33 (1949-51), 55-67; and Fox, "Field Systems of East and South Devon," 94-96. For one of the uplands within

151

the Midland zone, see D. Roden, "Field Systems of the Chiltern Hills and their Environs," in *Studies of Field Systems*, ed. Baker and Butlin, pp. 325-38.

[63] Some of these operational benefits are discussed in C. J. Dahlman, *The Open Field System and Beyond* (Cambridge: Cambridge Univ. Press, 1980), pp. 111-14.

[64] *The Book of Husbandry by Master Fitzherbert*, ed. W. W. Skeat, English Dialect Society Texts, 37 (London: Trübner and Co., 1882), p. 28; J. Lee, *Considerations Concerning Common Fields and Inclosures* (1654), cited in Nichols, *The History and Antiquities of the County of Leicester*, vol. 4, p. 86; and, from among the many nineteenth-century comments on this question, H. Stephens, *The Book of the Farm*, rev. ed. (Edinburgh: William Blackwood, 1887), vol. 2, pp. 454-55.

[65] W. J. Blake, "Hooker's Synopsis Chorographical of Devonshire," *Transactions of the Devonshire Association*, 47 (1915), 344. For the relationship between this type of husbandry and enclosed field systems, see H. S. A. Fox, "The Functioning of Bocage Landscapes in Devon and Cornwall Between 1500 and 1800," in *Les Bocages: histoire, écologie, économie*, ed. J. Missonnier (Rennes: Institut National de la Recherche Agronomique, 1977), pp. 55-61.

[66] *The Book of Husbandry*, p. 28.

[67] Sources for examples from Lincolnshire, Buckinghamshire, Derbyshire, and Bedfordshire are given in H. S. A. Fox, "Approaches to the Adoption of the Midland System," in *The Origins of Open-field Agriculture*, ed. T. Rowley (London: Croom Helm, 1981), p. 82 and n. 35. For a further example from Oxfordshire, see *Manorial Records of Cuxham, Oxfordshire circa 1200-1359*, ed. P. D. A. Harvey, Historical Manuscripts Commission Joint Publication 23 (London, 1976), pp. 94-95.

[68] Particularly those favored Midland townships where low-lying land gave way abruptly to downland, like the Chiltern-edge township of South Stoke in Oxford shire or the down-side township of Teffont Magna in Wiltshire: *VCH Oxfordshire*, VII (London: Oxford Univ. Press, 1962), p. 102; *VCH Wiltshire*, VIII (London: Oxford Univ. Press for the Institute of Historical Research, 1965), p. 75. In an earlier discussion I made too much of the function of the fallow field in providing space for stock and not enough of the function of stock in the fallow field ecosystem: Fox, "Approaches," pp. 66, 68. This question of relative emphasis raises a further query: was the genesis of the Midland system occasioned by a desire to maximize numbers of livestock, particularly sheep, or by a desire to increase arable output through provision of the benefits of regular fallows? For a comment see P. D. A. Harvey, "The English Trade in Wool and Cloth, 1150-1250: Some Problems and Suggestions," in *Produzione, Commercio e Consumo dei Panni di Lana XII-XVIII secolo* (Florence: Olschki, 1976), p. 372 n. 20.

[69] For example, Trow-Smith, *Livestock Husbandry*, p. 158; Dahlman, *Open Field System*, p. 114.

[70] Oschinsky, *Walter of Henley*, p. 329; see also "The Seneschaucy", p. 277, for reference to the fold, although again a not very specific one.

[71] E. Kerridge, "The Sheepfold in Wiltshire and the Floating of the Water

meadows," *Economic History Review*, 2nd ser., 6 (1953-54), 282-89.

[72] For example, custumals of some Wiltshire manors and of Puddletown in Dorset: R. Scott, "Medieval Agriculture," in *VCH Wiltshire*, IV, ed. E. Crittall (London: Oxford Univ. Press, 1959), p. 22; BL Cott. Tib. D. vi, fol. 118.

[73] There are very few references to folding in Ault, "Open-field Husbandry." The incidence and distribution of the practice, particularly in relation to soil types, needs much further investigation which might well begin with the albeit very late county and regional reports produced by the Board of Agriculture and by William Marshall. In Gloucestershire, for example, it was found that folding on the vale lands invariably gave sheep the rot, while on the lighter lands of the Cotswolds it was essential in order to compact the soil: W. Marshall, *The Rural Economy of Gloucestershire* (Gloucester, 1789), vol. 1, p. 209; T. Rudge, *General View of the Agriculture of the County of Gloucester* (London, 1807), p. 15.

[74] On this point see Kerridge, "The Sheepfold in Wiltshire," pp. 283-84.

[75] A. N. May, "An Index of Thirteenth-century Peasant Impoverishment? Manor Court Fines," *Economic History Review*, 2nd ser., 26 (1973), 389-401.

[76] Hoffman, "Medieval Origins of the Common Fields," p. 50; this follows J. Thirsk, "The Common Fields," *Past and Present*, 29 (1964), 23.

[77] Fox, "Approaches," pp. 72-83.

[78] R. Lennard, *Rural England 1086-1135: A Study of Social and Agrarian Conditions* (Oxford: Clarendon Press, 1959), pp. 1, 3.

[79] M. Bloch, *Les Caractères originaux de l'histoire rurale française* (Oslo: H. Aschehoug, 1931), pp. 5-17.

[80] Bloch, *Les Caractérés originaux*, p. 16 and plate 2; C. Higounet, "L'Abate Suger e le campagne francesi," in *Paysages et villages neufs du moyen âge* (Bordeaux: Féderation Historique du Sud-Ouest, 1975), pp. 119-23.

[81] As first formally suggested by B. K. Roberts, "Village Plans in County Durham: A Preliminary Statement," *Medieval Archaeology*, 16 (1972), 33-56.

[82] PRO E. 132/152B.

[83] *Curia Regis Rolls*, 13 (London: HMSO, 1959), pp. 239-41. See also *Feet of Fines for the County of York from 1218 to 1231*, ed. J. Parker, Yorkshire Archaeological Society, 62 (Leeds, 1921), pp. 2-4.

[84] T. Hearne, *Adam de Domerham: Historia de Rebus Gestis Glastoniensibus*, 2 vols. (Oxford, 1727), pp. 307-08.

[85] These examples could, of course, be multiplied. For other cases of colonization from the three localities mentioned here, Dartmoor, the moorlands of northern England, and the Somerset marshes, see W. G. Hoskins, "Cholwich," in Hoskins and Finberg, *Devonshire Studies*, pp. 78-94; R. I. Hodgson, "Medieval Colonization in Northern Ryedale, Yorkshire," *Geographical Journal*, 135 (1969), 44-54; W. M. Williams, *The Draining of the Somerset Levels* (Cambridge: Cambridge Univ. Press, 1970), pp. 40-74.

[86] Examples of studies which make use of these last types of records are: B. K. Roberts, "A Study of Medieval Colonization in the Forest of Arden, Warwickshire," *Agricultural History Review*, 16 (1968), 111-13; Raftis, *Assart Data*, pp. 98-156.

153

[87] *Anastatic Drawing Society*, vol. for 1860, plate xlvi. See also "The Rydeware Chartulary," *Collections for a History of Staffordshire*, 16 (1896), 229-302; *Catalogue of Additions to the Manuscripts 1926-1930* (London: Trustees of the British Museum, 1959), pp. 222-23; and Nichols, *The History and Antiquities of the County of Leicester*, vol. 3, p. 1002.

[88] E. King, *Peterborough Abbey 1086-1310: A Study in the Land Market* (Cambridge: Cambridge Univ. Press, 1973), pp. 81-82.

[89] G. F. Farnham, *Charnwood Forest and its Historians and the Charnwood Manors* (Leicester: Edgar Backus for the Leicestershire Archeological Society, 1930), pp. 100, 110.

[90] The account for 1251-52 is transcribed in J. Z. Titow, *English Rural Society 1200-1350* (London: George Allen and Unwin, 1969), pp. 198-200.

[91] Fox, "Approaches," pp. 95-97.

[92] Spalding Gentlemen's Society, Wrest Park Cartulary, fols. 242-242r.

[93] H. C. Darby, *The Domesday Geography of Eastern England*, 3rd ed. (Cambridge: Cambridge Univ. Press, 1971), p. 299.

[94] *VCH Bedfordshire*, I (London: Constable, 1904), p. 251, which records woodland for three-hundred swine and ten rams per year from customary woodland dues; *A Digest of the Charters Preserved in the Cartulary of the Priory of Dunstable*, ed. G. H. Fowler, Bedfordshire Historical Record Society Publ. 10 (Aspley Guise, 1926), pp. 71, 213; BL Harl. MS. 1885, fol. 7.

[95] BL Harl. MS. 1885, fol. 7r.

[96] It is interesting to note that for two other places evidence, though slighter than that used here, has been put forward for the relatively late emergence of a Midland system; both belong to "intermediate" countrysides of the same type. They are Marden on the flanks of the Bromyard Upland in Herefordshire and Church Bickenhill on the borders of Arden in Warwickshire: J. A. Sheppard, *The Origins and Evolution of Field and Settlement Patterns in the Herefordshire Manor of Marden*, Dept. of Geography, Queen Mary College, London, Occasional Papers, 15 (London, 1979), p. 22; V. Skipp, "The Evolution of Settlement and Open-field Topography in North Arden Down to 1300," in *The Origins of Open-field Agriculture*, ed. Rowley, pp. 167-69. Some northern townships belong to this intermediate type, and there, too, it has been suggested that the Midland system was slow in maturing: E. Miller, "Farming in Northern England During the Twelfth and Thirteenth Centuries," *Northern History*, 11 (1975), 11.

[97] A. H. Smith, "The Hwicce," in *Franciplegius: Medieval and Linguistic Studies in Honor of Francis Peabody Magoun Jr.*, ed. J. B. Bessinger and R. P. Creed (London: George Allen and Unwin, 1965), pp. 56-65.

[98] D. Hooke, "Open-field Agriculture: The Evidence from the Pre-Conquest Charters of the West Midlands," in *The Origins of Open-field Agriculture*, ed. Rowley, p. 59; Ford, "Settlement Patterns in the Region of the Avon," pp. 292-94; H. P. R. Finberg, "Anglo-Saxon England to 1042," in *The Agrarian History of England and Wales*, Vol. I.ii, A.D. 43-1042, ed. Finberg (Cambridge: Cambridge Univ. Press, 1972), p. 495.

[99] P. Liddle, *Leicestershire Archaeology: The Present State of Knowledge, Vol. I, To the End of the Roman Period*, Leicestershire Museums, Art

Galleries and Record Service, Archaeological Repts., 4 (Leicester: Leicester-shire County Council, 1982), pp. 22, 44.

[100] As by K. Cameron, "Scandinavian Settlement in the Territory of the Five Boroughs: The Place-name Evidence," in *Place-name Evidence for the Anglo-Saxon Invasion and Scandinavian Settlements*, ed. K. Cameron (Notting-ham: English Place-Name Society, 1975), pp. 121, 133.

[101] *Midland England*, ed. Darby, p. 334, and compare pp. 24, 80, 134, 188, 242, 288, 374, 398.

[102] Favored parts of the North of England must not be forgotten here: see J. A. Sheppard, "Pre-Conquest Yorkshire: Fiscal Carucates as an Index of Land Exploitation," *Transactions of the Institute of British Geographers*, 65 (1975), 67-78.

[103] C. Renfrew, *Before Civilization: The Radiocarbon Revolution and Prehistoric Europe* (London: Jonathan Cape, 1973).

[104] *The Pioneers and Progess of English Farming* (London: Longmans, Green and Co, 1888), p. 4.

[105] W. Cunningham, *The Growth of English Industry and Commerce during the Early and Middle Ages*, 4th ed. (Cambridge: Cambridge Univ. Press, 1905), pp. 74-75; F. W. Maitland, *Domesday Book and Beyond*, new ed. (London: Fontana, 1960), pp. 425-26.

[106] Gray, *English Field Systems*, pp. 74-82, 406.

[107] "The Economic Foundations of Medieval Society" (first pub. 1950), in *Essays on Medieval Agriculture and General Problems of the Medieval Economy* (Cambridge: Cambridge Univ. Press, 1973), p. 18. See also Postan, "Medieval Agrarian Society in its Prime: England," in *Cambridge Economic History of Europe*, vol. 1, ed. Postan, p. 583.

[108] For example, L. White, *Medieval Technology and Social Change* (Oxford: Oxford Univ. Press, 1962), pp. 74-75; D. C. North and R. P. Thomas, *The Rise of the Western World: A New Economic History* (Cambridge: Cambridge Univ. Press, 1973), p. 41.

[109] H. S. A. Fox, "Podimore, Somerset, and the Transformation from Two to Three Fields in Medieval England," forthcoming paper.

[110] The best discussion of the flexibility of the Midland system is J. Thirsk's "Field Systems of the East Midlands," pp. 255-62. For the tendency for the fallow field to be inviolable, a tendency which limited this flexibility, see Fox, "Approaches," pp. 74-75 and the sources there cited.

[111] E. Kerridge, *The Agricultural Revolution* (London: George Allen and Unwin, 1967), p. 95.

[112] Gray, *English Field Systems*, p. 73; E. Miller and J. Hatcher, *Medieval England: Rural Society and Economic Change 1086-1348* (London: Longman, 1978), p. 90. See also Titow, *English Rural Society*, p. 40.

[113] H. P. R. Finberg, *Gloucestershire: An Illustrated Essay on the History of the Landscape* (London: Hodder and Stoughton, 1955), p. 40; Thirsk, "Field Systems of the East Midlands," p. 257.

[114] The assumptions here are very simplistic, for crop courses did not everywhere coincide with field courses.

[115] B. A. Lees, "Social and Economic History," in *VCH Oxfordshire II,* ed. W. Page (London: Constable, 1907), p. 171.

[116] S. Bolin, "Medieval Agrarian Society in its Prime: Scandinavia," in *Cambridge Economic History of Europe,* vol. 1, ed. Postan, p. 647; Maitland, *Domesday Book and Beyond,* p. 426 n. 2; *Lincolnshire Notes and Queries,* III (1892-93), p. 177.

[117] This was one device by which the Midland system maintained its flexibility of cropping. The best description, which makes clear that *inhoks* were temporary expedients rather than fundamental long-term modifications to field systems, is in G. C. Homans, *English Villagers of the Thirteenth Century* (Cambridge: Harvard Univ. Press, 1941), pp. 57-58.

[118] N. S. B. Gras and E. C. Gras, *The Economic and Social History of an English Village (Crawley, Hampshire) A.D. 909-1928* (Cambridge: Harvard Univ. Press, 1930), p. 35.

[119] This misreading of Walter is frequently quoted and may stem from Sir John Clapham, *A Concise Economic History of Britain from the Earliest Times to 1750* (Cambridge: Cambridge Univ. Press, 1949), p. 81.

[120] Oschinsky, *Walter of Henley,* pp. 313-15, 321, 323, 327.

[121] The argument advanced here—that awareness of the more demanding nature of the three-field system discouraged its spread to environments not suited to it—seems more convincing than other explanations, for instance, those which stress the "psychological and transactions costs of instituting the three-field system": North and Thomas, *Rise of the Western World,* p. 42. Psychological "costs" would have been minimal, for the change did not introduce an entirely new system but merely a shift from one variant of the Midland system to another; the principal of fallow grazing was maintained. Nor was the change a capital-intensive one, a point which I discuss in "Podimore, Somerset, and the Transformation from Two to Three Fields in Medieval England."

[122] H. L. Gray was the first to provide details of these developments, which were often accompanied by modifications to field systems: *English Field Systems,* pp. 125-37. See also M. Havinden, "Agricultural Progress in Open-field Oxfordshire," *Agricultural History Review,* 9 (1961), 73-83; and, for the relationship of these changes to demand and prices, E. L. Jones, "Agriculture and Economic Growth in England, 1660-1750: Agricultural Change," *Journal of Economic History,* 25 (1965), 1-18.

[123] B. M. S. Campbell, "Agricultural Progress in Medieval England: Some Evidence from Eastern Norfolk," *Economic History Review,* 2nd ser., 36 (1983), 26-46. I am most grateful to Dr. Campbell for allowing me to use the findings of his paper in advance of its publication.

[124] Campbell, "Agricultural Progress," table 3.

[125] See n. 131.

[126] B. M. S. Campbell, "The Regional Uniqueness of English Field Systems? Some Evidence from Eastern Norfolk," *Agricultural History Review,* 29 (1981), 21.

[127] Campbell, "Agricultural Progress," table 2, and J. Z. Titow, *Winchester Yields: A Study in Medieval Agricultural Productivity* (Cambridge: Cam-

bridge Univ. Press, 1972), p. 4.

[128] "Demesne Arable Farming in Coastal Sussex During the Later Middle Ages," *Agricultural History Review*, 19 (1971), 123-30; *Thirteen Custumals of the Sussex Manors of the Bishop of Chichester*, ed. W. D. Peckham, Sussex Record Society Publ., 31 (Lewes, 1925), pp. 5, 15, 35, 43, 64, 71, 81, 101, 113.

[129] Longleat House MSS. 10655 and 11216. My work, in progress, on the Glastonbury estate in Somerset shows that before 1350 figures as high as these were restricted to marsh-edge manors.

[130] *Liber Henrici de Soliaco Abbatis Glaston*, ed. J. E. Jackson, (London: Roxburghe Club Publ., 1882), pp. 68, 72, 76. It is interesting to note that in their study of grain and other impressions on prehistoric pottery, Jessen and Helbaek recognized only three sites producing evidence of beans, all of them near the Somerset Levels: see P. J. Fowler, "Later Prehistory," in *The Agrarian History of England and Wales, Vol. I.i, Prehistory*, ed. S. Piggott (Cambridge: Cambridge Univ. Press, 1981), p. 207.

[131] White, *Medieval Technology*, p. 75. Titow, *English Rural Society*, pp. 41-44, gives the following figures: 0.5% of the sown area under legumes on the estate of the Bishopric of Winchester in 1208; 8.3% in 1345; 1.8% on the estate of the Earl of Cornwall in 1296; and 18% on the estate of Christ Church, Canterbury, in 1322, a figure inflated by particularly high plantings of legumes on a few of the Priory's manors. These data come from demesnes. For the lack of large plantings of legumes on peasant holdings see: *The Taxation of 1297*, ed. A. T. Gaydon, Bedfordshire Historical Record Society Publ., 39 (Luton, 1959), p. 108; and *A Suffolk Hundred in the Year 1283: The Assessment of the Hundred of Blackbourne*, ed. E. Powell (Cambridge: Cambridge Univ. Press, 1910), pp. xxx-xxxi.

[132] By the sixteenth century some parts of the Midlands, Leicestershire for example, were notable for the growth of peas and beans. Several writers have remarked on a trend in this direction in the century after the Black Death, when pressures on field systems were reduced: Hilton, "Medieval Agrarian History," p. 160; D. Roden, "Demesne Farming in the Chiltern Hills," *Agricultural History Review*, 17 (1969), 14.

[133] *Calendar of Inquisitions Post Mortem*, 4 (London: HMSO, 1913), pp. 290-310.

[134] N. Denholm-Young, *Seignorial Administration in England* (Oxford: Oxford Univ. Press, 1937), pp. 66-85.

[135] H. C. Darby, *Domesday England* (Cambridge: Cambridge Univ. Press, 1977), p. 90.

[136] Cooter, "Ecological Dimensions," pp. 470-71; M. M. Postan, *The Medieval Economy and Society: An Economic History of Britain in the Middle Ages* (London: Weidenfeld and Nicolson, 1972), pp. 64-65.

[137] There are signs of deterioration of the land in some parts of the zone of Midland field systems: A. R. H. Baker, "Evidence in the 'Nonarum Inquisitiones' of Contracting Arable Lands in England During the Early Fourteenth Century," *Economic History Review*, 2nd ser., 19 (1966), 518-32. The Winchester estate, which has always provided much evidence for the crisis of the thirteenth century, contains some manors with Midland field systems, as well as

157

some with more eccentric arrangements. But we must not rule out the possibility that, to a degree, the Midland system operated as a brake on very rapid population growth. Above all, there is need for detailed studies *in situ*, in which all of the interrelated variables are taken into account, for at the moment too much reliance is placed on relating trends in one variable, garnered from a particular local study, to those derived from some other place or estate. And on that note we must leave it.

ENVIRONMENTAL, ECOLOGICAL, AND AGRICULTURAL SYSTEMS: APPROACHES TO SIMULATION MODELING APPLICATIONS FOR MEDIEVAL TEMPERATE EUROPE

William S. Cooter

Models are constructs which provide a serviceable reflection of phenomena that may be vastly more complex than the model itself. Let us take, for example, an ordinary map. The map is a two-dimensional representation of features on the surface of the earth, which is in actuality an irregular sphere. The map-model will, therefore, contain distortions; it will not show everything on the real globe; and, in addition, one can anticipate insuperable geometrical problems in reducing a three-dimensional spherical shape to a two-dimensional rendering.

Most modeling exercises are even more complex. Imagine a situation in which the shape of the earth is the product of a number of variables, where the variables change, sometimes randomly, where not all variables are known, where, even when known, data about the variables cannot be acquired, and where, finally, there are unavoidable errors in measurement. To map such a shape would be extraordinarily complex. Techniques for developing serviceable models of such complex situations do exist,[1] however, and my purpose here is to explore some of the more promising of these techniques, particularly as they elucidate the marked contrast in medieval historiography between the richness with which it describes superstructural aspects like political and military affairs, and the sparseness with which it treats associated agricultural systems.

Documentary sources often fail to provide more than a skeletal picture of agrarian, ecological, and environmental relationships, even when supplemented by archaeological and palynological materials. This has encouraged a somewhat static picture of medieval agricultural systems. Especially for the early Middle Ages, agricultural systems are often portrayed as mere trait complexes[2]—infield-outfield systems, two-field systems, and three-field systems are typical examples. While a range of attributes may be used to define these complexes, and considerable effort expended in outlining such functional relationships as bear on environmental restraints, technological features, or economic, demographic, and social-structural patterns, these trait-complex representations still cannot address basic questions such as the stability, viability, or sustainability of such systems. For given regions and over reasonably short periods of time, only the most general of statements can be made concerning the prevailing types of environmental patterns, ecological settings, and agricultural practices.[3] One can usually be certain that some form of mixed agriculture was involved, but this leaves considerable latitude in the types of crops and livestock present and, more importantly, the relative emphases accorded the crops and livestock within an overall management pattern. To complicate matters, one is often uncertain as to the nature of the ecosystemic backdrop of vegetation and soils. Finally, there may even be uncertainty as to the basic patterns and variabilities of regional climatic and weather systems.

A wide variety of combinations and contingencies may need to be explored to approach the problems of the short- and medium-term performances of early medieval agricultural systems. For the period after approximately the twelfth century, it is often possible to delimit more explicitly the pertinent environmental, ecological, and agrarian variables,[4] but substantial problems still remain. The use of formal modeling techniques, therefore, offers one promising avenue to enhance attempts to relate regional agrarian, ecological, and environmental processes to the dynamics of overall societal systems.

The types of models envisioned are simulation models,[5] whose growing range of applications owes much to the development of modern high-speed computers. Thanks to computers, it is feasible to join together a variety of sub-models, each of which describes a portion of phenomena. The resulting model, a hybrid, can then be subjected to numerous trials.

Various portions of the model can be varied or held constant to help determine the relative importance of different relationships, variables, parameters, or components. As the features underlying the mathematical or logical behavior of the model become well-known through repeated simulation runs and analysis, hypotheses may be supported or unsuspected features may be suggested. Eventually, a detailed evaluation and validation of the model may give one confidence that a reasonable "map" has been obtained.

Here, the phenomena of interest are environmental, ecological, and agricultural systems. The ultimate goal is to isolate a set of submodels that describes these real-world systems, and then to link them to study their inter-related behaviors with an eye to a variety of specific historical contexts. An ideal situation would be one where an abundant historical data base is available. If a reasonably long series of crop yield estimates is available for a specific area in medieval temperate Europe, for example, accompanied by logical data for variables such as temperatures and precipitation, it might be possible to develop a multivariate regression model relating weather variables to crop yields.[6] Unfortunately, one cannot obtain the needed yield series for any region in temperate Europe before the thirteenth century,[7] and meteorological information is only sporadically recorded in the sources. For medieval Europe, then, the available historical data is seldom sufficient to permit the straightforward development of a model or its rigorous validation.

A frank acknowledgement of this situation need not be taken as a counsel of despair. One can assume that processes whose features are well-known can be used to account for similar processes operating in less well-documented contexts, and, since many of the phenomena of interest involve basic physical and biological principles, this approach provokes far less suspicion than if applied to social, political, or economic affairs.

Consider briefly the array of modeling approaches or existing models that have been developed for environmental systems. Whereas elementary statistical approaches can be implemented to describe separate variables like temperatures and precipitation, the joint occurrences of a range of meteorological variables will usually show conspicuous interdependencies. The ultimate rationale is based on principles of atmospheric physics: for instance, rainfall is impossible without clouds, and the presence of clouds is associated with the passage of large-scale air masses and fronts, or local heating and convection. The same physical processes that influence the occurrence of rainfall will also control local temperature patterns. Two types of modeling approaches have been developed to simulate regional weather patterns: global circulation models, which explicitly attend to atmospheric physics and thermodynamics, have proved useful in simulating large-scale continental or hemispheric patterns;[8] and stochastic climate generators, based on a more thorough-going statistical formulation, currently have a greater potential in simulating patterns for smaller-scale regions and incorporating predictions for a much wider array of meteorological variables.[9] To this latter, hydrological models which combine physical and statistical principles to simulate the water budgets of streams and smaller riverine watersheds, can be linked.[10] Thus, the magnitude and frequency of flooding can be estimated and predictions made about soil moisture balances and erosion rates throughout the watersheds.

Such environmental models can obviously supply critical inputs for ecological models. Research in this area has been centered in the United States, and while the models have, understandably, been calibrated to specific ecosystems in this country, they are extendable to other, similar ecosystems.[11] There is available an excellent body of data on European biomes that would greatly facilitate the needed recalibrations. Currently under development are constructs and kindred models that can simulate the short-term dynamics of plant and animal communities, the productivity of major ecosystem species, the nutrient status of soils, and a wealth of other information. Many of these models have been developed specifically to measure the impact of such human manipulations of the ecosystems as the pasturing of livestock or the harvesting of timber.

Finally, a wealth of models and modeling methods exist for major field crops, especially cereals,[12] and for livestock production. Many of the livestock models are linked to grassland and pasture models, with the more complicated versions similar in many respects to the ecosystems discussed above.[13] Such models integrate data collected over a century with analysis carried out primarily at agricultural colleges and experimental stations in this country and in Europe. With few exceptions, medieval historians have neglected the massive literature produced by specialists in agronomy, plant physiology, animal husbandry, and soil science.

Some of the models described above can probably be applied directly to medieval contexts following a strict, uniformitarian approach. In many instances, though, judicious alterations or recalibrations would be necessary. For instance, mean climatic regimes were not uniform throughout the Middle Ages. Although physical causes for these shifts remain obscure, there is a fair scholarly consensus on the magnitude of the changes as reflected, say, in shifts in mean temperatures and precipitation.[14] Such information can provide an objective basis for recalibrating stochastic climate generators and other environmental system models.

For ecological models, difficulties may be faced in adapting constructs developed for North American ecosystems to the plant and animal communities typical of Europe. A more basic problem, though, lies in deciding what sorts of ecosystemic backgrounds typified specific regions during various phases of the Middle Ages. The general trend was for forests to be supplanted by grasslands, moorlands, heaths, or boglands, with human intervention figuring as a major causative factor. Palynological research is making an increasingly important contribution to the understanding of regional vegetational changes,[15] for which, by the central Middle Ages, documentary evidence provides valuable clues. In the last analysis, a variety of ecosystem types may need to be experimentally simulated to compensate for an ignorance of the general ecosystem patterns. Such an approach may also be necessary to cope with situations where human intervention had transformed a region into a mosaic of different vegetational zones, all linked together in a common system of agrarian exploitation.

A major difficulty in agricultural modeling involves specifying the types of crop and livestock, for considerable changes in cereal strains and livestock breeds have taken place since about the sixteenth century. Modern cultigens and domesticated animals must be used with caution in assessing the performance of medieval crop and livestock types. Careful scrutiny of available historical documentation can often provide a useful basis for comparison.[16] Agricultural experimental stations can often provide detailed documentation of so-called old-field experiments, for cereal crops in particular.[17] Records of fairly traditional methods of seed-bed preparation, rotations, manuring, and harvesting, combined with the use of fairly unimproved cereal varieties, are often available in long data series. The yield series are often matched by detailed information on meteorological variables, soil chemistry, and other data that facilitate the development of good crop yield models. In the last decade or so, a variety of experimental archaeology projects have also been undertaken in Europe.[18] Many unimproved cereal varieties have been cropped under various sorts of prehistoric husbandry patterns that are analogous to medieval practices. Some of these experimental programs, along with a number of related projects, have endeavored to reconstitute ancient livestock breeds. Through these efforts, a solid experimental data base may soon be available for the development of both crop and livestock production models.

The foregoing discussion does not seek to downplay the inherent problems but, rather, proposes that it may be possible to construct sub-model components for overall models of environmental, ecological, and agricultural systems. It remains to suggest how the sub-models could

163

be combined to address substantive historical questions. Were it not for the factor of human intervention, one could simply piece together the sub-models for the environmental and ecological systems; environmental aspects, like weather systems, may not be affected by man, but the ecological sub-models certainly will be. One must also specify a host of features pertinent to the agricultural sub-models. Physical and biological regularities will also be reflected in agricultural systems, but a host of human factors—political, economic, and social—now come into play. These features are, in the jargon of modeling, largely exogenous: they must be supplied by someone and could logically best be supplied by historians.

A point of departure could be to make the best of the fairly static and stereotyped representations that still fill the literature. Two- and three- field open-field systems are likely candidates; others would include swiddening systems or infield-outfield systems.[19] Such generalized exemplars will not provide all the information needed to conduct a simulation, but at least they provide some frame of reference.

The open-field systems are classically envisioned as occupying fairly open landscapes. Grassland would be the predominant vegetative type in an ecosystem model, with some allowance made for remnant stands of woodland or high forest. The range of livestock types, mainly cattle, sheep, and swine, could be specified in a general fashion. For infield-outfield systems, the crop and livestock components would be analogous to open-field systems. The hinterland of the arable complex would probably contain grasslands, although heath associations, secondary forest, and even high forest might be represented as well. In swiddening systems, one would be dealing with temporary arable intakes in forest communities in various phases of succession. Many of the same livestock types, particularly cattle and swine, would be expected.

This may be as far as the textbook representations will carry one, leaving a number of critical features still to be supplied. Assumptions would be required as to the size, demographic composition, and minimal dietary needs of the human population. Target values would have to be assumed for the planted acreages set aside for each type of crop and, where appropriate, their sequence in a set of rotations. Assumptions would have to be made concerning the sizes of the different animal populations. The sources of their food supplies throughout an annual cycle would need to be clarified. The population dynamics of the livestock would depend, in part, on such natural factors as, for instance, inherent demographic rates of increase, the incidence of diseases, and other natural variables affecting mortality such as the carry capacities of pasture areas. Management practices would also come into play, with selective culling and related operations altering natural demographic processes. Whether sheep and cattle were exploited for meat only or for dairy products would critically affect the performance of the livestock and the way in which they were husbanded. For infield-outfield and open-field systems, livestock and arable husbandry would be intimately linked. Obviously, draft animals would be needed for hauling and tillage operations. More importantly, perhaps, from an ecological perspective, animals of all types would be a potential source of manure to boost arable productivity. Information on all these matters would be needed to calibrate the agricultural sub-models.

Once a set of initial environmental, ecological, and agricultural conditions have been determined, a simulation run could begin. Quite possibly, something catastrophic could befall the hypothetical human population after only a year or so of simulated history—one could be grimly Malthusian and let the population perish. A more fruitful approach, however, would be to add sets of contingency controls[20] to maintain the human population within certain bounds of relative poverty or affluence. Such control features could involve changes in livestock husbandry, say, through slaughtering more than the normal number of animals. Crop failure early in the season could be countered, where at all feasible, by replanting. If the human population were subject to tributes in kind or taxation, these might be judiciously relaxed. Livestock and foodstuffs might have to be periodically borrowed or bought from outside the area. Portions of the local population could be allowed to out-migrate. Thus, through the addition of such regulatory protocols, the initial simulations should eventually be capable of sustaining the human population for a number of years.

While such trial models may yield many fruitful insights, it might be difficult to validate them against our knowledge of any particular historical contexts. To do so one must, of course, design the trial models which take account of time and place in medieval temperate Europe. When the environmental and ecological settings, as well as the main features of the agricultural system, can be specified, the model can be adjusted until its performance imitates the historical context. When there are fundamental gaps in our knowledge, however, as is true for the early Middle Ages and for more of the later period than historians care to admit, the findings of environmental archaeology can be used to narrow the gaps, and one can, at least, establish a simulation model.

Simulation modeling lends itself best to just such problematical cases. Usually, enough would be known or reasonably surmised to suggest resemblances to one of the trial models for swiddening, infield-outfield, or open-field systems. Using one of the trial models as a starting point, a variety of modified versions can be constructed to reflect the probable range of ecological and agricultural conditions. Each variant could be subjected to extensive simulations; alternative control features could be experimented with; and on the basis of the simulation runs, some models could likely be eliminated. Even if a number of models remained in contention, careful scrutiny of, for instance, documentary sources, should suggest the types of information necessary to narrow the field. It would also be possible to suggest the types of information to be sought in future palynological and archaeological research.

The greatest challenge in developing such simulation models would probably lie in the elaboration of features pertaining to agriculture. The immediate objectives would involve determining, for instance, how much acreage to place in a certain crop, or how many livestock to overwinter, for even the best laid plans may be undone by inclement weather, disease, or other factors. In addition, a control hierarchy of alternative responses and strategies would be necessary, keyed to the fluctuating performances of the agricultural and ecological systems. The organizational aspects of the agricultural systems, then, would constitute both a source of variability and a set of regulatory responses. Such self-regulatory properties are built into natural environmental and eco-logical systems. With the addition of agricultural components to an overall model, it cannot be overstressed that regulation can become a largely human artifact. To one degree or another, the stability and integrity of the model and the historical phenomena mapped by the model will hinge on ongoing human intervention and manipulation.

Solid ecological reasons determine this need for constant human attention.[21] In temperate Europe, agricultural systems involve crop plants that could not sustain their habitat requirements in the face of succession-al processes; they would be choked out by native grasses, shrubs, or trees. Cultural handling of crop plants resulted in modifications as well. Thousands of years of domestication have deprived most cereals of the capacity to disperse their seeds efficiently, making for easier harvesting but requiring purposeful sowing. The cereals, furthermore, require fertile soils; their rates of nutrient turnover and biomass production rival or surpass the potentials of natural, climax vegetation. The cereals, with their special, cleared habitats, however, are not capable of sustaining the complicated food chains and material cycles required to maintain the needed fertile soils. Livestock, too, display the need for artificial props, a key factor being the extra demands of milk or tractive power placed upon them by human populations. Careful manipulation of herd demographies and of forage and fodder availability, say, through haymaking, are usually required to underwrite these extra demands.

To sustain the crop and livestock components of an agricultural complex requires intervention in the successional processes leading to the establishment of climax forested habitats. The new habitat types may demand ongoing manipulation, such as controlled grazing, mowing, or burning. The new landscapes are in large measure anthropogenic, in that human activities have created them and are required to sustain them on a regular basis.

The production of such anthropogenic landscapes involves a subtle interweaving of demographic, political, economic, and social processes. The superstructural processes obviously and manifestly involve short-term events and sequences of events. The ability of the agricultural systems to underwrite the superstructural systems will hinge on the short- and medium-term productivities of crops and livestock, factors that are not static, but variable. Formal modeling is proposed here as one tool that can enlarge and refine one's grasp of the extent and degree of this variability. No such historically oriented models now exist, but a large number of the needed components are available, and many of them are now in use for the analysis of contemporary problems. Particularly valuable guidelines are provided by the various biome modeling projects sponsored during the International Biological Program.[22] There is considerable opportunity for smaller groups, even single researchers, to develop the sub-model building blocks.

Our ultimate goal, in summary, is to provide serviceable maps to elucidate particular historical problems and contexts. The desired maps should enlarge our grasp of the short- and medium-term performances of the basic agrarian underpinnings of the medieval societies. Greater understanding of the dynamics of these fundamental processes would improve our grasp of the patternings and regularities of the broader political, economic, and social superstructures. Simulation modeling is one promising tool in achieving this end.

NOTES

[1] The cartography analogy is adapted from G. L. S. Shackle, "Marginalism: The Harvest," in *The Marginal Revolution in Economics: Interpretation and Evaluation*, ed. R. D. Collison Black and D. W. Craufurd Goodwin (Durham, NC: Duke Univ. Press, 1973), p. 336. For good discussions of the philosophical bases of modeling methodologies, see: Clyde H. Coombs, Robyn M. Dawes, and Amos Tversky, *Mathematical Psychology: An Elementary Introduction* (Englewood Cliffs, NJ: Prentice-Hall, 1970), pp 7-30; Wesley C. Salmon, Richard C. Jeffrey, and James G. Greeno, *Statistical Explanation and Statistical Relevance* (Pittsburgh, PA: Univ. of Pittsburgh Press, 1971); and Peter D. McClelland, *Causal Explanation and Model Building in History, Economics, and*

the New Economic History (Ithaca, NY: Cornell Univ. Press, 1979), pp. 21-104. In this and the notes that follow, the author can only attempt to provide useful points of entry to massive topical literatures.

    ² For a discussion of this tendency and its implications, see William S. Cooter, "Ecological Dimensions of Medieval Agrarian Systems," *Agricultural History*, 52 (1978), 458-77.

    ³ See P. J. Fowler, "Agriculture and Rural Settlement," in *The Archaeology of Anglo-Saxon England*, ed. David M. Wilson (London: Methuen and Co., 1976), for a typical and frank assessment.

    ⁴ This is due, understandably, to the abundance of surviving estate documents pertaining to the early medieval period. The conclusion that this relative wealth of documentation automatically guarantees an adequate picture of post-twelfth century medieval landscapes, however, should be resisted. See, for instance, Christopher Taylor, *Fields in the English Landscape* (London: J. M. Dent and Sons, 1975), pp. 87-88 for a pointed reminder of our fundamental ignorance of the functions of many technical features of open-field systems.

    ⁵ For introductions to the basic ideas underlying simulation modeling, see: Don T. Phillips, A. Ravindran, and James J. Solberg, *Operations Research: Principles and Practice* (New York: John Wiley and Sons, 1976), pp. 359-67; and, more extensively, Robert E. Shannon, *Systems Simulation: The Art and Science* (Englewood Cliffs, NJ: Prentice-Hall, 1975). A good sampling of the different types of simulation modeling can be found in such journals as *Simulation*, published by Simulation Councils, Inc., La Jolla, CA. For background on the development of simulation and systems applications in ecology, see *Systems Ecology*, vol. 9 of *Benchmark Papers in Ecology*, ed. H. H. Shugart and R. V. O'Neill (Stroudsburg, PA: Dowden, Hutchinson and Ross, 1979). For an excellent general introduction to the mathematical tools underlying many types of modeling approaches, see Kenneth L. Cooke, "Mathematical Approaches to Culture Change," in *Transformations: Mathematical Approaches to Culture Change*, ed. Colin Refrew and Kenneth L. Cooke (New York: Academic Press, 1979).

    ⁶ For a convenient review of state-of-the-art weather sensitive crop yield models, see *Proceedings of the Crop Modeling Workshop, Columbia, Missouri, October 3-5, 1977* (Washington, D.C.: Environmental Data and Information Service, National Oceanic and Atmospheric Administration, U.S. Dept. of Commerce, 1979).

    ⁷ See J. Z. Titow, *Winchester Yields: A Study in Medieval Agricultural Productivity* (Cambridge: Cambridge Univ. Press, 1972), for an excellent presentation of the most extensive of these early yield series.

    ⁸ For representative examples of recent modeling applications, see: B. J. Mason, "Some Results of Climate Experiments with Numerical Models," in *Proceedings of the World Climate Conference: A Conference of Experts on Climate and Mankind* (Geneva: World Meteorological Organization, 1979); S. Manabe and D. T. Wetherald, "The Effect of Doubling the CO_2 Concentration on the Climate of a General Circulation Model," *Journal of Atmospheric Sciences*, 38 (1978), 3-15; and R. Cess, "Biosphere-Albedo Feedback and Climatic Model-

ing," *Journal of Atmospheric Sciences*, 35 (1975), 1765-68.

[9] See, for example, G. Amos Eddy, *A Multivariate Climate Generator: Final Report to Battelle Columbus Laboratories Supported Under Contract No. D. O. 1384* (Norman, OK: Amos Eddy, 1980).

[10] See, for example: H. N. Holtan, G. J. Stiltner, W. H. Henson, and N. C. Lopez, *USDAHL-74 Revised Model of Watershed Hydrology: A United States Contribution to the International Hydrological Decade*, U. S. D. A., Agricultural Research Service, Tech. Bull. No. 1518 (Washington, D.C.: G.P.O., 1975); or *CREAMS: A Field-Scale Model for Chemicals, Runoff, and Erosion from Agricultural Management Systems*, ed. Walter G. Knisel, U. S. D. A., Conservation Research Rept., 26 (Washington, D.C.: G.P.O., 1980).

[11] Major impetus by the International Biological Program encouraged the development of a number of large-scale models for such major biome types as forests and grasslands. See the convenient syntheses in *Systems Analysis and Simulation in Ecology*, ed. Bernard C. Patten, vol. 3 (New York: Academic Press, 1975). For recent advances in forest ecosystem modeling, see *Forests: Fresh Perspectives from Ecosystem Analysis*, ed. Richard H. Waring, Proc. of the 40th Annual Biology Colloquium (Corvallis, OR: Oregon State Univ. Press, 1979). Similarly, for grasslands, see *Grassland Simulation Model*, ed. George S. Innis, Ecological Studies, vol. 26 (New York: Springer-Verlag, 1978).

[12] See the set of abstracts assembled in *Proceedings of the Workshop on Crop Simulation, 4-6 April, 1978* (Clemson, SC: Biological Systems Simulation Group and Dept. of Agricultural Engineering, Clemson Univ., 1978).

[13] See, for example: *Systems Analysis in Agricultural Management*, ed. J. B. Dent and J. R. Anderson (New York: John Wiley and Sons, 1971); or C. R. W. Spedding, *Grassland Ecology* (Oxford: Clarendon Press, 1971).

[14] See the excellent synthesis by Charles Stockton, "Interpretation of Past Climatic Variability from Paleoenvironmental Indicators," in *Climate, Climatic Change, and Water Supply* (Washington, D.C.: National Academy of Sciences, 1977). A useful set of bibliographies with the series title "A Bibliography of Recent Works Regarding Climatic Variation and Its Effects in Historic Times" have been assembled under the direction of Robert H. Claxton, Coordinator of Environmental Studies, West Georgia College, Carrollton, GA. Copies of these manuscripts are available through Dr. Claxton upon request.

[15] For the British Isles, see: pertinent sections in Frank (G.F.) Mitchell, *The Irish Landscape* (London: Collins, 1976); *The Effect of Man on the Landscape: The Highland Zone*, ed. J. G. Evans, Susan Limbrey, and Henry Cleere, C. B. A. Research Rept. No. 11 (London: Council for British Archaeology, 1975); and *The Effect of Man on the Landscape: The Lowland Zone*, ed. Susan Limbrey and J. G. Evans, C. B. A. Research Rept. No. 21 (London: Council for British Archaeology, 1978). For the continent, see Elsbeth Lange, *Botanische Beiträge zur mitteleuropäischen Siedlungsgeschichte: Ergebnisse zur Wirtschaft- und Kulturlandschaft in frühgeschichtlicher Zeit* (Berlin: Akademie-Verlag, 1971).

[16] See, for example: Titow, *Winchester Yields*; or B. H. Slicher van Bath, *The Agrarian History of Western Europe, A.D. 500 - 1850*, trans. Olive Ordish

(London: Edward Arnold, 1963).

[17] See, for example, C. E. Millar, *Soil Fertility* (New York: John Wiley and Sons, 1955), pp. 395-422, for a discussion of several such experimental series. Perhaps the most famous were the Broadbalk experiments at England's Rothamstead Station. For more information, see Alfred Daniel Hall, *The Book of the Rothamstead Experiments*, rev. E. J. Russell, 2nd ed. (New York: E. P. Dutton, 1917).

[18] An excellent overview of such projects is provided by John Coles, in *Experimental Archaeology* (New York: Academic Press, 1979).

[19] "Swiddening" was popularized as a technical term in Harold C. Conklin, *The Study of Shifting Cultivation*, Pan American Union, Dept. of Social Affairs, Studies and Monographs 6 (Washington, D.C.: Pan American Union, 1963). See also Cooter, "Ecological Dimensions of Medieval Agrarian Systems." On infield-outfield systems, see Francois Sigaut, *L'agriculture et le feu: role et place du feu dans les techniques de preparation du champ de l'ancienne agriculture Européene* (Paris: Mouton and Co., 1975). See also the critical remarks in F. H. A. Aalen, *Man and the Landscape in Ireland* (New York: Academic Press, 1978), esp. pp. 93-96; and Ian Whyte, *Agriculture and Society in Seventeenth-Century Scotland* (Edinburgh: J. Donald, 1979), pp. 60 ff. A useful overview of infield-outfield and open-field systems is contained in Taylor, *Fields in the English Landscape*.

[20] Such control hierarchies or regulator (feedback) processes are discussed in Roy A. Rappaport, "The Sacred in Human Evolution," *Annual Review of Ecology and Systematics*, 2 (1971), 23-44; and Rappaport, *Pigs for the Ancestors: Ritual in the Ecology of a New Guinea People* (New Haven: Yale Univ. Press, 1968). Control phenomena may be couched in highly elaborate terms, drawing on information theory and electronic-circuit control theory. For this, see H. Kalmus, "Control Hierarchies," in *Regulation and Control of Living Systems*, ed. H. Kalmus (New York: John Wiley and Sons, 1966). Much simpler formulations are also possible, as in Henry Wright and Melinda Zeder, "The Simulation of a Linear Exchange System Under Equilibrium Conditions," in *Exchange Systems in Prehistory*, ed. Timothy K. Earle and Jonathan E. Ericson (New York: Academic Press, 1977).

[21] Cooter, "Ecological Dimensions."

[22] See the excellent discussion in R. G. Woodmansee, "Critique and Analyses of the Grassland Model ELM," in *Grassland Simulation Model*, ed. George S. Innis, Ecological Studies, vol. 26 (New York: Springer-Verlag, 1978).

170

EARLY MEDIEVAL AGRICULTURE IN COASTAL HOLLAND: THE EVIDENCE FROM ARCHAEOLOGY AND ECOLOGY

WILLIAM TEBRAKE

Medieval Europe was overwhelmingly agrarian. Even at the height of urban development in the later Middle Ages, agriculture touched the lives of nearly everyone in an economy fueled almost exclusively by the production, distribution, and consumption of agricultural products. Yet, despite the importance of agriculture to medieval studies, our present state of knowledge is far from perfect. While recent village and regional studies based on archival research, especially for the later Middle Ages and for certain areas, have measurably improved this situation, this type of inquiry cannot be applied to earlier periods for which there is but a paucity of documentation.

These gaps in our knowledge became all too clear to me several years ago while making a study of changes in settlement, land use, and social patterns associated with peat-bog reclamation in a part of coastal Holland after 950. I found that I could not describe with accuracy the pre-950 situation, as existing documents had very little to say about the agricultural activities of the early-medieval community.

The problems affecting that study ranged beyond a simple lack of information, however, for the conceptual framework in which early-medieval agricultural data is normally placed proved inadequate.[1] Traditional studies are confined almost exclusively to field systems, an approach that makes a certain amount of sense if the data is interpreted strictly from an economic perspective: fields loomed large in early-medieval society because control of the cereals they produced, the primary storable surplus, formed the basis of all wealth and power. Yet, it appears that fields produced only a small proportion of the total diet, since early-medieval crop yields could be appallingly low. Particularly if one perceives agriculture from the standpoint of food provisioning, it becomes evident that crop production could not have been practiced by itself. This point is verified by the early ninth-century capitulary, *De Villis*, which shows that food provisioning, at least in the rather idealized settings of royal estates, could be broadly based and that the actual production of the fields was but a part of total food production.[2] There was, in short, more to agrarian life than activity in the fields, and, therefore, any inquiry into early-medieval agriculture should include the context in which crop production fits, including the entire set of subsistence strategies practiced by communities and individuals.

It is desirable then, to abandon the traditional framework used in medieval agricultural research and to recognize that agrarian practices constituted, first and foremost, a set of relationships between human communities and their environments. Close attention must be paid to the natural environment of an area, for its character can reveal much about these varied relationships. Recast in such terms, early-medieval agriculture becomes somewhat more explicable; and it is in this context that I have examined the information derived from written and archaeological sources for parts of coastal Holland.

Place Names Mentioned in the Text
(Numbers refer to locations on the map in Figure 1.)

1. Aartswoud	12. Katwijk	22. Valkenburg
2. Alkmaar	13. Langeveld	23. Veenenburg
3. Alphen	14. Leiden	24. Velsen
4. Andijk	15. Leidschendam	25. Vlaardingen
5. Bergschenhoek	16. Medemblik	26. Vogelenzang
6. Bovenkarspel	17. Molenaarsgraff	27. Voorburg
7. Castricum	18. Monster	28. Voorschoten
8. Haamstede	19. Oostwoud	29. Wevershoef
9. Hazendonk	20. Rijnsburg	30. Zandwerven
10. Hekelingen	21. Rijswijk	31. Zwaagdijk
11. Hoogkarspel		

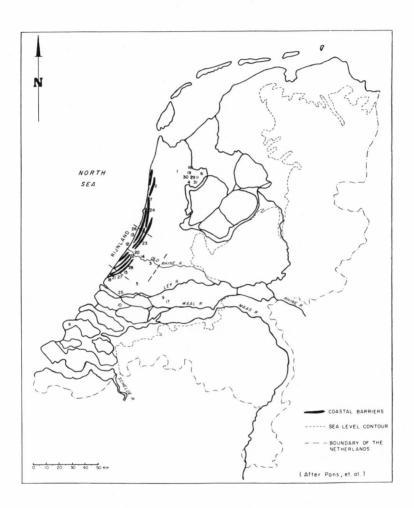

Figure 1
Location of Sites in the Western Netherlands
(numbers refer to accompanying alphabetized list of Place Names)

173

Rijnland: The Setting

The focus of my study is Rijnland, an area of nearly twenty-five kilometers by twenty-five kilometers surrounding the city of Leiden and bordering on the North Sea, which, by the late Middle Ages, had become an integral and important part of the County of Holland. It took its name from what was formerly the main branch of the Rhine, still referred to as Oude Rijn or Old Rhine, even though it is now totally controlled by a system of dams, dikes, sluices, and pumps. In the modern Netherlands, Rijnland constitutes the northwestern corner of the province of South Holland.

The early-medieval residents of Rijnland obtained most of the things they needed for existence from their environment. Exactly how they did so is difficult to establish, however, for documentary sources provide only scattered bits of information. We do know that early settlements in Rijnland, and in coastal areas generally, were associated with fields, meadows, pastures, woods, waters, and ditches and that their inhabitants carried out cropraising, livestock keeping, fishing, hunting, and gathering in addition to drying peat for use as fuel.

While it is possible from the documents to assemble a simple list of landscape features and subsistence strategies, establishing a context for the latter is far more complex and requires going beyond documentation to such non-documentary sources as, for instance, archaeological reports. Here, too, there is a problem, for although archaeological research for medieval coastal Holland has increased considerably in recent years,[3] its findings still are too scattered to systematically describe the pattern of subsistence in Rijnland. We can, however, broaden our scope of inquiry to include, in addition to archaeological data, a review of the entire post-glacial natural history of the region and surrounding coastal areas, not only to establish its major physical and geographical features— location and distribution of water, soil, and vegetation types, for instance—but also the relationship of human settlement to such features.[4] Against such a backdrop can be placed the results of an extensive survey of pre- and proto-historic archaeological literature. A study of this scope, which is both temporal and spatial, can delineate an ecological tradition that, evolving from neolithic origins, persisted well into the early Middle Ages[5]—and, because of this high degree of continuity in patterns of settlement and land use, it is possible to fill some early-medieval lacunae by analogy to earlier, often better known, situations.

Physical Geography of Rijnland

In geological terms, the physical landscape of early-medieval Rijnland, and coastal Holland in general, was young, formed during the 10,000 years of the post-glacial era. A series of low sand dune ridges at the coast, with a low flat peat and clay expanse behind it, were the basic features of this landscape; underlying, older soils, mostly sands, reached the surface only somewhat east of Rijnland, in the vicinity of the city of Utrecht. To the west, these soils were covered by more recent sediments ranging in depth from about ten meters at Rijnland's eastern edge to approximately eighteen meters at the coast.[6]

The primary mechanism producing this landscape was a world-wide rise in sea level linked to the melting of glaciers and ice sheets in late glacial times, a process which had proceeded so far by about 6,000 B.C. that the shore of the North Sea approximated the present coastline in the western Netherlands. The continued rise in sea level thereafter constituted a marine invasion of the western Netherlands, creating broad shore flats and salt marsh where marine clays and sands were deposited. Sometime between 3,600 and 3,000 B.C., an offshore barrier ridge or sandbar began to form where the eastern edge of the dune system is found today, six to eight kilometers inland from the modern coast. As sand accumulated along this barrier, a low sand dune began to protrude above tide and waves. Another offshore barrier developed some time later to the west of the first and eventually became a dune ridge as well. This cycle repeated itself a number of times until the completed dune system, consisting of at least four parallel barrier ridges with dunes, emerged by 1600 B.C. By the early Middle Ages, portions of these dunes had become covered by a well-developed hardwood forest.[7]

The coastal dunes reduced the influence of the sea on the area to the east, which gradually became a fresh-water swamp intersected by rivers such as the Old Rhine. Though the tides continued to introduce saltwater and marine sediments into the immediate river mouth areas, tidal influence to the east resulted in the rise and fall of fresh water levels and the deposition of riverine sands and clays along the river courses. Away from the rivers, drainage became so sluggish that soggy conditions prevailed, resulting, especially after 1800 B.C., in a substantial accumulation of partially decomposed plant material or peat. Although virtually uninterrupted for the next two millennia, by the early Middle Ages this peat growth had produced rather substantial bogs. These bogs extended as much as forty kilometers from the coastal dunes to higher-lying areas to the east and in Rijnland appeared to the north and south of the Old

175

Rhine. Peat also accumulated between the dune ridges at the coast.[8]

The large bogs resembled huge sponges that absorbed water, which in turn was kept at the surface by capillary action within the bogs. As a result, their centers gradually became raised, and water that could not be absorbed slowly flowed off their surfaces—which always remained soggy—via radial networks of streams into the major rivers such as the Old Rhine. At times of high water in the main rivers, flood waters could flow by way of the radial networks of streams into the bogs and leave behind marine and riverine sediments. These deposits provided the only relatively stable ground within the raised bogs as well as the nutrients that made possible the appearance of differing types of vegetation. Where regular flooding occurred, as, for instance, along the major rivers and the lower courses of some of the small bog streams, clay was deposited, on which grew a tall gallery forest of oak, ash, and willow. Laterally away from the rivers or further upstream into the bogs, where silt-carrying water came less frequently, the vegetation shaded into a lower growth of reed, sedge, birch, and alder. Finally, beyond the reach of river flooding and stretching across the raised centers of the bogs, there was a vast, treeless expanse interspersed by pools and ponds of standing water which contained only such species as could survive on nutrient-poor precipitation—peat moss, heath, and cotton grass.[9]

Before the land reclamation schemes of the late tenth century, Rijnland, as well as the entire western Netherlands, offered only limited opportunities for permanent occupation. The primary consideration for selecting sites for settlement and agriculture in this area was surface moisture: those places which could dry out between floods or episodes of precipitation were most favored; those which remained constantly or periodically water-logged, such as the peat areas, were simply unsuitable for settlement and agriculture, except under the most exceptional conditions.

Outside the peat areas, however, the degree of dryness or sogginess of a specific location was determined by such factors as elevation, slope, proximity to water courses, and types of soil. A sandy ridge protruding above the surrounding landscape and sloping towards a nearby stream would dry out most quickly; dense clay, barely above the ground water level, with little or no slope, lacked easy avenues of drainage and would remain water-logged for long periods of time. Between these two extremes were a number of possible combinations conducive to settlement, such as sandy clay, clay on top of sand, clay with good slope near a stream, and others.

The suitability of a particular location could change according to shifts in drainage patterns as a result of modifications in river courses,

176

sediment transport of rivers, tidal ranges, precipitation amounts, and storm surge frequency.[10] Thus, although no specific sites saw continuous occupation, the conditions determining settlement location were the same from neolithic through early medieval times; settlements and agricultural activities were found exclusively on well-drained sites.

The Human Geography of Rijnland

The first human occupation of the post-glacial landscape of the western Netherlands was apparently founded on sandy outcrops and stream ridges before completion of the first coastal barrier and dune ridge.[11] With the gradual establishment of the barrier and dune system, however, settlement became possible along its interior ridges as well as on the natural clay and sand levees of tidal rivers and creeks. Beginning around 2,450 B.C., a number of such sites were settled by groups of migrants from the higher-lying regions further inland. Their presence is known from numerous sites, ranging from Haamstede (Zeeland) in the south, to Zandwerven (North-Holland) in the north, to the central Netherlands river clay area in the east. Towards the center of this distribution, in and near what became Rijnland, settlements were established at Vlaardingen and Hekelingen (on the north and south sides of the Maas estuary respectively), at Voorburg just south of Rijnland, and at Leidschendam and Voorschoten in Rijnland. The Vaardingen and Hekelingen sites were located on tidal creek banks, and those at Voorburg, Leidschendam, and Voorschoten formed along the innermost dune ridge at a time when a new ridge was developing further westward.[12]

Excavations of these late-neolithic settlements have yielded considerable information about their natural settings and the uses the residents made of them. The creek bank locations of the Vlaardingen and Hekelingen settlements were adjacent to extensive and at least partially wooded swamp that provided excellent habitats for red deer, wild pig, and many other species of game, species prominent among the remains of animal bones that have been analyzed. Also found were the skeletal remains of beaver and pike, which indicate the presence of fresh, running water in the vicinity. Further, these people consumed many varieties of waterfowl and evidently hunted sea mammals along the nearby shore. Between one-quarter and one-third of all the bones uncovered, however, came from various species of domesticated animals, the most numerous being cattle, with evidence of sheep, goat, pig, horse, and dog or wolf as well. The residents of the Vlaardingen and Hekelingen sites seem to have

177

had little opportunity for raising cereals or other crops, but they may have been able to import them from inland areas with which they apparently maintained trading contacts.[13]

Natural conditions were different enough along the dune ridges to allow slight modifications in food provisioning. The evidence from Leidschendam and Voorschoten, and less clearly from Voorburg, shows that from the initial occupation phase onward, settlers placed greater emphasis on livestock keeping. Over eighty-five percent of all animal remains came from domesticates, chiefly cattle, but also pigs, sheep, goats, and dogs. Presumably, the cattle grazed on the extensive natural grasslands between the dune ridges, while the residents hunted along the wooded dunes, the streams, and the nearby beach for aurochs, wild pig, red deer, roe deer, pine martin, grey seal, sperm whale, and beaver. Faunal remains further indicate that birds and fish (especially sturgeon at Voorschoten) could be important items in the diet, even though their bones are more susceptible to the ravages of time and are, thus, likely to be underrepresented in most archaeological samples. Finally, the presence of cereal pollen in local pollen profiles shows that residents practiced arable agriculture nearby. Though there is no evidence for establishing their exact location, the fields were most likely laid out along the dune ridge, since the adjacent peat and clay areas would have been too soggy for most crops.[14]

As the late neolithic progressed, pottery and other artifacts used by prehistorians to indicate cultural affiliations changed periodically as a result of acculturation processes, or migration, or both.[15] Forms of environmental exploitation, in contrast, remained relatively unchanged during the same period, for, with the exception of the earliest occupation phase at Vlaardingen and Hekelingen, all other late neolithic settlements display essentially the same basic subsistence patterns known from the Voorschoten and Leidschendam sites: a greater emphasis on livestock keeping than on hunting, considerable reliance on fishing and fowling, and a small but important crop raising component. In fact, cattle raising grew in importance and, in time, became the primary means of subsistence in the western Netherlands.

At Voorschoten and Leidschendam, for example, the first settlers grazed their cattle on natural pastures along and between the dune ridges. Somewhat later, during a second occupation stage, residents of the same sites used fire to clear the forest vegetation of the dunes as pastures for their presumably larger herds of cattle, a coastal version of a practice known to culturally-related groups on the higher-lying sandy areas in the eastern Netherlands. In any case, there was a substantial increase in the pollen of plants associated with grazing and possibly burning.[16]

As livestock keeping became increasingly important, crop raising, too, advanced; at least it figures more prominently in the archaeological record. While the pollen record for Voorschoten, Leidschendam,
and Voorburg merely indicates cereal raising in the vicinity, excavations
of contemporaneous and culturally-related sites in the northeastern section of North-Holland—better known in earlier times as Westfriesland—
offer a variety of indicators for arable agriculture. For example, the
distinct traces of ploughings found at Zandwerven, on a sandy ridge in a
salt marsh, are among the earliest evidence for the practice in the
Netherlands.[17] At nearby Aartswoud, located on a sandy ridge, thousands
of seeds of mostly barley, but also emmer wheat, flax, and other species,
were found.[18] Excavation at a later, neolithic Westfrisian site at Oostwoud revealed many sets of ploughing and cross-ploughing marks, some
of which may have been made by an evolved type of plough capable of
making furrows wider and deeper than those normally encountered for
the period and locale.[19]

During the late neolithic and at various times during the succeeding Bronze Age, a number of shifts occurred in settlement location. Sites
in such estuarine areas as Vlaardingen and Hekelingen began to suffer
deteriorating drainage conditions; thus, after 1950 B.C., Vlaardingen
knew only occasional, temporary encampments. Occupation continued
in the dunes at Voorschoten, however, and a new settlement is known
from Velsen. Some sites remained habitable in Westfriesland to the north
and in the river clay areas in the central Netherlands. During the early
Bronze Age, beginning c. 1700 B.C., further shifts in settlement location
took place. Dunal sites are known from Monster, Veenenburg, and
Velsen, but the river clay areas to the east were abandoned before long as
was much of the Westfrisian area.

The middle Bronze Age, c. 1500 to 1000 B.C., saw a heightened
intensity of settlement in the Westfrisian area and in a number of sites
from the central river clay areas. The dunes, in contrast, appear to have
been relatively empty for this period, though settlement probably would
have shifted westward to more recently-formed dune ridges as peat
growth engulfed the original dunes. The more westerly ridges were
largely covered by more recent dune formation or obliterated by coastal
erosion during the Middle Ages.

A considerable decline in human presence occurred in the western
Netherlands during the late Bronze Age, between 1000 and 700 B.C. A
wetter, stormier period and accelerated peat growth caused a deterioration of drainage in many places, resulting in the abandonment of many
sites in the estuarine, marine clay, and river clay areas. Only in the dunes
and on the most favorable sites in Westfriesland did settlement continue

179

into the Iron Age.[20]

The Low Countries as a whole first achieved fully effective food production during the Bronze Age; from then on, pastoral and arable agriculture became the predominant means of subsistence, with a secondary reliance on fishing, fowling, and occasional hunting.[21] This is true for the marine clay, river clay, and dune environments of the western Netherlands as well. Inventories of faunal remains from eight Bronze Age sites in North and South Holland indicate that more than 99% (in some cases 100%) came from domesticated animals.[22] The inhabitants of the western Netherlands also raised crops wherever possible along the sandy ridges on which they lived, as evidenced by fossilized plough marks in the soil, traces of field systems surrounded by ditches, numerous finds of cereal kernels, and raised circular areas for storing grain or sheaves constructed of soil dug from an encircling ditch.[23]

These patterns of settlement and land use, established in the neolithic and Bronze Ages, persisted with little change until the tenth century. Even though changes in climate and drainage patterns would alter the habitability of specific sites, the criteria for selection remained the same: those locales with the best drainage were most likely to see settlement.

What did change through time, however, was the density or degree of settlement. During the early Iron Age, few sites were known outside the dunes; by the late pre-Roman Age (the last two centuries B.C.), occupation reached an unprecedented intensity. The western Netherlands experienced unusually dry conditions between c. 200 B.C. and A.D. 250. As a result, settlements were established along tidal creeks in estuarine areas, in the river clay areas, along the dunes, and even on the edges of some peat bogs.[24] Consequently, at the beginning of our era, when the Romans arrived and built the fortifications of their *limes* system along the left bank of the Old Rhine, the western Netherlands was already densely settled. Although Rijnland, bisected as it was by the imperial boundary, was essentially militarily occupied during the Roman period, considerable civilian agricultural activity is known from the Maas river area and the region around Velsen.[25] In fact, recent excavations of a settlement near Rijswijk show a thriving agricultural community, whose expansion was, undoubtedly, a result of its ability to sell its surplus production to the nearby military masters.[26] Even the Romans, however, could do little to affect the prerequisites for settlement and agriculture. By the end of the third century A.D., they abandoned the soggy western Netherlands which was experiencing another episode of deterioration in climate and drainage.[27]

The favorable conditions for extensive settlement during the

Roman period gradually disappeared, and many a site was abandoned as a rising ground water table and the resumption of extensive peat growth aggravated good drainage.[28] In fact, there is almost a complete lack of archaeological or written evidence for occupation in the area between the third and sixth centuries A.D. For Rijnland, the possibility of continued settlement is suggested only for the neighborhood of Katwijk, near the mouth of the Old Rhine,[29] where some indirect evidence points to limited continuity. Further, a group of place and water names surviving in the coastal regions, including Rijnland, displays characteristics of name-giving that predate the early Middle Ages.[30] Had there been a complete interruption in occupation, these old names would have fallen into disuse. Nevertheless, the western Netherlands appears to have been largely uninhabited until the sixth century, when drier conditions again permitted occupation; traces of settlement in Zeeland and in an area north of Alkmaar, as well as an arable field near Castricum, can be ascribed to this period. Settlement extended throughout the western Netherlands during the seventh century.[31]

In Rijnland, improved drainage led to the establishment of new population centers at the mouth of the Old Rhine, near Katwijk, Valkenburg, and, particularly, Rijnsburg, where archaeological investigations have uncovered many signs of occupation dating from the seventh to tenth centuries along a sandy ridge in the Old Rhine estuary. The evidence includes ploughing marks, buildings, and small dams or bridges across a narrow tidal creek.[32] Both written and archaeological evidence attests to a gradual increase in the density of settlement over time: by the early tenth century, there were between forty and fifty small settlements in Rijnland alone. Many were concentrated at the mouth of the Old Rhine, with rows of settlements stretching northward and southward along the sand dunes as well as eastward along the slightly elevated riverbanks.[33]

Early Medieval Agriculture in Rijnland: A Model

The residents of early-medieval settlements in the western Netherlands were known as Frisians by virtue of language and customs.[34] Unfortunately the written evidence of the period says very little about the ways in which these Frisians exploited their soggy environment. There are early administrative documents that mention items of property: charters, cartularies, and lists of possessions confirm the existence of fields, pastures, meadows, and combinations of these in manors and villas, and also mention woods and waters and the rights to exploit them. There are also a

181

few, brief descriptions of unspecified portions of the coastal regions surviving in various histories, sagas, saints' lives, and other narrative sources, which are of little help in reconstructing the early-medieval agrarian scene.[35]

These scattered bits of historical information for coastal Holland are not of much use until they can be placed within a meaningful framework. Here, the normal medieval pattern prevailing in higher-lying areas to the south—manors, open fields, and tenant farmers tied to the soil—is not acceptable, since the environmental differences are too great. We must, therefore, look for a pattern that conforms more closely to the special environmental qualities of the western Netherlands which have been outlined above.

The most detailed picture we have of agrarian life in the western Netherlands before reclamation is the one that has been reconstructed for Westfriesland during the middle to late Bronze Age,[36] where subsistence is most clearly seen as an ongoing process of adaptation. Migrants from the sandy areas to the southeast, and also perhaps from the dunes to the southwest, recolonized the area c. 1300 B.C. They already possessed agrarian knowledge and skills, which they quickly applied to the somewhat wetter environment of the Westfrisian marine clay area: these settlers learned to read drainage and soil patterns accurately and established their fields on the highest portions of the sandy and sandy clay ridges emerging above the surrounding clay. They placed their farmyards at the edges of the fields on the flanks of the ridges, and they used the lower and wetter clay lands for grazing livestock and cutting hay.[37]

The wetter conditions of the landscape required the Frisians to encircle their farmyards and fields with ditches to aid drainage, the coastal equivalent of hedges and fences. At first, cattle made up about sixty-five percent of the livestock, but ample grazing opportunities on the clay soils promoted growth of cattle herds, which later made up over eighty-five percent of the domesticated stock. The domestic population also consisted of sheep or goat, pig, dog, and chicken, but cattle, by supplying meat, milk, and traction, became central to the local economy. As time progressed, there was also a gradual expansion of the area of crop lands during a relatively dry period. Crops consisted of hulled barley and emmer wheat, sometimes sown separately and at other times mixed, as well as some flax. Summer weeds in cereal samples suggest summer planting and harvesting, and the appearance of weeds associated with fallowing, along with other indicators, suggests the use of a long-fallow cropping system.[38]

The Westfrisian settlements consisted of small groups of large, rectangular houses (thirty meters by seven meters), occupied by an average family of perhaps six members and containing, under the same roof, stalls for twenty to thirty head of cattle, with space for smaller livestock, such as pigs and sheep or goats. For crops and pasture, a two-homestead settlement would use about eighty hectares of land, worked by the family labor-force, with occasional help from neighbors. An ard pulled by cattle was used for tilling the soil, and a wide variety of stone and bronze implements was available for other tasks. Approximately one-half of all food consumed was meat from domesticated animals; about 40% came from cereals; the remainder was supplied by milk and vegetables.[39]

Towards the end of the Bronze Age, Westfriesland experienced deteriorating drainage conditions caused by a rising ground water table, to which the residents once again had to adapt. They began to place their houses higher on the ridges and to dig deeper and wider ditches around their farmyards and fields. The area of cropland declined while livestock breeding became even more important. At the same time, the livestock began to be represented by more sheep or goats; perhaps they were less likely than cattle to sink into waterlogged pastures and reduce them to muck and mire. Fishing, too—sometimes in the ditches of the settlement complexes—became a more important, though still minor, activity. As the water levels continued to rise, much of the area was abandoned by c. 700 B.C. With a still rather simple technology and no compelling reasons for taking a stand, the population left for more suitable areas.[40]

With only slight modifications to suit local conditions, Bronze Age settlement and land use in Westfriesland could apply to early medieval Rijnland as well, for the picture fits the natural conditions of pre-reclamation Rijnland much more closely than do the discussions of manors and field systems for monasteries at St. Germain-des-Prés or elsewhere. Only after the reclamation of the peat bogs and the placement of hydraulics under human control in the late tenth century were the patterns of agriculture known from higher and drier areas applied with any consistency to Rijnland and adjacent portions of coastal Holland.[41]

NOTES

[1] William S. Cooter, "Ecological Dimensions of Medieval Agrarian Systems," *Agricultural History*, 52 (1978), 458-77, provides some interesting perspectives. See also the responses of R. S. Loomis and J. A. Raftis, in the same publication, 478-83 and 484-87.

[2] For a general introduction to early medieval agriculture, see: B. H. Slicher van Bath, *The Agrarian History of Western Europe A.D. 500-1850,*

trans. Olive Ordish (London: Edward Arnold, 1963), pp. 3-74; and Georges Duby, *The Early Growth of the European Economy: Warriors and Peasants from the Seventh to the Twelfth Century*, trans. H. B. Carke (London and Ithaca: Cornell Univ. Press, 1974), pp. 1-111. For the low productive capacity of crop raising and its limited dietary role, see: Guy Fourquin, *Le paysan d'occident au moyen âge* (Paris: F. Nathan, 1972), pp. 13-15; Andrew M. Watson, "Towards Denser and More Continuous Settlement: New Crops and Farming Techniques in the Early Middle Ages," in *Pathways to Medieval Peasants*, ed. J. A. Raftis, Papers in Mediaeval Studies 2 (Toronto: Pontifical Institute of Mediaeval Studies, 1981), pp. 69 and 80, n. 8; William S. Cooter, "Preindustrial Frontiers and Interaction Spheres: Aspects of the Human Ecology of Roman Frontier Regions in Northwest Europe," Diss. Univ. of Oklahoma 1976, pp. 34-59; and his "Ecological Dimensions of Medieval Agrarian Systems," 475-76.

[3] See, for example, the wide range of medieval archaeological publications referred to in the recent bibliography of J. C. Besteman and H. Sarfatij, "Bibliographie zur Archäologie des Mittelalters in den Niederlanden 1945 bis 1975," *Zeitschrift für Archäologie des Mittelalters*, 5 (1977), 163-231.

[4] H. T. Waterbolk, "Siedlungskontinuität im Küstengebiet der Nordsee zwischen Rhein und Elbe," *Probleme der Küstenforschung im südlichen Nordseegebiet*, 13 (1979), 3, recommends looking beyond one's immediate area to compensate for the uneveness in archaeological research.

[5] L. P. Louwe Kooijmans, *The Rhine/Meuse Delta: Four Studies on its Prehistoric Occupation and Holocene Geology*, Analecta Praehistorica Leidensia 7 (Leiden: Leiden Univ. Press, 1974), p. 42: "no fundamental changes in the relations men-natural environment occurred before A.D. c. 1000, the start of the embankments."

[6] William H. TeBrake, "The Making of a Humanized Landscape in the Dutch Rijnland, 950-1350: Ecological Change in a Coastal Lowland," Diss. Univ. of Texas at Austin, 1975 pp. 43-67.

[7] Louwe Kooijmans, *The Rhine/Meuse Delta*, pp. 7, 38-42; S. Jelgersma, et al., "The Coastal Dunes of the Western Netherlands: Geology, Vegetational History and Archaeology," *Mededelingen van de Rijks Geologische Dienst*, n.s., 21 (1970), 97-100, 147, and plate 1; and S. Jelgersma and J. F. van Regteren Altena, "An Outline of the Geological History of the Coastal Dunes in the Western Netherlands," *Geologie en mijnbouw*, 47 (1969), 237.

[8] B. P. Hageman, "Development of the Western Part of the Netherlands During the Holocene," *Geologie en mijnbouw*, 48 (1969), 379. See also enclosures 7-9 in L. P. Pons, et al., "Evolution of the Netherlands Coastal Area During the Holocene," in *Transactions of the Jubilee Convention*, Verhandelingen van het Koninklijk Nederlands Geologisch Mijnbouwkundig Genootschap, geologische ser., 21 (Maastricht: Geologisch Mijnbouwkundig Genootschap, 1973); and L. J. Pons, "De veengronden," in *De bodem van Nederland: toelichting bij de bodemkaart van Nederland schaal 1:200,000*, comp. Stichting voor Bodemkaartering (Wageningen: Stichting voor Bodemkaartering, 1965), p. 146, fig. 60.

[9] Pons, "De veengronden," pp. 145-47; C. van Wallenburg and W. C.

Markus, "Toemaakdekken in het Oude Rijngebied," *Boor en spade*, 17 (1971), 64-66; J. Bennema, "Het opervlakteveen in West-Nederland," *Boor en spade*, 3 (1949), 139-41, 144; C. H. Edelman, *Soils of the Netherlands* (Amsterdam: North Holland Publishing Co., 1950), pp. 68-71; Z. van Doorn, "Enkele waarnemingen van oorspronkelijke Indonesische veenmoerassen ter vergelijking met de Hollands- Utrechtse venen," *Boor en spade*, 10 (1959), 158; Louwe Kooijmans, *The Rhine/Meuse Delta*, p. 84; and W. H. Zagwijn, "De ontwikkeling van het 'Oer-IJ' estuarium en zijn omgeving," *Westerheem*, 20 (1971), 14.

[10] Louwe Kooijmans, *The Rhine/Meuse Delta*, pp. 37-38.

[11] Louwe Kooijmans, *The Rhine/Meuse Delta*, pp. 17-20, 78-124, and see esp. his discussion of the middle neolithic occupation of Hazendonk, about fifty kilometers east of the coast in the central Netherlands river area, pp. 125-68. See further the reports on L. P. Louwe Kooijmans' recent investigation of the early neolithic (c. 3500 B.C.) fishing and duck-hunting camp discovered near the modern community of Bergschenhoek, between Rijnland and Rotterdam, near what was then a small, fresh-water lake, in H. Sarfatij, "Archeologische Kroniek van Zuid-Holland over 1976," *Holland: regionaal-historisch tijdschrift*, 9 (1977), 248-52; Sarfatij's "Archeologische kroniek van Zuid-Holland over 1977," *Holland: regionaal-historisch tijdschrift*, 10 (1978), 197-299; and L. P. Louwe Kooijmans, "Het onderzoek van neolithische nederzettings terreinen in Nederland anno 1979," *Westerheem*, 29 (1980), 108-10, 112.

[12] A. T. Clason, *Animal and Man in Holland's Past: An Investigation of the Animal World Surrounding Man in Prehistoric and Early Historical Times in the Provinces of North and South Holland*, Palaeohistoria: Acta et Communicationes Instituti Bio-Archaeologici Universitatis Groninganae 13 (Groningen: J. B. Wolters, 1967), p. 4-7, 10-26, 105; Louwe Kooijmans, *The Rhine/Meuse Delta*, pp. 4-5, 8, 10-11, 20-45, 49, 118, 281; E. J. Helderman, "Enige resultaten van vijftien jaar archaeologisch onderzoek in de Zaanstreek," *Westerheem*, 20 (1971), 42; Jelgersma, et al., "The Coastal Dunes of the Western Netherlands," pp. 133-38; W. Glasbergen, et al., "Settlements of the Vlaardingen Culture at Voorschoten and Leidschendam (1 and 2)," *Helinium*, 7 (1967), 3-31, 97-120; and W. Groenman-van Waateringe, et al., "Settlements of the Vlaardingen Culture at Voorscheten and Leidschendam (Ecology)," *Helinium*, 8 (1968), 105-30.

[13] W. Glasbergen, et al., "Da neolithische nederzettingen te Vlaardingen (Z.H.)" in *In het voetspoor van A. E. van Giffen*, Universiteit van Amsterdam, Instituut voor Prae- and Protohistorie, 2nd ed. (Groningen: J. B. Wolters, 1966), pp. 41-65, 157-58, 173; Clason, *Animal and Man in Holland's Past*, pp. 10-12, 102; H. T. Waterbolk, "The Lower Rhine Basin," in *Courses Toward Urban Life: Archaeological Considerations of Some Cultural Alternates*, ed. R. J. Braidwood and G. R. Wiley (Chicago: Aldine, 1962), p. 242; J. A. Brongers, et al., "Prehistory in the Netherlands: An Economic-Technological Approach," *Berichten van de Rijkdienst voor het Oudheidkundig Bodemonderzoek*, 23 (1973), 12-13; and Jelgersma, et al., "The Coastal Dunes of the Western Netherlands," pp. 133-38.

[14] Glasbergen, et al., "Settlements of the Vlaardingen Culture," pp. 5-26,

185

98-112, 114; Groenman-van Waateringe, et al., "Settlements of the Vlaardingen Culture," pp. 109-18; and Louwe Kooijmans, *The Rhine/Meuse Delta*, pp. 23-26. See also the cautions about the greater vulnerability to decay of bird and fish remains in Wietske Prummel, "Vlees, gevogelte en vis," *Spieghel historiael*, 13 (1978), 285.

[15] L. P. Louwe Kooijmans, "The Neolithic at the Lower Rhine: Its Structure in Chronological and Geographical Respect," in *Acculturation and Continuity in Atlantic Europe Mainly During the Neolithic Period and the Bronze Age*, ed. S. J. de Laet, Dissertationes Archaeologicae Gandenses 16 (Brugge: De Tempel, 1976), pp. 150-73; his *The Rhine/Meuse Delta*, pp. 20-35; and Jelgersma, et al., "The Coastal Dunes of the Western Netherlands," pp. 133-46.

[16] Groenman-van Waateringe, et al., "Settlements of the Vlaardingen Culture," pp. 107-10; H. T. Waterbolk, "The Occupation of Friesland in the Prehistoric Period," *Berichten van de Rijksdienst voor het Oudheidkundig Bodemonderzoek*, 15-16 (1965-66), 19; Brongers, et al., "Prehistory in the Netherlands," p. 10; Jelgersma, et al., "The Coastal Dunes of the Western Netherlands," p. 131; and Louwe Kooijmans, *The Rhine/Meuse Delta*, p. 26.

[17] H. H. van Regteren Altena and J. A. Bakker, "De neo lithische woonplaats te Zandwerven (N.H.)," in *In het voetspoor van A. E. van Giffen*, pp. 34, 38-39.

[18] Communications by F. F. van Iterson Scholten in P. J. Woltering, "Archeologische kroniek van Noord-Holland over 1975," *Holland: regionaal-historisch tijdschrift*, 8 (1976), 239-41; in his "Archeologische kroniek van Noord-Holland over 1977," *Holland: regionaal-historisch tijdschrift*, 10 (1978), 254-55; and in his "Archeologische kroniek van Noord-Holland over 1978," *Holland: regionaal-historisch tijdschrift*, 11 (1979), 249-50.

[19] A. E. van Giffen, "Nederzettingssporen van de vroege Klokbekercultuur bij Oostwoud (N.H.), in *In het voetspoor van A. E. van Giffen*, pp. 66, 68; and Woltering, "Archeologische kroniek van Noord-Holland over 1978", pp. 250-51. For early ploughs, their evolution, and their uses, see Bernard Wailes, "Plow and Population in Temperate Europe," in *Population Growth: Anthropological Implications*, ed. Brian Spooner (Cambridge, MA: MIT Press, 1972), pp. 154-79.

[20] Louwe Kooijmans, *The Rhine/Meuse Delta*, pp. 30-35; and Jelgersma, et al., "The Coastal Dunes of the Western Netherlands," pp. 139-40.

[21] Waterbolk, "The Lower Rhine Basin," pp. 246-47; Brongers, et al., "Prehistory in the Netherlands," p. 12; and Clason, *Animal and Man in Holland's Past*, pp. 5-6, 206. This was true for central Europe as well; see H. Jankuhn, *Vor- und Frügeschichte vom Neolithikum bis zur Völkerwanderungzeit*, Deutsche Agrargeschichte 1 (Stuttgart: Eugen Ulmer, 1969), pp. 68-69.

[22] For Langeveld and Vogelenzang along the dunes, for Zwaagdijk, Wevershoef, Oostwoud, Hoogkarspel, and Bovenkarspel in Westfriesland, and for Molenaarsgraff in the central river clay area, see Clason, *Animal and Man in Holland's Past*, pp. 12-15; Louwe Kooijmans, *The Rhine/Meuse Delta*, pp. 274, 278; Woltering, "Archeologische Kroniek van Noord-Holland over 1977," pp. 255-56; W. Groenman- van Waateringe, "Nederzettingen van de Hilversumcul-

tuur te Vogelenzang (N.H.), en Den Haag (Z.H.)," in *In het voetspoor van A. E. van Giffen*, p. 170; and J. A. Bakker, et al., "Hoogkarspel-Watertoren: Towards a Reconstruction of Ecology and Archaeology of an Agrarian Settlement of 1000 B.C.," in *Ex horreo, I.P.P. 1951-1976*, ed. B. L. van Beek, et al., Univ. of Amsterdam, Albert Egges van Giffen Instituut vor Prae- en Protohistorie, Cingula 4 (Amsterdam: I.P.P., 1977), pp. 204-08.

[23] For Monster and Velsen along the dunes, for Wevershoef, Andijk, Bovenkarspel, Hoogkarspel, and Medemblik in Westfriesland, and for Molenaarsgraaf in the central river area, see P. J. Woltering, "Archeologische kroniek van Noord-Holland over 1976," *Holland: regionaal-historisch tijdschrift*, 9 (1977), 193; his "Archeologische kroniek van Noord-Holland over 1977," 256-57; his "Archeologische kroniek van Nord-Holland over 1978," 246-49, 253; Jelgersma, et al., "The Coastal Dunes of the Western Netherlands," p. 143; Louwe Kooijmans, *The Rhine/Meuse Delta*, pp. 30, 109, 277, 328; Janneke Buurman, "Cereals in Circles: Crop Processing Activities in Bronze Age Bovenkarspel (the Netherlands)," in *Festschrift Maria Hopf zum 65. Geburtstag am 14. September 1979*, ed. U. Körber-Grohne, Rheinischen Landesmuseum Bonn, Archaeo-Physika 8 (Cologne and Bonn: Rudolf Habelt Verlag, 1979), pp. 21-37; F. Baars, "Afdelingnieuws: afdeling Noord-Holland Noord," *Westerheem*, 27 (1978), 337; J. A. Bakker, "Een grafheuvel en oud akkerland te Hoogkarspel (N.H.)," in *In het voetspoor van A. E. van Giffen*, pp. 104, 108; Bakker et al., "Hoogkarspel- Watertoren," pp. 187-225; and J. C. Besteman, "Carolingian Medemblik," *Berichten van de Rijksdienst voor het Oudheidkundig Bodemonderzoek*, 24 (1974), 53.

[24] W. A. van Es, "Friesland in Roman Times," *Berichten van de Rijksdienst voor het Oudheidkundig Bodemonderzoek*, 15-16 (1965-66), 40, 44; W. Haarnagel, "De Prähistorischen Siedlungsformen im Küstengebiet der Nordsee," in *Beiträge zur Genese der Siedlungs- und Agrarlandschaft in Europa*, Geographische Zeitschrift: Beihefte (Wiesbaden: Franz Steiner Verlag, 1968), pp. 67-71; and William H. TeBrake, "Ecology and Economy in Early Medieval Frisia," *Viator: Medieval and Renaissance Studies*, 9 (1978), 7-8. On the relative dryness of the period, see H. T. Waterbolk, *De praechistorische mens en zijn milieu: een palynologisch onderzoek naar de menselijke invloed op de plantengroei van de diluviale gronden in Nederland* (Assen: Van Gorcum, 1954), pp. 16, 131.

[25] The best general treatment of the Roman period is W. A. van Es, *De Romeinen in Nederland*, Grote Fibula serie (Bussum: Fibula-van Dishoeck, 1972). Though the Rijnland saw essentially a military occupation, there was an agricultural component to it. The castellum at Valkenburg, for example, seems to have been particularly important as a storage and shipping point for grain emanating from the dune, estuarine, and riverbank areas of the western Netherlands as well as from England: See W. Groenman-van Waateringe, "Grain Storage and Supply in the Valkenburg Castella and Pretorium Aggripinae," in *Ex horreo: I.P.P. 1951-1976*, pp. 226-40.

[26] J. H. F. Bloemers, "Rijswijk (Z.H.) 'De Bult', een nederzetting van de Cananefaten," *Hermeneus: tijdschrift voor antieke cultuur*, 52 (1980), 95-106.

[27] Van es, *De Romeinen in Nederland*, pp. 96-97; and H. Sarfatij, "Friezen- Romeinen-Cananefaten," *Holland: regionaal-historisch tijdschrift*, 3 (1971), 175.

[28] Bloemers, "Rijswijk," p. 106, considers this a factor contributing to the abandonment of the settlement at Rijswijk.

[29] S. J. Fockema Andreae, "De Rijnlandse kastelen en landhuizen in hun maatschappelijk verband," in S. J. Fockema Andreae, et al., *Kastelen, ridderhofsteden en buitenplaatsen in Rijnland* (Leiden: Vereniging "Oud-Leiden," 1952), p. 1; and Sarfatij, "Friezen-Romeinen-Cananefaten," pp. 175-76.

[30] D. P. Blok, "De vestigingsgeschiedenis van Holland en Utrecht in het licht van de plaatsnamen," in M. Gyselling and D. P. Blok, *Studies over de oudste plaatsnamen van Holland en Utrecht*, Bijdragen en Mededelingen der Naamkunde- Commissie van de Koninklijke Nederlandse Akademie van Wetenschappen te Amsterdam, no. 17 (Amsterdam, 1959), pp. 13-15; and J. K. de Cock, *Bijdrage tot de historische geografie van Kennemerland in de middeleeuwen op fisisch- geografische grondslag* (Groningen: J. B. Wolters, 1965), p. 252. In Rijnland, water names such as Aar, Vennep, and Wilk, and the place-name Alphen, are of this type.

[31] Jelgersma, et al., "The Coastal Dunes of the Western Netherlands," p. 144; and Sarfatij, "Friezen-Romeinen-Cananefaten," p. 20.

[32] W. A. van Es, "Early Medieval Settlements," *Berichten van de Rijksdienst voor het Oudhiedkundig Bodemondersoek*, 23 (1973), 281-85; and H. Sarfatij, "Die Frühgeschichte von Rijnsburg (8.-12. Jahrhundert), ein historisch-archäologischer Bericht," in *Ex horreo: I.P.P. 1951-1976*, pp. 295-97.

[33] TeBrake, "The Making of a Humanized Landscape in the Dutch Rijnland," pp. 80-87.

[34] TeBrake, "Ecology and Economy in Early Medieval Frisia," 10-15.

[35] TeBrake, "The Making of a Humanized Landscape in the Dutch Rijnland," pp. 80-87.

[36] R. W. Brandt, "De kolonisatie van West-Friesland in de bronstijd," *Westerheem*, 29 (1980), 141; and Waterbolk, "Siedlungskontinuität im Küstengebiet der Nordsee," 7. There has been extensive archaeological research in Westfriesland since World War II, but the efforts of the State Service for Archaeological Investigations of Amersfoort (Rijksdienst voor het Oudheidkundig Bodemonderzoek) and the Institute for Pre- and Protohistory of the University of Amsterdam (Albert Egges van Giffen Instituut voor Prae- en Protohistorie) have been particularly fruitful during the last fifteen years. Numerous excavations and extensive mapping have taken place in the neighborhood of Hoogkarspel and Bovenkarspel in particular.

[37] Waterbolk, "The Occupation of Friesland in the Prehistoric Period," 25; Buurman, "Cereals in Circles," p. 22; Bakker, et al., "Hoogkarspel-Wateren," p. 222; and Brandt, "De kolonisatie van West-Friesland in de bronstijd," p. 143.

[38] Brandt, "De kolonisatie van West-Friesland in de bronstijd," p. 148.

[39] R. W. Brandt of the Institute for Pre- and Protohistory established this general picture of Bronze Age occupation in Westfriesland. See his "Landbouw en veeteelt in de late bronstijd van West-Friesland," *Westerheem*, 25 (1976),

58-66. The author presupposed a family similar to that which has been postulated for other places during the Bronze Age and later: six members, with a high ratio of children because of short life expectancy. The average calorie needs were estimated at about 2,000 per person per day or about 12,000 per family per day. He concluded, therefore, that a diet of fifty percent meat and forty percent cereals was supplied by the following quantities each year: either 1160 kilograms of beef or 780 kilograms of pork or 750 kilograms of mutton (actually some sort of combination of these was likely), plus 550 kilograms of cereals. The estimated herd sizes based on stalling facilities accord well with these quantities of meat. The amount of arable land required to produce the cereals was conservatively estimated in the following fashion: 170 kilograms of seed would be sown per hectare which would yield a modest 340 kilograms at harvest; about 3.5 hectares were, therefore, needed each year. Since fallowing was perhaps the only means of maintaining soil fertility, as little as one-fifth of the potential arable may have been planted at any time. A total of 17.5 hectares of potential arable was, therefore, required for each homestead. All of these estimates fit well the amount of arable land available along the sand ridges and outcrops and the labor potential of a six member family using the cattle-drawn ard, various stone and bronze tools, and other implements.

[40] Waterbolk, "Siedlungskontinuität im Küstengebiet der Nordsee," 8, 12; and his "The Occupation of Friesland in the Prehistoric Period," 26.

[41] William H. TeBrake, "Ecology of Village Settlement in the Dutch Rijnland," in *Pathways to Medieval Peasants*, ed. J. A. Raftis, pp. 13-18.
(This list of place names must accompany figure 1; may be placed on a facing page, if necessary.)

PART III:
RECONSTRUCTING MATERIAL WORLDS FROM
ARTIFACTS

NORTH SEA TRADE BEFORE THE VIKINGS

RICHARD HODGES

In *Mohammed and Charlemagne*, Henri Pirenne lay great emphasis on the isolation of northern Europe from the Mediterranean following the seventh century and upon the subsequent growth of trade in and around the North Sea.[1] He believed it was this North Sea commerce—trade between the Rhineland and the Low Countries, the Scandinavian territories and Anglo-Saxon England—that provided the modest economic foundations for Charlemagne's great triumph at the end of the eighth century and for the Carolingian Empire as a whole. This trade, he argued, continued until the Viking raids of the mid-ninth century disrupted all aspects of European life.

Even though Pirenne's theories have been scrutinized by hosts of scholars over the years, none has really gone beyond his generalizations.[2] Here, I wish to speculate briefly on this series of issues, using archaeological evidence to outline the chronology of North Sea trade before the Vikings, to illustrate the evidence for trading zones during this period, and, finally, to question Pirenne's basic propositions for the economic basis of the Carolingian Renaissance. Such evidence stems not from a fresh analysis of existing documentation but from a growing body of archaeological data collected over a twenty-year period.

The Chronology of North Sea Trade

Between 400-600 A.D., the scale of long-distance trade around the North Sea seems to have been small and directed from one court to another. The imported goods that enriched the burials of this period have been found clustered close to royal centers, with a sharp decrease in these imports beyond the well-known core areas.[3] The first evidence of a more constant source of commerce has been traced to Ipswich in Suffolk, where the material remains of Merovingian traders—undoubtedly attracted to King Redwald's kingdom of East Anglia—have been excavated.[4] These artifacts—Merovingian pots dated to the early seventh century—are contemporaneous with the cemetery site of Sutton Hoo, just fourteen kilometers east of Ipswich. This material evidence suggests that significant numbers of aliens were being detained deliberately at a coastal point, possibly because they represented a threat to the social equilibrium of the community.[5] A similar site may have also existed in Kent at this time, probably on or close to the Wantsum Channel; but so far only charter references to a settlement at Sarre[6] and a range of imported commodities characteristic of the later sixth and seventh century cemeteries in the vicinity support this hypothesis.

Whether trade between England and the Merovingian kingdoms of Neustria, in northern France, and Austrasia, in the Rhineland, persisted throughout the seventh century is still unknown, although the minting of English gold coins towards the middle of the seventh century, for example, may imply some isolation or regionalization in contrast to the early seventh century when Frankish gold coins were imported into Kent in large numbers.[7] We know that a new impetus was given to North Sea commerce in the last quarter of the century with the foundations of new settlements at Dorestad and Quentovic. Dorestad was located where the river Rhine meets the river Lek in central Holland, and Quentovic somewhere near Boulogne.[8] Recent archaeological excavations at these sites provide new insights into this commerce. The earliest wheel-thrown (Rhenish) pots known at Dorestad have not yet been found at Ipswich. We cannot be certain, therefore, of the direction of the trade through Dorestad, but the striking similarity between the earliest Frisian silver coins of this period and the earliest Kentish coins points tenuously to commercial contact between these areas, possibly to the detriment of the kingdom of East Anglia.

The earliest eighth-century evidence for trade between Neustria and southern England comes from Hamwih, Saxon Southampton. This site served as the centralized trading outlet for the kingdom of Wessex

194

and possibly for the large kingdom of Mercia in central England. Excavations at Hamwih have shown that the settlement grew slowly between c. 700-720/25 and flourished between c. 720/25- 50. Then a hiatus in major commercial activity occurred which lasted until about 790, when its third phase began, ending c. 820-30.[9]

The excavators of Dorestad are confident that it functioned throughout the eighth century. A significant upturn in commerce occurred there between c. 775-830, dates which correlate with the years of Carolingian expansion and dominance.[10] At Ipswich we can only point to a massive increase in trade with the Rhineland, via Dorestad, and with Flanders during the later eighth and ninth centuries, though it is important to note that Rhenish imports of all kinds were definitely fewer in number than those from areas to the south of the Rhine.[11] Similarly, there is increased evidence for trade between Carolingia (again via Dorestad) and Haithabu, the trading station at the base of Jutland. The first phase of this emporium, planned in the early ninth century and attributed to King Godfred of the Danes, contained many imported Rhenish pots, whereas the earlier eighth century "south settlement" at Haithabu contained virtually none.[12]

There are now signs that there were dramatic changes in the North Sea economy before the main burst of Viking raids in the late 830s and 840s. Dendrochronological evidence from Dorestad confirms C14, numismatic, and ceramic evidence that the emporium was in decline after approximately 830. Hamwih also appears to have been in decline by this decade, if not before, at a time when, ironically, the West Saxon dynasty was reimposing itself over the Mercians. All the evidence suggests a downswing in international trade until the tenth century, with a related growth in regional markets[13] (Fig. 1).

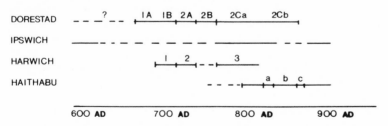

Figure 1
The Chronology of Four Major North Sea Emporia

195

The Trading Zones

All the archaeological and historical evidence points to the centralized control of long-distance trade by either the aristocracy or, to a lesser extent, members of the church.[14] This accounts for the great discrepancies in settlement size between the enormous emporia on the one hand, and the small villages, royal sites, and monasteries on the other—a difference, on average, between sites measuring roughly fifty ha. and about two ha. area. The emporia were points where trade was controlled and traders settled for short lengths of time. The restrictiveness of the trade reflects its social purpose: the Merovingians and later Carolingians traded manufactured goods such as wine, pottery, glasses, and quernstones to acquire certain luxuries like textiles to accentuate social prestige; the West Saxons and Danes, in contrast, exchanged their local raw materials for these manufactured goods to sustain political prestige in their own delicately balanced tribal systems. The scale of this trade was also delimited by the boats employed in the early medieval period. All these crafts had to be rowed, with only small sails for extra assistance, and, including the rowers, had a maximum capacity of about eight to ten tons.

The western Frankish traders were probably Carolingian noblemen (*negociatores*) acting on behalf of specific courts. The best-known merchants, however, were the famous Frisians.[15] To what extent was there competition between these entrepreneurs from Dorestad and *negociatores* from other parts of the Empire? An answer to this question can be found by analyzing the material remains from the emporia discussed so far.

In most Roman or medieval contexts, broken pottery is thought to represent traded goods. The imported wares in Dorestad were clearly used by its inhabitants as well as traded, however, while the miscellaneous imports to Hamwih and Ipswich were largely restricted to those emporia.[16] The marked clustering of imported Carolingian pottery at Hamwih and Ipswich would seem to reflect traders prepared to await business but not prepared to wine and dine from native hand-made pots when their own well-thrown wares might easily be brought along. Similarly, if we plot the distribution of Rhenish imports known from the Dorestad excavations, we should get some perspective on the wares traded and used by the Frisians. The same can be done in the case of the Hamwih and Ipswich imported pottery, as illustrated in Figure 2. To the north of the river Scheldt, even up to Jutland, the majority of imports are Rhenish in origin, although Rhenish wares are scarce around the Baltic Sea. To the south of the line, the variety of imports from several western

Frankish pottery centers seemingly illuminates the activities of many different merchants north of the Loire and east of Brittany.

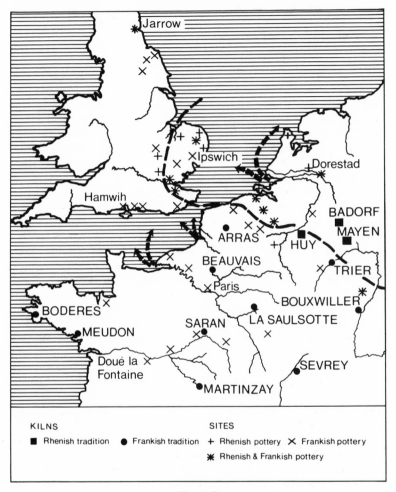

Figure 2
Map showing trade competition in areas of the Frisians and Franks, based on the products of Carolingian pottery kilns

    This evidence points to at least two different trading zones in the North Sea, with the Frisians controlling the more northerly one. It is likely that the same picture might be deduced from glass finds; but it is not so clear in the case of vital utilitarian objects like lava quernstones quarried near Coblenz in the Eifel, for this material is found in most regions around the North Sea.[17] It seems, therefore, that it was as romantic strangers and occasional traders to western settlements that the Frisians won their reputations—as the exception rather than the rule.

The Bolin Thesis

Thirty years ago, Sture Bolin argued that the Carolingian Renaissance in the early ninth century was not financed by slow economic growth, as Pirenne speculated, but by a swift and powerful injection of wealth from the Orient via the Baltic Sea.[18] In particular, Bolin skillfully asserted that the Emperor Charlemagne may have tapped the Viking link to the Caspian Sea which was bringing large amounts of newly-mined Persian and Afghan silver to the Scandinavians. Many scholars, however, have contested Bolin's argument on the grounds that Arabic coins are extremely rare in Carolingia.[19] Bolin himself had a ready explanation for this negative evidence: he was certain that the silver dirhems would have been melted down upon entering the Empire if they had not been already melted down by the Viking entrepreneurs. It seems possible to evaluate this dispute in the light of the significant assemblages of archaeological data now available.

Following from the discussion of North Sea trade and traders outlined above, it is possible to find much in favor of Bolin's hypothesis.[20] First, it appears that the bulk of the products manufactured on the important estates of Charlemagne and Louis the Pious in the Rhineland were being shipped via Dorestad along the Frisian coastline to Haithabu, not to other parts of the Empire or to the Christian Anglo-Saxon kingdoms. Second, the strategy employed by King Godfred, who founded Haithabu close to Denmark's southern border with Carolingia's allies, suggests that the settlement was deliberately envisaged as an *entrepôt* to link the North Sea trading system to the Baltic one—a very advantageous strategy. Third, this last point is reinforced by the very deliberate planning of the first settlement at Haithabu with a street grid and tenements laid out neatly on the shores of the Schlei.[21] Lastly, the very size of Dorestad—the *entrepôt* servicing the empire's core region—strongly suggests its purpose. This point is now strengthened by the evidence for economic collapse there and elsewhere in the North Sea in the 830s, before the Viking raids and at the time of a substantial decline, lasting about fifty years, in Viking trade with the Orient. As a result of

198

this decline, fewer silver hoards were deposited around the Baltic Sea, and the Scandinavians, as Randsborg has shown, turned from "trade" to "raid."[22] Clearly, this new archaeological information calls into question one of the major theses concerning the Carolingian Empire, as well as the timing of the Viking raids, the Carolingian civil war, and the mid-ninth century expansion of Wessex.

Conclusions

It is evident how archaeology can illuminate this Dark Age controversy raised more than fifty years ago by Henri Pirenne. Archaeological evidence points to the existence of trade between various parts of the continent and the less complex kingdoms to the North and West. The pattern of this pre-market trade was in all probability defined by individual agreements between kings, as anthropologists have shown in other pre-market contexts.[23] From archaeological data, different zones in which traders operated may be reconstructed; this, in turn, indicates the restricted role played by the Frisians from Dorestad in the development of European commerce. Conversely, there is no doubt that Frisian traders handled the bulk of the mass-produced goods from the Imperial estates in the Rhineland and that these goods were apparently destined for northern clientele. The Frisians, it seems, may have acted as a buffer between the Christian Carolingians and the predominately pagan Norsemen who offered, among other things, Arabic silver in exchange for Rhenish wine. Yet, because the merchants were so embedded in the fortunes of the Carolingian aristocracy, it is not surprising that the socio-economic stress on the political system caused the stunning collapse of long-distance trade. Thus, an impressive trading system operating between undefended emporia gave way, first to unremitting Viking raids and, ultimately, to regional market economies and the birth of the European States.

NOTES

I am indebted to Kathy Biddick for the invitation to write this paper; to Klavs Randsborg for discussions concerning it, and to Andrea Penney and Dorothy Cruse for typing the various versions of it.
 [1] Henri Pirenne, *Mohammed and Charlemagne* (London: Allen and Unwin, 1939).
 [2] A. R. Bridbury, "The Dark Ages," *Economic History Review*, 22 (1969), 526-37.

[3] Chris Arnold, "Wealth and Social Structure: A Matter of Life and Death," in *Anglo-Saxon Cemeteries*, ed. P. Rahtz, T. Dickinson, and L. Watts (Oxford, 1979). British Archaeological Reports, 82 (Oxford, 1980), 81-142 gives an interesting example of rich imports being clustered in a seventh-century kingdom.

[4] See Richard Hodges, *Dark Age Economics* (London: Duckworths, 1982); Keith Wade, "Excavations in Ipswich, 1974-78," *East Anglian Archaeology*, 10 (1984).

[5] Hodges, chap. 3.

[6] Martin Biddle, "The Towns," in *The Archaeology of Anglo-Saxon England*, ed. David M. Wilson (London: Methuen and Co., 1976), p. 115.

[7] S. E. Rigold, "The Sutton Hoo Coins in the Light of the Contemporary Background of Coinage in England," in *The Sutton Hoo Ship Burial*, ed. R. L. S. Bruce-Mitford (London: British Museum, 1975), vol. 1, pp. 635-77.

[8] W. A. van Es and W. J. H. Verwers, *Excavations at Dorestad 1. The Harbour: Hoogstraat 1* (Amersfoort: Nederlandse Oudheden, 1980); Jan Dhondt, "Le problème de Quentovic," *Studi in Onore D'Amintore Farfani*, (Milan, 1962), pp. 185-248.

[9] J. F. Cherry and Richard Hodges, "The Chronology of Hamwih, Saxon Southampton Reconsidered," *Antiquaries Journal*, 58 (1978), 299-309; Richard Hodges, *The Hamwih Pottery—The Local and Imported Wares from Thirty Years Excavations in Middle Saxon Southampton and Their European Context*, Council for British Archaeology Research Rept. 37 (London, 1981).

[10] Van Es and Verwers, pp. 300-03.

[11] Richard Hodges, "The Pottery," in Wade, "Excavations in Ipswich, 1974-78."

[12] Klavs Randsborg, *The Viking Age in Denmark* (London: Duckworths, 1980), pp. 71-72.

[13] Hodges, *The Hamwih Pottery*, chap. 8.

[14] P. Sawyer, "Kings and Merchants," in *Early Medieval Kingship*, ed. P. Sawyer and I. N. Wood (Leeds: Dept. of History, 1977), pp. 139-58; Hodges, *Dark Age Economics*, chap. 3.

[15] D. Jellema, "Frisian Trade in the Dark Ages," *Speculum*, 30 (1955), 15-36.

[16] Hodges, *The Hamwih Pottery*, chap. 4.

[17] Hodges, *The Hamwih Pottery*, chap. 6.

[18] Sture Bolin, "Mohammed, Charlemagne and Ruric," *Scandinavian Economic History Review*, 1 (1953), 5-39.

[19] Karl F. Morrison, "Numismatics and Carolingian Trade: A Critique of the Evidence," *Speculum*, 38 (1963), 403-83.

[20] Richard Hodges, "Trade and Market Origins in the Ninth Century: An Archaeological perspective of Anglo-Carolingian Relations," in *Charles the Bald: Court and Kingdom*, ed. Margaret Gibson and Janet Nelson, British Archaeological Repts. 101 (Oxford, 1981), pp. 213-33; see also Richard Hodges and David Whitehouse, *Mohammed, Charlemagne and the Origins of Europe. Archaeology and the Pirenne Thesis* (Ithaca: Cornell Univ. Press, 1983).

[21] Herbert Jankuhn, *Haithabu. Ein Handelsplatz der Wikingerseit*, 6th ed. (Neumünster: Karl Wachholtz, 1976), App. 66.

[22] Randsborg, pp. 152-53.

[23] Marshall Sahlins, *Stone Age Economics* (London: Tavistock Press, 1974), pp. 227-314; George Dalton, "Karl Polanyi's Analysis of Long-Distance Trade and His Wider Paradigm," in *Ancient Civilisation and Trade*, ed. J. Sabloff and C. C. Lamberg-Karlovsky, (Albuquerque: Univ. of New Mexico, 1975), pp. 63-132.

MORPHOLOGICAL ANALYSIS OF MEDIEVAL FINE POTTERY: PROVENANCE AND TRADE PATTERNS IN THE MEDITERRANEAN WORLD

JANET E. BUERGER

Late-medieval glazed pottery in the Mediterranean area has long been regarded as a clue to daily life, but it has not been fully studied as an indicator of cultural cross-currents and economic ebb and flow. As an indicator of these processes, only fine wares—mostly glazed wares—are relevant. Cooking pots or other ceramic types that did not circulate beyond a local area (twenty miles was the average distance between pottery-producing centers in North and South Italy) are obviously not suitable for such a study. Fine pottery, in contrast, has special character-istics that make it ideal for this kind of research: it displays a sophistica-tion of craftsmanship generally associated with the arts in a broader sense and was potentially desirable outside the area of its manufacture.

The quality of glazed pottery production in various Mediterranean cities was of such refinement that the commodity was exported and imported to a surprising degree. The trade patterns for glazed pottery correspond closely not only to political activity and to emigrations, but to the interchange of styles and influences found in art and architecture in the Mediterranean area.

The study of international trade and intellectual cross-currents in the Mediterranean during the late Middle Ages is highly complex, but at present, our means of establishing the nature of the various levels of communications are still sketchy. It is, therefore, helpful to draw upon archaeological materials with a "peripatetic" nature as we begin a systematic analysis of this question.

Fine glazed pottery provides an excellent starting point. This essay refers only to glazed pottery in Italy, Yugoslavia, Greece, and Southern France, produced from about A.D. 1200-1400.[1] In order for the evidence to yield maximum information, however, this study must be expanded in the future to include the entire Mediterranean basin, and slightly earlier periods as well, in order to encompass the precocious Islamic and Byzantine wares that were circulated prior to the flourishing of Italian maiolicas. This must be an "interdisciplinary" effort, bridging the Western Medieval, Byzantine, and Arab cultures that surrounded the Sea.

In the past, scholars have studied late-medieval Italian pottery primarily through its decoration. This research, while establishing some basic and useful information, presents a number of hazards. First, there is no "decoration" on plain glazed pottery, which provides some of the most valuable evidence of trade. Green glazed pottery, for instance, was often considered a luxurious imitation metal vessel and enjoyed great popularity among affluent populations throughout the Mediterranean. Unfortunately, it is this type of pottery that especially falls prey to sloppy cataloguing procedures when found in undated strata on pre-medieval sites and is classified as "modern." Thus, parallels to the finely refined forms of Metallic Ware and related green or brown glazed pottery, such as were found in the excavations of Diocletian's Palace in Split, on the Dalmatian Coast, are difficult to find (see Figs. 1 and 2 at end of essay).[2]

Decorative analysis, when used by itself, can also mislead. Many decorative motifs were ubiquitous and do not, therefore, necessarily prove any specific origin. Provenance can be more precisely determined by using morphological analysis of, for instance, the shape of the pot. This method has proven to be a powerful tool in the study of Classical Greek vases, and it has adapted well to my own research on medieval pottery.[3] The problems differ in medieval Italy from Classical Greece, yet pottery forms still indicate provenance, if not specific workshop.

Morphological analysis not only has advantages over decorative analysis but also is more accessible and often more precise than the scientific techniques of mineralogical and neutron analysis. It can be carried out by a pottery expert on the site, with a handful of readily-available tools. Mineralogical analysis can be too general to help find a specific origin, and neutron analysis—aside from its expense and general unavailability—can require the archaeologist to know already the information sought. The technique demands clay samples from specific river beds and comparative samples of pottery, presupposing the possibility of carry-away examples that may be unavailable from museums housing material from related sites.

A few examples will suffice to suggest the possibilities of the morphological method. In Italy, two major categories of late-medieval maiolica have been distinguished by students in the field: the Proto-Maiolica of the South of Italy and the Archaic Maiolica from the North. The latter usually carries decoration in green and brown on a white ground and is ubiquitous in all the northern provinces of Italy. The forms, however, frequently vary in each province. Thus, for example, a characteristic form in the Romagna-Marches area is a carenated jug with a strap handle that is pinched to the body of the jug at the lower end (Fig. 3). This form was not produced in Liguria, Tuscany, or Lazio, so when it appeared on an imported jug found in the excavations at Split, it could be identified as from the Romagna-Marches region (Figs. 4, 5). The Split piece could not have been identified as accurately by decorative analysis alone (Figs. 6, 7).

A further example can be seen in Sicilian Gela Ware. Gela Ware, a typical Proto-Maiolica bearing various colors in its decoration, was originally defined as a pottery (named after one of its find spots, Gela, in Sicily) with a flaring rim and characteristic yellow, green, and brown design on a white ground. After an examination of the forms of Gela Ware in both the Archaeological Museum in Gela and the State Museum of Ceramics in Caltagirone, Sicily, it was apparent that the ware could be more usefully defined in terms of its highly regularized forms (Figs. 8-11), which are marked by ridged rims and a distinctive grooved, disk-roofed ring-based foot.[4] These forms—evidently done by the same workshop or group of workshops—encompass not only yellow, green, and brown decorated pottery but also examples with red, green, and brown decoration, and plain green glazed pottery as well.

As a result of defining the ware by form rather than decoration, its identification on sites outside of Sicily is simplified. In addition, copies of the ware, perhaps indicating some kind of indirect influence, can be separated easily into a different category. Similarly decorated bowls found at Split and Corinth (where they were tentatively identified as Gela Ware pieces) do not have the same forms. Bowls found at Atlit and identified as Gela Ware, however, do have the Gela Ware forms; attibution can be confirmed, suggesting some kind of direct relation between this Sicilian community and that of Atlit.[5] Further investigation into the

205

sgraffito pottery that was found at the port of San Simeon in Syria, which has a Gela Ware form, might turn up valuable evidence regarding the pottery of southeast Sicily.[6]

Again, Split provides an ideal location for linking cultural cross-currents with trade patterns and pottery evidence. The Adriatic area, like Spain and Sicily, was a meeting point between the East and the West in the Mediterranean. Split is among many sites on the Adriatic where an influx of different types of pottery from around the Mediterranean is a prominent feature of its archaeological finds, and it must reflect the cosmopolitan character of the other major Adriatic and Italian port cities of Venice, Dubrovnik, Durazzo, and Naples, where archaeological investigations have not yet revealed supporting materials (Figs. 12-17).

Sadly, much has been lost of the medieval aspects of the Adriatic *metropoles*—by a seventeenth-century earthquake in Dubrovnik, and general deterioration in Split and Venice. It is hard to appreciate from standing monuments just how cosmopolitan their culture was. In Split, we have lost the multi-colored striped arches of the campanile to a dry nineteenth-century restoration in white monochrome limestone, but many small monuments remain as testaments to the cultural cross-currents that existed: for example, the polygonal pulpit in the Cathedral and a similar one in the nearby town of Trogir with Byzantine-style capitals; Andrija Buvina's carved wooden doors on the Cathedral (A.D. 1214), suggesting Byzantine influence; and the proto-Renaissance sculptures at the base of the campanile, which come from an Italian tradition. The pottery reflects this complex atmosphere in influences and can offer several concrete clues as to the origin of the influx of ideas that fed the city (Figs. 18-19). Clearly, then, morphological analysis can aid not only the historian but also the art historian in reconstructing the important international exchange that made this period one of the most fascinating in the history of modern Europe.

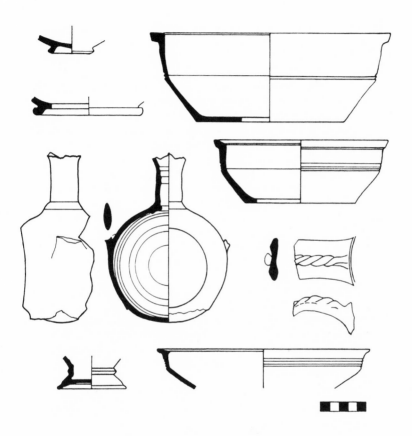

Figure 1
Plain brown or green glazed pottery, including "Metallic Ware," found in
Split, Yugoslavia. (13th - early 15th centuries.)

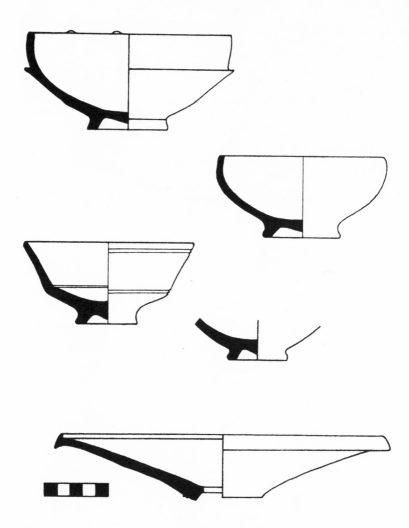

Figure 2
Brown glazed pottery, related to "Metallic Ware," found in Split,
Yugoslavia. (13th - early 15th centuries.)

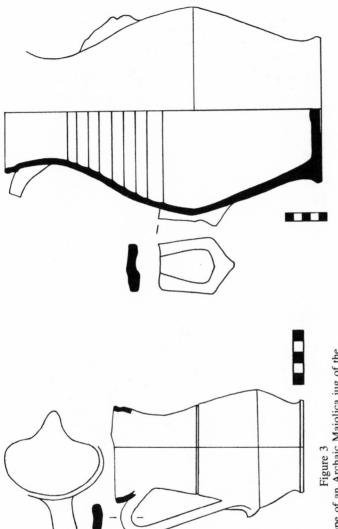

Figure 4
An Archaic Maiolica jug with a typical Romagna-Marche area form. Split, Yugoslavia. (Ca. 1350-1400.)

Figure 3
Typical shape of an Archaic Maiolica jug of the Romagna-Marches area of North Italy, with a carenated body and a handle pinched at the lower end. (Scorza Collection Pesaro, ca. 1350.)

209

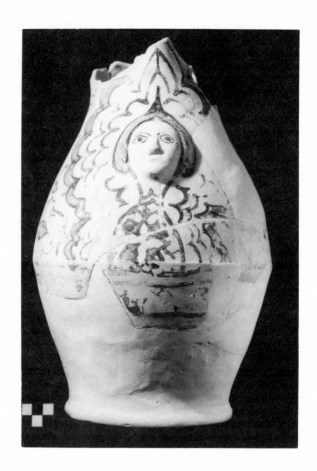

Figure 5
Photograph of the pot in Figure 4.

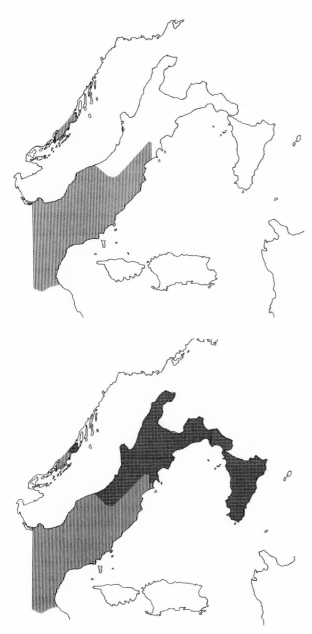

Figure 7
Italy, showing distribution of Archai Maiolica.

Figure 6
Italy, showing distribution of North Italian Archai
Maiolica (striped area) and South Italian Proto-Maiolica
(cross-hatched area).

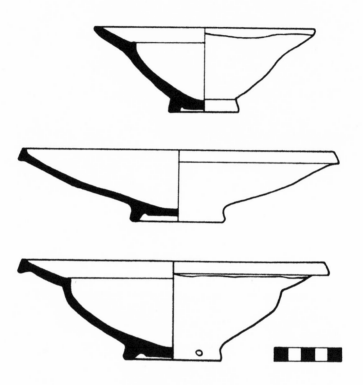

Figure 8
Gela Ware, with its characteristic disk-roofed, ring-based foot,
which can identify the pottery in the absence of decoration.

Figure 9
Gela Ware, State Museum of Ceramics, Caltagirone, Sicily.
(Ca. 13th century.)

Figure 10
Gela Ware, State Museum of Ceramics, Caltagirone, Sicily.
(Ca. 13th century.)

213

Figure 11
Gela Ware, State Museum of Ceramics, Caltagirone, Sicily.
(Ca. 13th century.)

Figure 12
Fragment of a Syrian alkaline-glazed bowl
found in Split, Yugoslavia. (Ca. 1350-1400.)

Figure 13
Fragment of a Spanish Lustreware plate,
found in Split, Yugoslavia. (Ca. 1400.)

215

Figure 14
Tunisian bowl, found in Sicily. Archaeological Museum, Gela. (Ca. 14th century.) The type is also found as decoration on church walls (bacini) in Pisa.

216

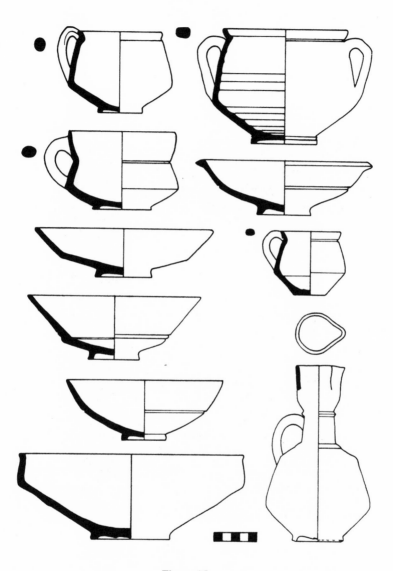

Figure 15
Characteristic forms of Arab pottery, found in Sicily. State Museum of
Ceramics, Caltagirone. Similar forms are found in coastal cities in Apulia
and in Frederick the Second's castle at Lucera in Apulia.

217

Figure 16
Near Eastern or Nagreb bowl used as decoration on the exterior wall of the Vladadon Monastery in Thessaloniki, Greece. (14th century.)

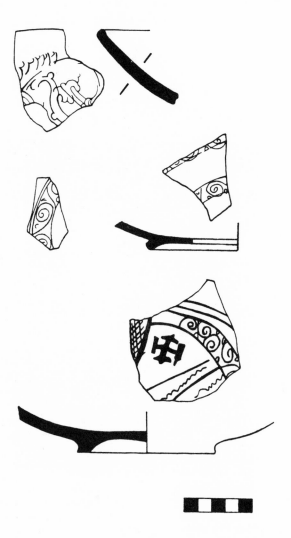

Figure 17
Byzantine pottery found at Split, Yugoslavia. (Ca. 12th century.) Similar
fragments have been found on coastal sites in Apulia and at Canosa in
Apulia.

219

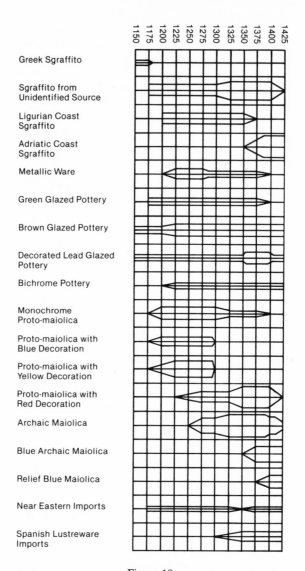

Figure 18
Pottery types at Split. The wide variety of pottery types found at the Adriatic seaport city of Split on the Dalmation coast contrasts with the more restricted range yielded by protected inland centers, e.g., Florence, Italy (see Fig. 19).

220

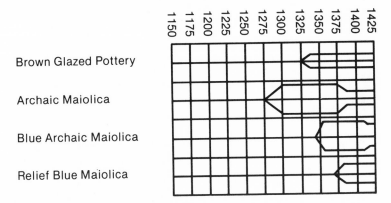

Figure 19
Pottery types at Florence. The narrow range of pottery types found in
Florence, Italy, where import restrictions protected local potters, contrasts
with the wide variety found at free trading port cities such as Split, on the
Dalmation coast (see Fig. 18).

NOTES

[1] The morphological method was used extensively in my "Medieval
Glazed Pottery," in *Diocletian's Palace: American Yugoslav Joint Excavations*,
ed. Sheila McNally, Jerko Marasović, Tomislav Marasović, Urbanisticki zavod
Dalmacije (Split, 1979), pp. 5-123. The background for the Split report and many
comparative Italian pottery examples can be found in my dissertation, "Late
Medieval Glazed Pottery in Italy and Surrounding Areas: With Specific Detail
from the Excavations in the Cathedral in Florence and in Diocletian's Palace in
Split," Diss. Columbia University 1978. The maps in this essay take into account
the pottery types found in the excavations in the Florence Cathedral. [I wish to
thank Franklin Toker, who directed the work from a Committee to Rescue Italian
Art fellowship and who kindly invited me to study the finds when I arrived for my
CRIA grant in 1972.] A full pottery bibliography is in the Split report and in my
dissertation, but a major study of Pisan Medieval pottery has been published
since: Graziella Berti and Liana Tongiorgi, *Ceramica Pisana* (Pisa: Pacini Edi-
tore, 1977).

[2] Occasional pieces have been noted at Corinth and Lucera, in Apulia. For
Corinth, see Charles Morgan, *Corinth XI, The Byzantine Pottery* (Cambridge,
MA, 1942), chap. 3, Fig. 46b and cat. no. 300. For Lucera, see David White-
house, "Ceramiche e vetri medievali provenienti dal castello di Lucera," *Bollet-*

tino d'Arte, 51 (1966), 171-78 and his "Medieval Pottery of South Italy," Diss. Cambridge University 1967.

[3] The method was suggested to me by Hanjörg Bloesch's division of Greek kylikes in his seminal work, *Formen Attischer Schalen von Exekias bis zum Ende des Strengen Stils* (Bern, 1940).

[4] I am grateful to the director of the Caltagirone Museum, Antonio Ragona, for facilitating my research there, and to Segretario Tuccio Biagio at the Gela Museum.

[5] For Corinth, see Morgan, *Corinth XI*; for Split, Buerger, *Diocletian's Palace*, 3; for Atlit, see C. Johns, "Medieval Slip Ware from Pilgrim's Castle Atlit, *Quarterly of the Department of Antiquities in Palestine*, 3 (1934), 137-44. In all these cases, the pieces were discovered in thirteenth-century contexts. Gela Ware has also been noted at Tunisia: see J. Ferron and M. Pinard, "Ceramique musulmane à Carthage," *Cahiers de Byrsa* 4 (1954), 44-65; "Les fouilles de Byrsa," *Cahiers de Byrsa* 5 (1955), 31-81; "Les fouilles de Byrsa," *Cahiers de Byrsa* 6 (1960-61), 77-170. On Gela Ware in Sicily, see Antonio Ragona, "La ceramica del periodo della monarchia aragonese in Sicilia," *Faenza*, 42 (1956), 52 ff.

[6] A San Simeon bowl from Dumbarton Oaks was displayed at the exhibition "The Meeting of the Two Worlds: The Crusades and the Mediterranean Context," organized at the University of Michigan Museum of Art at Ann Arbor in connection with the Medieval Institute's Congress in 1981. See the handbook for the exhibition, *The Meeting of the Two Worlds*, illus. 17, pp. 39-40, where the bowl is compared to Gela Ware, presumably based on the comparative form drawings (here Fig. 8) that were published in my report for *Diocletian's Palace*, 3.

THE ARCHAEOZOOLOGY OF THE ANGLO-SAXON SITE AT WEST STOW, SUFFOLK

PAMELA CRABTREE

Introduction

The study described here is part of an analysis of animal bone remains from the early Anglo-Saxon settlement of West Stow in England. The site—located on sandy soil overlooking the river Lark in the northern part of Suffolk, East Anglia—was continually occupied through three successive chronological phases which correspond roughly to the fifth, sixth, and seventh centuries A.D.

The West Stow site was almost completely excavated between 1965 and 1972 and is to date the only such settlement to have been so extensively studied.[1] Excavation there has revealed approximately seventy sunken-featured buildings, or *grubenhäuser*, clustered around six small, rectangular timber halls, as well as a small Iron-Age farming settlement and a number of Romano-British pottery kilns. Even more remarkable, however, was the discovery of approximately 200,000 fragments of excellently preserved animal bone which comprise the largest archaeozoological collection examined in Britain to date. Thus, West Stow afforded an opportunity to examine a very large and virtually intact faunal assemblage and to reconstruct the patterns of animal exploitation at the site.

In the enormous task of identifying, recording, and analyzing the West Stow faunal materials, particular attention was given to the bone measurements, ages at death, and kill-patterns of domestic mammals as key sources of evidence for either continuity or change in animal husbandry in early Anglo-Saxon Britain.

Species Identified

The West Stow site produced the remains of a wide range of animal species, domestic mammals, wild mammals, birds, and fish, among others. Domestic mammal bones—from cattle, sheep, goats, pigs, horses, dogs, and cats—made up over 99% of the assemblage. From the faunal material recovered, it can be seen that cattle, sheep, and pigs were the most common domesticates. Numerically, sheep were always predominant, followed by cattle and pigs, even though cattle would have produced the greatest weight of meat. Although some goat bone fragments were present in all three Saxon phases, sheep bones outnumbered those of goats by a fifty to one margin throughout the Saxon period. We can, therefore, assume that most indeterminate fragments belong to sheep rather than goats.

Ages at Death

It was clear that sheep, cattle, and pigs were vital to the West Stow animal economy. To determine more precisely the economic use to which they were put, however, a detailed study of ages at death was undertaken. Age estimates were based primarily on the system of dental eruption and wear proposed by Grant for mandibles of cattle, sheep, and pigs.[2] This system is similar to the one proposed by Payne for sheep and goat mandibles:[3] initially, each tooth in each mandible is scored for state of dental eruption or wear using a twenty-stage system; then an age estimate or "numerical value" for the entire jaw is derived by summing the scores for the first, second, and third molars. The resulting distribution of values indicates the relative age at death. Although numerical values can be calculated precisely, it is somewhat more difficult to translate them into years, for variations in the conditions under which domestic stock were kept could affect rates of dental eruption and wear to some extent. Here, ages in years have been estimated following Silver.[4]

Cattle

The distribution of numerical values for Saxon West Stow cattle mandibles showed that a significant number of neonates, or very young calves (numerical values = 1-4), died early in their first year (see fig. 1 at end of essay). A sizeable number was killed just as the second molar was coming into wear (numerical value = ca. 20), which suggests death at about two years. Almost half the cattle survived to maturity, as about 44% of the specimens had a fully-erupted, permanent dentition. Among the mature cattle was a significant number well over five years of age (numerical value = 44-47). These statistics—high mortality within the first two years of life combined with the presence of older cattle—suggest that milk production may have been an important element in West Stow husbandry. One would, therefore, expect most of the adult cattle to be female, and, indeed, measurements on cattle metacarpals[5] have shown that this was the case. Thus, the large number of animals killed in the second year (mid-adolescence) was probably male.

The West Stow age distribution appears unique when compared to kill-patterns of cattle from later Saxon sites. West Stow cattle were significantly younger than those from all other large Anglo-Saxon sites. The Middle Saxon town of Hamwih, modern Southampton, produced cattle that were significantly older, on the average, than the West Stow stock, and the faunal assemblages from Saxon Portchester Castle and from the Middle Saxon features at North Elmham in Norfolk[6] also produced a majority of mature cattle. Maltby noted that the majority of cattle from earlier Roman urban and military sites were mature, while rural and villa sites husbanded cattle of all ages. He suggested that this was because rural sites may have been relatively self-sufficient, "and therefore their deposits include a higher percentage of immature cattle not required for breeding or working but also not in demand for redistribution to other centres."[7] The military and urban sites, in contrast, contained cattle of specific ages which had been brought to town for slaughter. The West Stow community fits well the model of a self-sufficient rural community husbanding cattle from a wide age range.

We find the closest equivalents to West Stow cattle in small, self-sufficient, Iron-Age sites in southern Britain such as Gussage All Saints, which produced a sizeable faunal sample and where cattle age distribution most closely paralleled that of West Stow.[8] At Gussage Phase I, 36% of the cattle were killed before approximately two years of age, having

225

only the milk dentition and first molars in wear; at West Stow 32.1% of the Saxon cattle were less than two years old at death. The Iron-Age sample from Ashville, in rural Oxfordshire, also produced substantial numbers of young cattle.[9]

Sheep

Sheep were abundant sources of meat, milk, and wool, and analysis of mortality patterns may shed light on the relative importance of these economic uses. A distribution of ages at death calculated for all sheep from Saxon West Stow (Fig. 2) was polymodal, showing a primary mode late in the first year of life (numerical value = 11); a secondary mode in the second year (numerical values = 24-25); and minor modes in adulthood (numerical values = 34, 41). A small but significant number of sheep was killed before the first molar came into wear, that is, between about two and six months of age (numerical value less than or equal to six), but not before. Most of these immature animals show some wear on the milk dentition, indicating that they were more likely victims of seasonal cullings in the first year of life than neonatal mortalities. It appears that very few Saxon sheep survived to old age. The major modes indicate a substantial kill-off in both the first and second years of life; the minor modes (at numerical values = 34 and 41) probably represent three to four and four to six year-olds, respectively.

In his interpretation of these data, Payne argued that dairying populations may kill surplus lambs at six to nine months, while shepherds emphasizing meat tend to kill a large number of their flock at two to three years of age.[10] That West Stow sheep show a high mortality in both the first and second years suggests that both meat production and dairying may have been practiced. Despite minor mortality peaks within the three to six year age range, however, fewer sheep survived to maturity than one would expect from a wool-producing flock. It is, therefore, likely that while some wool was produced for domestic consumption, it was not on a large scale. This is especially revealing, since a few of the sunken-featured buildings at West Stow seem to have served as weaving huts,[11] and preliminary analysis of the data from the first excavation seasons suggested that textile production may have played an important role in the West Stow economy.[12]

The pattern of sheep mortality at West Stow contrasts markedly with age patterns at other Anglo-Saxon sites. West Stow sheep were killed at significantly younger ages than those at Saxon Hamwih, Portchester Castle, and North Elmham.[13] Barbara Noddle, who studied the

226

North Elmham fauna, suggested that most of the North Elmham sheep were kept for wool production.[14] Other smaller Saxon faunal samples, including Ramsbury in Wessex and Durham,[15] included substantial proportions of adult sheep; this led Maltby to propose that large-scale wool production became important in the Saxon period and that the roots of this development may be early Saxon.[16] However, the West Stow ageing data provide no evidence to support this contention.

To find parallels for the West Stow pattern of sheep exploitation, we must again look to British Iron-Age sites. Early sites such as the hillfort of Baulksbury Camp in Wessex yielded the remains of sheep killed in their first year of life along with a broad clustering of older sheep. While this pattern might suggest milk production, as in West Stow, it may simply indicate inefficient husbandry, as it resembles the natural mortality pattern among unimproved Soay sheep.[17] In contrast, a number of later Iron-Age sites—the later levels of Gussage All Saints in Dorset, Micheldever Down in Hampshire, and Ashville in Oxfordshire, among others—produced high numbers of first and second year cullings. These findings suggest that meat production, as well as dairying, may have been important in sheep exploitation.[18] The West Stow pattern of sheep exploitation more closely resembles that found in later Iron-Age sites.

Pigs

Unlike sheep, cattle, and even horses, pigs have only one major economic use—food. Studies of pig mortality patterns can determine, however, whether pigs were raised for home consumption or, as is often the case on military and urban sites, were brought in from other areas at certain ages for slaughter. The distribution of age estimates or numerical values for the West Stow Saxon pigs is shown in Figure 3. As the pig mandibles were often quite heavily fragmented, numerical values were estimated within class intervals of five. The numerical values for modes of mortality are seen in the 21-25 and 31-35 age classes and correspond to the stages when the second and third molars were in early wear, representing pigs in approximately the second and third years of life. The highest mortality was indicated in the early third year, the period when the lower third molar was coming into wear; it was at about this stage that the pig reached bodily maturity, and continuing to feed the animal beyond this age could not substantially increase its body weight or meat yield. Thus, killing a sizeable number of pigs at this age maximized the meat yield to fodder input ratio. The second mode of mortality corresponds to mid-adolescence.

The Anglo-Saxon levels also produced the remains of pigs killed in the early stages of life (numerical values of less than ten). Pigs are fecund animals, often producing litters of ten or more piglets, many more than are needed to maintain the stock. In a self-sufficient agricultural community, one would expect sizeable kill-offs of neonates and young juveniles, as farmers select runts, weak, or sickly pigs for early slaughter. In addition, suckling pig has long been considered a delicacy, especially among the Romans.[19]

As is the case with sheep and cattle, West Stow pigs were substantially younger than those from other large Saxon sites: in particular, West Stow swine were consistently younger than the Middle Saxon pigs from Hamwih.[20] Two factors may account for these age differences. First, Hamwih, an urban center, may have been shipped pigs of selected age classes, such as adults, for slaughter. At rural West Stow, in contrast, one would expect to see a wide range of age classes, including a larger number of younger pigs not needed to maintain the breeding stock. Second, the West Stow area was not ideal pig country. Trees are scarce even today, and documentary evidence suggests that they were scarce in the Anglo-Saxon period also; the nearest extensively wooded area was located several miles from the site.[21] Thus, substantial amounts of feed would have been needed to supplement the pannage available, and the practice of sty husbandry would have provided a strong economic motive to eliminate excess animals.

The figures for ages at death of the West Stow pigs also contrast sharply with those from North Elmham. During the Middle Saxon period, 50-85% of North Elmham pigs were mature, more than four years at time of death; many were elderly, with heavy wear on all teeth. These figures dropped to 20% during the post-Medieval period, for, as Noddle observed, "...during the Saxon period the pigs were almost wild and were difficult to catch when young. Later pigs may well have been kept in stys."[22] At West Stow, the high proportion of young animals killed and the argued lack of available fodder may well indicate the practice of sty husbandry at an early date.

The data on ages at death for Iron-Age pigs are limited, for available samples are often inadequate. The mandible sample from Micheldever, for instance, was too small for detailed analysis.[23] Information from Ashville is based primarily on epiphyseal union of the long bones and suggests "a relatively high slaughtering rate."[24] Only 37% of the small, fragmented Ashville mandible sample showed wear on the third molar, indicating that a minority of pigs survived to adulthood. The evidence from Gussage likewise indicates that only about one-third of the pigs survived to maturity (as evidenced by wear on the third molar), but again, sample sizes are small.[25] Although the minority of adult specimens link Gussage and Ashville to West Stow, the samples are too small to permit detailed comparisons of ageing patterns. Given the inadequacy of the Iron-Age mandible fragments, it is not surprising to find the closest parallels to West Stow pig mortality patterns in Roman faunal samples, particularly those from the urban center at Exeter and from the later phases of the Roman palace at Fishbourne in southern Britain.[26] The Exeter pigs, in particular, show a steady mortality throughout the first three years of life, with only a small proportion of the swine surviving to advanced years. The Fishbourne sample also shows a high mortality in the first year of life.

In summary, the early Anglo-Saxon cattle, sheep, and pigs from West Stow were killed at consistently younger ages than were domestic stock from later Anglo- Saxon sites. The age distributions for West Stow sheep and cattle are most closely paralleled at rural Iron-Age sites, while pig kill-patterns are most similar to those at a number of Roman sites. That the West Stow domesticates may have been used in ways similar to domestic stock of the preceding Roman and Iron-Age periods suggests a continuity in exploitation practices. Such significant changes in animal exploitation as the development of sheep rearing for wool production may have taken place during the middle and later Saxon periods.

Measurements

Although the age distributions of the domestic stock link West Stow to the Iron Age and Roman periods, osteometric data present a different picture. All West Stow animal bones were measured following the recommendations of von den Driesch.[27] Standard factors were used to calculate shoulder heights from complete long bone measurements.[28]

Measurements of West Stow cattle remains indicated that early Saxon bovines were of moderate size, comparable to cattle whose remains have been recovered from later Anglo-Saxon sites in Britain. Shoulder height estimates for the West Stow cattle ranged from 104.6 to 121.4 cm., with an average of 112.9 cm. These estimates fell well within the Hamwih range of 101.7 to 137.7 cm.[29] When other long bone measurements from West Stow were compared to the extensive measurement series from Hamwih, the means and ranges were quite similar. The West Stow measurements also compared well with those from the Roman levels at Portchester Castle: the distal tibial width of the Portchester remains ranged from 50-69 mm., a figure virtually identical to the West

229

Stow range of 50.5-68.5 mm.[30] A recent archaeozoological survey showed that astragalus length was the measurement most commonly taken on cattle remains from Iron-Age, Romano-British, and Anglo-Saxon sites.[31] Lateral lengths of West Stow astragali ranged from 53.6 to 70.3 mm. with means of 61.1 for Period 1, 60.1 for Period 2, and 60.7 for Period 3. The West Stow data again compared well with the data from other Roman and Saxon sites: for example, 167 measured astragali from Hamwih provided a mean astragalus length of 60.9 mm. Astragali from Iron-Age sites were consistently smaller. It has been suggested that the Romans introduced larger breeds of cattle into Britain[32] and that later Saxon cattle, at Hamwih in particular, "were maintaining the general improvement ascribed to the Romans with their introduction of [these new breeds or types]."[33] The West Stow evidence indicates that cattle size remained relatively large throughout the early Saxon period.

Like West Stow cattle, West Stow sheep seem to have been relatively good-sized; shoulder height estimates ranged from 54.0 to 68.8 cm. This compared well with the Hamwih estimates based on radii and metapodials ranging from 53.5 to 70.9 cm.[34] West Stow sheep were apparently larger than Wessex Iron-Age sheep, which were 50-60 cm. in height. Distal tibial width is the commonly-taken measurement on archaeological sheep remains,[35] and for West Stow Saxon sheep they averaged 26.2 mm. for Period 1, 26.0 mm. for Period 2, and 26.1 mm. for Period 3. Mean distal tibial widths for other Saxon sites ranged from 25.2 to 26.3 mm. Thus, West Stow sheep were near the top of the Saxon range in size and were larger, on the average, than all Iron-Age and Romano-British samples studied to date. West Stow sheep compared most closely in size to the later Saxon sheep from North Elmham and Thetford in East Angia.

Since pig remains are less numerous at most Iron-Age, Roman, and Saxon sites in Britain, including West Stow, fewer measurements are available. For instance, no shoulder height estimates could be calculated for the pig bones from the West Stow huts, since no complete long bones were found. However, enough information was available from West Stow and other Anglo-Saxon sites to indicate that West Stow pigs were comparable in size to other Saxon swine: comparisons of proximal radial breadths showed no significant differences between West Stow and Hamwih, Ramsbury, and North Elmham. Unfortunately, we have little evidence to determine the differences or similarities in size between Anglo-Saxon, Iron-Age, and Romano-British pigs. Coy notes, however, that Saxon pigs, at least at Hamwih, seem to have had an upper size limit somewhat larger than Iron-Age pigs from Wessex: while withers height estimates for Hamwih pigs ranged from 50 to 70 cm., those from

230

Iron-Age sites ranged from 50 to 60 cm.[36]

In summary, the cattle, sheep, and pigs at West Stow were relatively large and fully comparable in size to the domestic stock from later Anglo-Saxon sites. The West Stow cattle remains were larger than those found at Iron-Age sites but similar in size to remains from Romano-British sites such as Portchester Castle. West Stow sheep were larger, on the average, than either Iron-Age or Romano- British sheep and comparable in size to later Saxon sheep from East Anglia. Although comparative data from Iron-Age and Romano-British sites are limited, it is clear that the West Stow swine were similar in size to pigs from later Anglo-Saxon sites.

Conclusions

The fifth- to seventh-century site of West Stow was intermediate in date between Iron-Age and Romano-British sites on the one hand, and later Saxon sites on the other, and it appears that animal husbandry patterns there were also intermediate in character. While the West Stow domesticates were comparable in size to later Saxon stock, the ageing distributions and probable patterns of exploitation were most similar to those of the later Iron Age, meaning that West Stow farmers exploited an improved stock in traditional ways. While stock size may have increased in Roman to early Saxon times, it is in the later Saxon periods that patterns of animal use show fundamental changes.

231

WEST STOW CATTLE KILL PATTERN

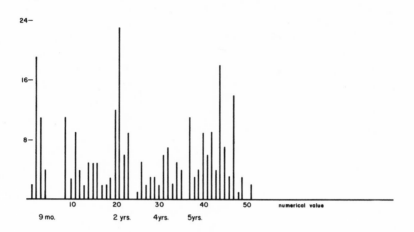

Figure 1

WEST STOW SHEEP KILL PATTERN

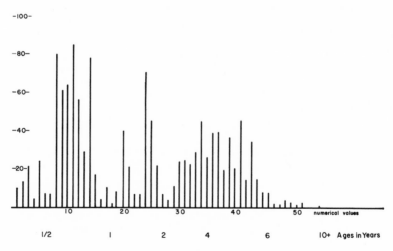

Figure 2

232

WEST STOW PIG KILL PATTERN

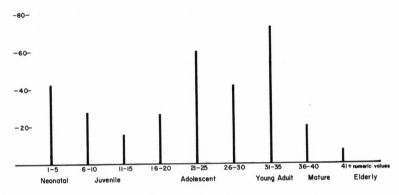

Figure 3

NOTES

This research was supported by grants from the U.S. National Science Foundation, the Wenner-Gren Foundation for Anthropological Research, and by a Fulbright- Hayes Full Grant and renewal. Special thanks are due to Jennie P. Coy, Research Fellow, Faunal Remains Unit, Department of Archaeology, University of Southampton, who has provided advice and support throughout the project, and to Roger Jones, Ancient Monuments Lab, Department of the Environment, London, who designed the computer-coding system used in this project.

[1] See Stanley West, "The Anglo-Saxon Village at West Stow: An Interim Report of the Excavations, 1965-68," *Medieval Archaeology*, 13 (1969), 1-20 for an interim report on the West Stow site.

[2] Annie Grant, "Appendix B: The Use of Toothwear as a Guide to the Age of Domestic Animals—A Brief Explanation," in *Roman*, vol. 1 of *Excavations at Portchester Castle*, ed. Barry Cunliffe (London: Society of Antiquaries, 1975), pp. 437-50.

[3] Sebastian Payne, "Kill-off Patterns in Sheep and Goats: The Mandibles from Asvan Kale," *Anatolian Studies*, 23 (1973), 281-303.

[4] I. A. Silver, "The Ageing of Domestic Animals," in *Science in Archaeology*, ed. D. Brothwell and E. S. Higgs, 2nd ed. (London: Thames and Hudson, 1969), pp. 283-302.

[5] Following M. Howard, "The Metrical Determination of the Metapodials

233

and Skulls of Cattle," in *Man and Cattle*, ed. A. E. Mourant and F. E. Zeuner (London: Royal Anthropological Society, 1963), pp. 92-100.

[6] For Hamwih, see: J. Bourdillon and J. Coy, "Statistical Appendix to Accompany the Animal Bone Report on Material from Melbourne Street (Sites I, IV, V, VI, and XX) Excavated by the Southampton Archaeological Research Committee between 1971 and 1976," TS, p. 25, available from the Southampton Archeological Research Committee; for Portchester, see: Annie Grant, "Animal Bones," in *Saxon*, vol. 2 of *Excavations at Portchester Castle*, p. 276; and for North Elmham, see: Barbara Noddle, "The Animal Bones," in *Excavations at North Elmham Park, 1967-72*, ed. P. Wade-Martins, East Anglian Archaeology Rept. no. 9, vol. 2 (Norfolk, 1980), pp. 375-412.

[7] M. Maltby, "Iron Age, Romano-British and Anglo-Saxon Animal Husbandry—A Review of the Faunal Evidence," TS, p. 37, available from the Faunal Remains Unit, Univ. of Southampton. (Hereafter cited as "Review.")

[8] R. Harcourt, "The Animal Bones," in *Gussage All Saints: An Iron Age Settlement in Dorset*, ed. G. J. Wainwright (London: HMSO, 1979), p. 151.

[9] Julie Hamilton, "A Comparison of the Age Structure at Mortality of Some Iron Age and Romano-British Sheep and Cattle Populations," in *The Excavation of an Iron Age Settlement, Bronze Age Ring-Ditches and Roman Features at Ashville Trading Estate, Abingdon (Oxfordshire) 1974-76*, ed. M. Parrington, Council for British Archaeology Research Rept. no. 28 (London: C. B. A., 1978), p. 133.

[10] Payne, p. 282.

[11] West, p. 5.

[12] (No author), "West Stow," *Current Archaeology*, 4, no. 5 (1973), 154.

[13] Bourdillon and Coy, p. 25; Grant, *Saxon*, p. 278; and Noddle, p. 396.

[14] Noddle, p. 396.

[15] For Wessex, see: Jennie P. Coy, "The Animal Bones," in section three of "Excavations of a Middle Saxon Iron Smelting Site at Ramsbury, Wiltshire," ed. J. Halsam, et al., *Medieval Archaeology*, 24 (1980), 41-51; for Durham, see: J. Rackham, "Animal Resources," a contribution to "Three Saxo-Norman Tenements in Durham City," ed. M. O. H. Carver, *Medieval Archaeology*, 23 (1979), 53.

[16] Maltby, "Review," p. 32.

[17] Maltby, "Review," pp. 27, 26.

[18] Harcourt, p. 152; Hamilton, pp. 126-31; Coy, "Animal Bones from Micheldever Wood Banjo, Hampshire, R27 M3 Motorway Rescue Excavations," TS, p. 159, Department of the Environment, Ancient Monuments Lab, Rept. no. 3288.

[19] K. D. White, *Roman Farming* (London: Thames and Hudson, 1970), pp. 318-20.

[20] Bourdillon and Coy, p. 25.

[21] Personal communication from Stanley West, 3 January 1979.

[22] Noddle, p. 400.

[23] Coy, "Micheldever," p. 159.

[24] R. Wilson, "General Conclusions and Discussion of the Bone Sample,"

in *The Excavation of an Iron Age Settlement*, p. 135.

[25] Harcourt, p. 153.

[26] M. Maltby, *Faunal Studies on Urban Sites: The Animal Bones from Exeter, 1971-1975*, Exeter Archaeological Repts., vol. 2 (Sheffield: Dept. of Prehistory and Archaeology, 1979), pp. 55-57; Grant, "The Animal Bones," in *Excavations at Fishbourne 1961-69*, vol. 2, ed. Barry Cunliffe (London: Society of Antiquaries, 1971), p. 383.

[27] Angela von den Driesch, *A Guide to the Measurement of Animal Bones from Archaeological Sites*, Peabody Museum Bulletins no. 1 (Cambridge, MA: Harvard Univ. Press, 1976).

[28] Angela von den Driesch and J. Boessneck, "Kritische Anmerkung zur Widerristhöhenberechnung aus Längenmasses vor- und frühgeschichtlicher Tierknochen," *Säugetierkundliche Mitteilungen*, 22 (1974), 325-48.

[29] Bourdillon and Coy, p. 23.

[30] Grant, "The Animal Bones," in *Roman*, p. 401.

[31] Maltby, "Review," pp. 41-42.

[32] Grant, *Roman*, p. 402.

[33] J. Bourdillon and J. Coy, "The Animal Bones," in *Excavations at Melbourne Street, Southampton, 1971-1976*, ed. P. Holdsworth, Council for British Archaeology Research Rept. no. 33 (London: C. B. A., 1980), p. 106.

[34] Bourdillon and Coy, "Animal Bones," p. 109.

[35] Maltby, "Review," pp. 43-49.

[36] "Animal Husbandry and Faunal Exploitation in Hampshire," TS, available from the Faunal Remains Unit, Univ. of Southampton.

PART IV:
TIME-DEPTH AND SETTLEMENT:
OVERVIEW AND CASE STUDIES

A DIACHRONIC MODEL FOR
SETTLEMENT AND LAND USE
IN SOUTHERN BURGUNDY

CAROLE L. CRUMLEY

Before two devastating world wars took their toll, the brilliance and promise of new research in medieval history dazzled the European intellectual community. Particularly in France one saw, in the work of Bloch and his colleagues, a long and distinguished tradition of historical geography on the eve of rapprochement with the humanities and social sciences. More than a half century later, the study of medieval society in Western Europe is moving once again toward a blending of the social sciences and the humanities, with a new and vital element added: the natural sciences.

Our research team, based at the University of North Carolina (Chapel Hill), is committed to broadening the scope of medieval studies through such interdisciplinary means. Drawing on scholarship in the humanities, social sciences, and natural sciences, and integrating these with the comparative, theoretical, and field-work oriented approach of anthropology, our study in southern Burgundy has been able to trace the shifting, intimate relationships between society and economy, economy and ecology. Furthermore, it is our contention that in order to study a period effectively, regional change must be understood within a broad, flexible, spatial, and temporal framework, for only in this manner can the

239

respective fluctuations of climate, long-distance trade, the effects of social, political, and economic shifts, population movements, and defense be integrated into a systemic framework in which change can be observed through time. The fluctuations of a variety of factors may be individually collated, and their changing relations through time collectively assessed. We are thus engaged in a regional, diachronic, interdisciplinary study of southern Burgundy from the first century B.C. (the late Iron Age) to the present.

Nowhere in the world can one find a region that can supply an ideal range of information necessary to reconstruct medieval society; nevertheless, it is possible to construct a regional model of medieval society and then test it against data from elsewhere. Under the umbrella of the anthropological concept of culture, such a model can assimilate a variety of information from numerous sources and build a cohesive group of interlocking models—of climate, settlement, family structure, political organization, and the like. For these reasons, we chose southern Burgundy for our study, a region with varied physiography, considerable time depth, the absence of elements destructive to previous spatial configurations, and an unambiguous cultural affiliation at the beginning of the period of study.

In the late Iron Age, southern Burgundy was the territory of the powerful Aedui, who played an important military and economic role in pre- and post- conquest Gaul. The region lies between the Loire and Saône rivers; at the north and south ends of its eastern boundary are breaks in the Côtes du Challonais and Mâconnais, through which trade, traveling between the Rhône-Saône corridor and the Loire, would be obliged to pass. Instrumental in almost every period in the regulation of commerce between Britain, France, and the Mediterranean, southern Burgundy is distinctive, yet extremely diverse in terms of its physiography, drainage, climate, sub-surface geology, and pedology. Furthermore, our research indicates that it was a distinctive political, social, economic, and demographic region from the late Iron Age until the tenth century. Bounded in so many ways by such different data, the region offers a superb opportunity to understand forces of continuity and change in society and economy while holding constant (or at least controlling the variation in) the natural environment. In addition, the area is rich in the spatial data critical to the evaluation of relationships between spatial organization (population agglomeration and dispersal, shifts in settlement size and function, land use, exploitative patterns of natural resources, and the like) and cultural change.

Actually, the study of settlement and land use in the region is relatively easy, given the wealth of documents in Burgundian archives.

Much information concerning climatic conditions, crops, comparative crop yields, field size, imports and exports, sex ratio, fertility/mortality rates, and the function, nature, and location of settlement has been obtained from written sources referring to the region. Classical writers (Julius Caesar is perhaps the most famous) as well as medieval chroniclers give useful quantitative and qualitative information. In addition, we have carried out five years of ground and aerial survey in the Arroux valley (the heartland of the Celtic Aedui; the Arroux, with the city of Autun at its headwaters, is a tributary of the Loire) and excavated the important hill fortress of Mont Dardon and several smaller sites.

We have been able to establish, with the excavation of Mont Dardon, a chronology for the region which may be the longest historic chronology in France. The site was occupied at least by the late Bronze Age (1000 B.C.), was fortified first in the early Iron Age and again at the time of the Roman conquest, and continued to be occupied until the eleventh century. Bronze and Iron Age components in the plateau area of the site were explored during the 1975-77 seasons.[1] The Gallo-Roman, Merovingian, and Carolingian components of the citadel, whose features include a Gallo-Roman *fanum* dating from the fourth century and a tenth-century Carolingian church overlying an eighth-century Merovingian chapel and cemetery, were excavated in the 1978 and 1979 seasons.[2]

The excavation of Mont Dardon has been instrumental in giving us a picture of factors affecting settlement and land use through time. Equally important has been our extensive site survey and aerial reconnaissance of the mountain and outlying areas which, along with the documentary research, has allowed us to construct models of settlement for the region in each major period of its history. The articulation of historical, archaeological, and ecological data by our interdisciplinary team has not always been simple, but the insight we have given one another is priceless. For example, in 1977 a ground survey team found and recorded a site, in a cornfield, which (judging from ceramics) might have been a fourth-century domestic structure, perhaps a villa. Aerial reconnaissance in the same year found no visible evidence of the same site, but our practice of flying the survey segments each year at different times of the day and in different seasons bore fruit in 1979; when planted in alfalfa, the field revealed the amazingly clear outlines of a large, late fourth-century villa. Analysis of the geomorphology of the site gave us an understanding of patterns of erosion and deposition in the river (thus, information on where other sites of that period might be found); analysis using satellite photography (LANDSAT) of the field containing the villa showed a half-dozen other locations throughout the valley with the same visual "signature"—along a Roman road known to us through

241

documentary evidence!

Other examples might also be mentioned, but Professor Berry's discussion in this volume will serve well to explore the power of interdisciplinary research. The tenth-century church itself was unknown to medieval historians before its discovery in the course of our excavations of the hillfort. Although we had originally hoped for a long chronology from prehistoric into historic times, we were not expecting to undertake any archaeological excavation of medieval sites, planning instead to rely on documentary and ecological evidence for selected periods. Fortunately, Professor Berry has been with the project from its inception, in the capacity of medieval historian, and he undertook the archaeological excavations when his protohistoric-specialist colleagues found themselves well beyond their chronological expertise and well into the excavation of an important early medieval church. The full importance of the church would not have been realized were it not for the project's emphasis on the multi-temporal, multi-disciplinary study of the region.[3]

The site of Mont Dardon retained its religious function from Celtic through Gallo-Roman times and well into the Middle Ages. The actual form of the place of worship varied with the needs and beliefs of the faithful it served. The location of a ritual center atop Mont Dardon assured that center's defense and (quite literally) its regional prominence. Similarly, an analysis of the setting of the Gallo-Roman villa on the banks of the Arroux, as well as other sites found in the survey, offers many insights into the system of settlement of each period.

Exactly how we have articulated these various models is discussed in an article on the model-building strategy and will be dealt with exhaustively in our forthcoming volume on the results of the project as a whole.[4] We can say that we are well along in integrating the research findings and are extremely excited at the power of these multiple operational models in the spatial and temporal study of a region. The particular attractiveness of a cluster of time- and space-sensitive models to an integrated study of medieval society is clear. We believe that it is an approach appropriate to both the history and the future of medieval studies.

NOTES

[1] See Carole L. Crumley, "Toward a Locational Definition of State Systems of Settlement," *American Anthropologist* 78, no. 1 (1976), 59-73; her "Les fouilles du Mont Dardon," *La physiophile*, 86 (June 1977), 93-102; and Carole L. Crumley and Walter E. Berry, "Rapport annuel: les fouilles du Mont Dardon—1977," *Echos du passé*, 39 (1978), 13-32.

² See Carole L. Crumley and Walter E. Berry, "Les fouilles du Mont Dar don—1978," *Echos du passé*, 41 (1979), 17-40; and their "Les fouilles du Mont Dardon—1979," *Echos du passé*, 43 (1980), 1-43.

³ See Crumley, "Toward a Locational Definition"; her "Reply to Smith," *American Anthropologist* 79, no. 4 (1977), 906-08; and esp. her "Three Locational Models: an Epistemological Assessment for Anthropology and Archaeology," in *Advances in Archaeological Method and Theory*, vol. 2, ed. M. B. Schiffer (New York: Academic Press, 1979), pp. 141-73. A volume reporting our research, which will be titled *Regional Dynamics: Burgundy from the Iron Age to the Present*, is in preparation; the volume will particularly stress the value of a multi-temporal, multi-disciplinary approach to region and culture.

⁴ See description of *Regional Dynamics* in n. 3.

AN EXPERIMENTAL MODEL FOR EARLY MEDIEVAL SETTLEMENT IN SOUTHWESTERN BURGUNDY

WALTER E. BERRY

For the medieval historian, the reconstruction of rural settlement patterns over time is a difficult, demanding task, even for those few areas where early documentation and extensive archaeological data are available. In most cases, the researcher can speak with assurance only of later rural settlement patterns, and remarks grow increasingly tentative the further back in time the researcher moves. Paradoxically, full understanding of any portion of a later period is tied intimately to knowledge of preceding rural settlement patterns. For this reason, a major goal must be to develop models that can describe the spatial relationships between early medieval rural centers and their outlying environments.

There is nothing new in this proposal, for, as E. M. Jope observed a decade ago, "model building, testing and remodelling [have] long been a procedure underlying all branches of medieval studies."[1] In recent years, however, it has become apparent that traditional approaches to rural settlement in the early medieval period throughout Europe and in the British Isles can no longer accommodate the breadth and complexity of the evidence now available. A better understanding of this new information can be reached through such techniques as spatial analysis and model building, developed by geographers and archaeologists for pre-medieval periods.[2]

These techniques are particularly useful when applied to a study of medieval Europe after about the eleventh century, a period for which, unlike earlier periods, our knowledge of the rural settlement pattern is not necessarily dependent on either site or artifactual data.[3] Considerable information, much of which is open to statistical investigation, can be drawn from documentary sources. And certain spatial models seem highly relevant to settlement in this period, especially on the regional scale.[4]

The early Middle Ages, however, present peculiar methodological problems for the building of models based on spatial analysis. For many regions, vital archaeological and documentary records of early settlement locations and types are limited.[5] This is certainly the case in rural southwestern Burgundy, the object of my research. Here, I will summarize the experimental methods I used in formulating a diachronic study of the region.[6] In my attempt to overcome methodological difficulties, I have integrated techniques drawn from spatial analysis with methods derived from historical geography and church history, using the scales of commune (parish) and region. My assumption—that the location and distribution of parish centers indicate concentrations of activity and, frequently, population, and that analysis of their spatial arrangement can lead to a knowledge of the settlement pattern to which they belonged—contains four basic parts:

(1) Burgundian parishes developed in a discernable fashion.
(2) The foundation dates of parishes indicate certain demonstrable facts about the settlements in which they were established.
(3) In many cases, the foundation dates of parishes can be determined or estimated.
(4) It is possible to reconstruct, in conjunction with other evidence, the essential outlines of the settlement pattern of a given period from the contemporary parochial pattern.

The development of parishes in southwestern Burgundy halted by c. 1300 outside urban areas, and the present day communal boundaries of the area preserve, to a large extent, the pre-revolutionary borders. Medieval parishes, of course, are not only convenient territorial units; they represented the basic social and cadastral entities of the countryside and have often been ascribed pre-medieval origins.[7] Their territories were not simply administrative divisions but may have comprised, at the time of their foundation, the domains of one or more villages and/or estates.[8]

Thus, the parish centers were central places, and their parochial territories were as hinterland to those centers.

Drawing on these assumptions and on knowledge of the processes through which the parish system took form, it is possible to produce an idealized model of parish formation for a hypothetical diocese.[9] The model has three major phases (see Fig. 1 at end of essay). In the earliest phase (late-third to mid-fourth century), the diocese was itself a parish, administered by its bishop from his residence in or just outside the chief city of the district. The bishop's authority conformed to the boundaries of that city's territory. Outside the episcopal city, cult services were exceptional; however, in larger towns along major routes, or in a few of the villas where Christian communities were of sufficient size, chapels or oratories might exist. Such self-styled *tituli minores* did not have permanent clergy; in theory, at least, the major feasts and the rights to baptize and bury remained the prerogatives of the episcopal church as *ecclesia mater*.

By the latter half of the fourth century, the growth of the Christian populations in outlying areas necessitated the assignment, by the bishop, of permanent clergy to centers beyond the chief city. Thus, the first parish churches—grown out of the *tituli minores* of the first period—were founded. The number of these early parishes was small and, consequently, the extent of their districts large. Operating from these new centers, the newly-established parochial clergy was responsible for the emerging Christian communities in the other towns and for the increasing numbers of the villas within its parish territory. The chapels and oratories of these secondary places formed a parochial group of *tituli minores*. This phase came to an end during the seventh century, when the power of the bishop declined.

The third phase was characterized by the breakup of the large Merovingian parishes. In a repetition of the process of the second phase, the parochial-level *tituli minores* achieved full parish status. Gradually, the number of "villas" becoming parishes greatly outnumbered all other types of sites. The causes of this development were complex and involved population expansion, colonization of marginal lands, and political changes, but one of the major causative factors was secularization. The latter had already been a problem in the sixth century,[10] and by the eighth century most of the rural parishes had fallen into the hands of the local landowners or other members of the aristocracy. The multiplication of parishes which constituted this third phase continued into the tenth and early eleventh centuries, but its essential features were formed by c. 900.

In its simplest form, then, the formation of the parochial system can be thought of as a geometric progression of parishes developing out of

247

chapels in a fixed order, first within urban centers, with a gradual decline toward smaller, more rural villas and their attached villages. For instance, if the settlement typology of the sites which became parish centers (as presented in the model) is arranged chronologically, a typological distribution by date of foundation emerges (Fig. 2). Moving forward in time, the types of sites becoming parishes changed, and there was a definite swing of new foundations away from the urban centers toward increasingly rural locations.

It is equally apparent that knowledge of the parish pattern is greatly limited as one moves back in time, a methodological difficulty caused by Christianity's slow penetration of rural areas[11] and by the nature of the early parish system itself. In Figure 3, curve A represents the total number of "functional centers"[12] which were parishes at a given time, while curve B depicts the hypothetical number of similar centers which existed but of which we know nothing because they had not yet become parishes. This problem can be overcome, however, if we reverse the operation of the parochial model previously described and implement a "building-down" approach; it thus becomes theoretically possible to use the model in a predictive locational mode.[13] The resulting predictive capacity of the model—particularly when it is used in conjunction with chronological data drawn from extant early documents, toponymic studies, and analysis of parochial patron saints—may then form the framework for both synchronic and diachronic reconstructions of the functional centers of the rural settlement pattern.[14] Admittedly, this proposition is risky, but if we begin with a fully-documented period and work backwards as carefully and objectively as possible, a reasonable approximation of the settlement patterns in selected periods from as early as the fifth or sixth century may be obtained.

The research area in which the method is now being tested consists of the Arroux River valley and the adjacent uplands between Autun and the Loire (Fig. 4). Geologically, the area is part of a finger-like extension of the Massif Central separating the Saône valley from the Loire valley and the tributaries of the Yonne. The city of Autun dominates the intersection of the natural routes connecting the Rhône-Saône corridor with the Loire and Paris basins. The region within the research area formed the core of the city territory of Augustodunum, of the Merovingian and Carolingian *pagus*, and of the diocese based on the same city.

Figure 5 shows the network of parishes within the region in the eleventh century, as known from fairly complete *pouillés* and other documents.[15] At that time the pattern was about eighty-five percent complete. Thiessen polygons have been used to suggest the possible relative sizes of the parish territories.[16]

A series of distribution maps (Figues 6-9) allows us to visualize the evolution of the parish system from the breakup of the large Merovingian territories in the seventh century, through the Carolingian period, to the onset of the High Middle Ages. The most hypothetical portion of the reconstruction, for pre-seventh-century periods, is represented in Figures 10 and 11. Lacking direct documentation, and dependent upon knowledge of the Gallo-Roman settlement pattern, toponyms, parochial patron saints, and the predictive model, the pattern must remain conjectural.[17]

These "time-slice" maps of the parish-level functional centers are the basis for identifying the significant factors associated with the development of these patterns. Individual centers and their immediate environments are investigated using a modified form of site catchment analysis;[18] factors relating to the physical setting and settlement typology, as well as political and ecclesiastical connections and patronage, are recorded and compared; where appropriate, the results are mapped in the form of trend surfaces[19] and are then compared synchronically and diachronically.

For example, when the trend surface map of parent geological material for all parish catchment areas (Fig. 12) is analyzed in terms of conjectured foundation dates, the general relationship of sub-surface geology to the developing parish pattern can be seen. During the Merovingian period, as shown in Fig. 15, the vast majority of parish centers were located on sites where alluvium or sand and gravel predominated. Between c. 650 and 950, however, this situation reversed: the formation of new parishes in these zones dropped off, while development in areas of granite and sandstone increased rapidly.

A similar analysis of the altitudes of parish centers is summarized in Figures 13 and 14. The latter shows Merovingian parishes, which tended to lie at altitudes between 250 and 300 meters; however, there is a marked upward movement for post-sixth-century Carolingian sites, which, in two out of three cases, tended to lie between 300 and 350 meters or even higher. From a comparison of such geological and altitudinal data, a tendency for early settlements in the region to move toward higher sites away from the valley slopes into areas with less fertile soil can be recognized.

The introduction of "cultural" data to the environmental evidence greatly enhances the descriptive value of the method. For instance, we may note that the growth in the number of upland sites during the early Middle Ages was paralleled by a steep decline in the percentage of parish centers on or near the major Roman routes of the region. Such data

249

suggest the transformation of the urban-based structure of Roman society through the by-products of ruralization, as few of the Carolingian period foundations had Roman era place-names, and by the eighth century, a sizable proportion of parishes were under the patronage of the larger monastic houses of the region. It should be noted, however, that while incorporation of such secondary social factors as these helps us grasp more fully the character of the changes in regional settlement patterns of the period, still, they do not in themselves explain why the changes occurred.

Explanation comes only with the re-introduction of the body of reduced and simplified data, products of the "building-down" process. The characteristics of individual sites, the relationships between one locality and another and between separate localities and the region as a whole, can be determined by comparing the results of trend surface analyses. Using a "building-up" approach—that is, re-combining the sets of variables and comparing the outcomes sequentially—"broad territorial trends"[20] underlying the changes in the settlement pattern through time are revealed. These trends can be expressed as one or more chronologically arranged spatial models, and these provide the basis for understanding the developmental features of the settlement system. When compared and/or contrasted to other, more theoretical, models of settlement systems, such as Central Place Theory,[21] the salient features as well as the peculiarities of the settlement model(s) for the research area are recognizable. For example, a classic Central Place hierarchy and distribution of centers is found in the region but is limited to those areas below four-hundred meters; further, fourteenth-century fiscal evidence suggests that the connections between centers were arranged along the lines of a dendritic pattern[22] rather than following the dictates of the Central Place model. These models are, to some degree, abstracted illustrations of a particular part of the real world, not explanations in themselves. But they do form "a conceptual prop . . . not the whole truth but a useful and comprehensible part of it,"[23] and they provide an objective framework for the evaluation and interpretation of a variety of sources.

While the method outlined above has its drawbacks and limitations, and parts will certainly require revision, it does call our attention both to the problems surrounding the diachronic reconstruction of a settlement system during a period for which there is little or no archaeological or primary evidence and to the need for a method with which to attack these problems.[24] As noted earlier, this is a difficult demand which must be met, for our full understanding of much of medieval society in general is dependent upon our knowledge of where people lived and why.

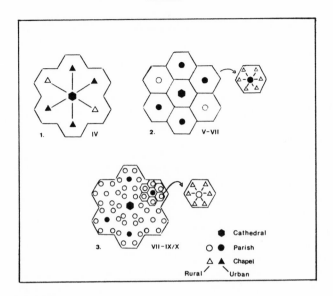

Figure 1
Idealized Model of Parish Formation for a Hypothetical Diocese

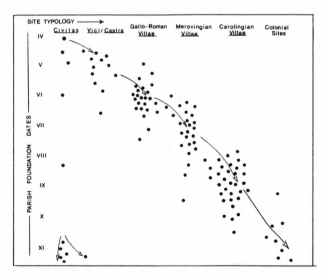

Figure 2
Typological Distribution of Parishes by Date of Foundation

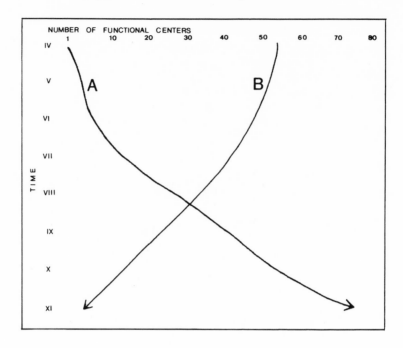

Figure 3
Number of Parishes (A) compared with the Number of "Functional Centers" existing at the same time but which are not parishes (B)

Figure 4
The Research Area

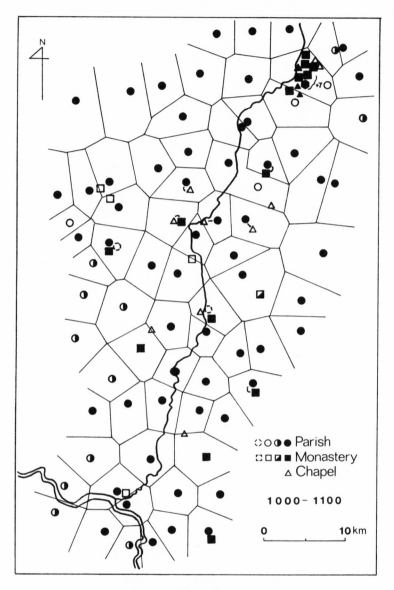

Figure 5
Distribution of Parishes in the Eleventh Century
($\overset{\cdot\cdot}{\bigcirc}$ = Hypothetical; $\bigcirc$ = Possible; $\bullet$ = Probable; $\bullet$ = Certain)

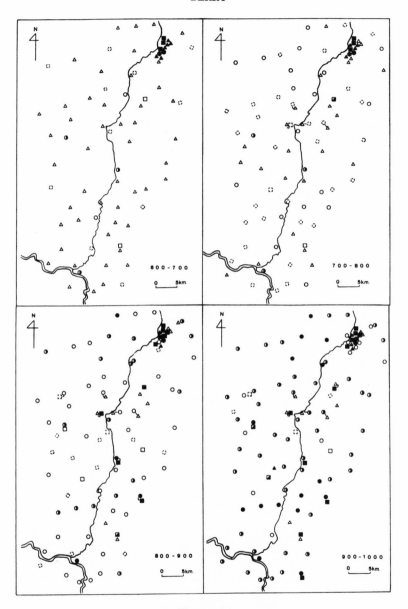

Figures 6-9
Distribution of Parishes, 600-1000

255

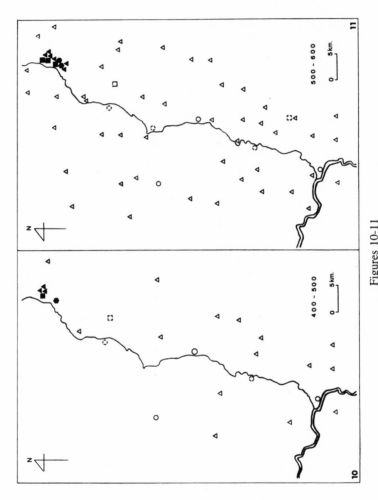

Figures 10-11
Conjectured Distribution of Parishes, 400-600

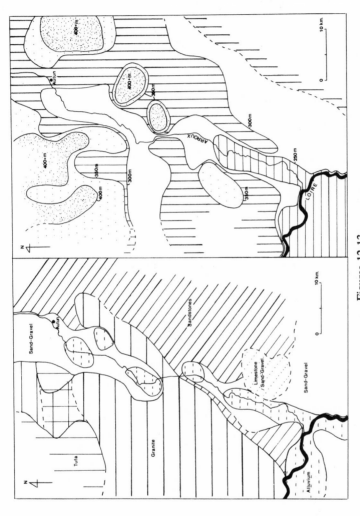

Figures 12-13

Subsurface Geology and Altitudes of Parishes of the Eleventh Century (Fig. 5) expressed as Trend Surfaces

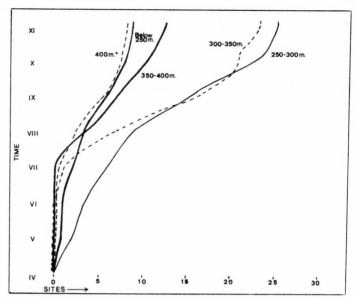

Figure 14
Chronological Distribution of Parish Altitudes (Fig. 13)

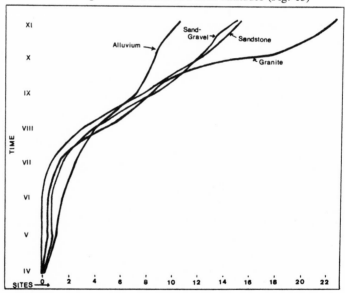

Figure 15
Chronological Distribution of Parish Subsurface Geology (Fig. 12)

NOTES

¹ E. M. Jope, "Models in Medieval Studies," in *Models in Archaeology*, ed. D. L. Clarke (London: Methuen and Co., 1972), p. 984.

² See in general, *Models in Geography*, ed. R. J. Chorley and P. Haggett (London: Methuen and Co., 1967); B. J. L. Berry, *Geography of Market Centers and Retail Distribution*, Prentice-Hall Foundations of Economic Geography (Englewood Cliffs, NJ: Prentice-Hall, 1967), pp. 59-73; D. L. Clarke, *Models in Archaeology* and his *Spatial Archaeology* (London and New York: Academic Press, 1977); and I. Hodder and C. Orton, *Spatial Analysis in Archaeology*, New Studies in Archaeology (Cambridge: Cambridge Univ. Press, 1976).

³ Two dilemmas face the historian or archaeologist who wishes to use spatial analysis: first, the possibility of unintentional bias entering into archaeological data due to variations in the preservation of the archaeological record; and, second, the potential inappropriateness of locational models borrowed from other fields. Recent responses to these difficulties include: the maintaining of rigorous and objective procedures (Hodder and Orton, *Spatial Analysis in Archaeology*, pp. 71 ff.); the use of "regional-spatial models" (C. A. Smith, "Regional Economic Systems: Linking Geographical Models and Socioeconomic Problems," in *Regional Analysis*, ed. C. A. Smith [New York: Academic Press, 1967], vol. 1, pp. 3-7); and the application of multiple, well-fitting locational models to highly-documented situations (C. L. Crumley, "Three Locational Models: An Epistemological Assessment for Anthropology and Archaeology," in *Advances in Archaeological Method and Theory*, ed. M. B. Schiffer [New York: Academic Press, 1979], vol. 2, pp. 157-66).

⁴ Jope, "Models in Medieval Studies," passim.

⁵ See note 16, below.

⁶ This forms part of an interdisciplinary study, "Spatial Aspects of Continuity and Change in Protohistoric and Historic Gaul," directed by Dr. Carole L. Crumley, Dept. of Anthropology, Univ. of North Carolina at Chapel Hill, and funded between 1975 and 1980 by grants from the National Science Foundation, the National Endowment for the Humanities, and from EARTHWATCH. See C. L. Crumley, "Les fouilles du Mont Dardon," *La Physiophile*, 86 (June, 1977), 93-102; and her "Three Locational Models," pp. 157 ff.

⁷ For example, M. Chaume, "Les anciens domaines gallo-romains de la région bourguignonne," *Mémoires de la Commission des antiquités de la Côte d'Or*, 20 (1934), 267 ff.

⁸ See G. R. J. Jones, "Multiple Estates and Early Settlement," in *Medieval Settlement*, ed. P. H. Sawyer (London: Edward Arnold, 1976), pp. 15-40. Though dealing with Great Britain, his conclusions seem largely applicable to French parishes as well.

⁹ The major source of the model is M. Chaume, "Le mode de constitution et de délimitation des paroisses rurales aux temps mérovingiens et carolingiens," *Revue Mabillon*, 27 (1937), 61-73 and 28 (1938), 1-9. Also of importance are Imbart de la Tour, "Les paroisses rurales dans l'ancienne France," *Revue Histori*

que, 60 (1896), 241 ff., 61 (1896), 1 ff., 63 (1897), 1 ff., 67 (1898), 1 ff. and 68 (1898), 1 ff. See also M. Chaume, *Les origines de Duché de Bourgogne*, 4 vols. (Dijon: Jobard, 1925-37), vol. 2, ch. 2, pp. 780-815; J. Lestocquoy, "De l'unité à la pluralité: le paysage en Gaule du Ve au IXe siècle," *Annales d'Histoire économique et sociale*, 8 (1953), 159-72; J.-F. Lemarignier, "Quelques remarques sur l'organisation écclesiastique de la Gaule de VIIe à la fin du IXe siècle principalement au nord de la Loire," *Settimane di Studio del Centro italiano di Studi sull'Alto Medioevo*, 13 (1966), 451-86; E. Griffe, *La Gaule chrétienne à l'époque romaine*, 2nd ed., rev., 3 vols. (Paris: Letouzey, 1964-65), vol. 3, pp. 260-98; and M. Roblin, *Le terroir de Paris aux époques gallo-romaine et franque*, preface by A. Grenier, 2nd ed., enlarged (Paris: Picard, 1971).

[10] For instance, canon 26 of the Fourth Synod of Orleans (541), which concerns episcopal control over the priests of *parochiae in potentum domibus* (Mansi, *Conciliorum*, 9.117-18).

[11] Griffe, *La Gaule chrétienne à l'époque romaine*, vol. 3, pp. 160-66.

[12] See C. L. Crumley, "Toward a Locational Definition of State Systems of Settlement," *American Anthropologist*, 78 (1976), 67-68, where she defines a functional center as "any spot/place/site/location which serves a function or functions not equally available elsewhere, i.e., that has a hinterland for which it provides a function or functions."

[13] D. L. Clarke, *Analytical Archaeology* (London: Methuen and Co., 1968), p. 444. A somewhat analogous example is found in G. W. Conrad, "Models of Compromise in Settlement Pattern Studies: An Example from Coastal Peru," *World Archaeology*, 9 (1977-78), 281-98, where a Central Place model is used in a predictive fashion. The model of parish development summarized above and illustrated in Fig. 1 is similar to Central Place models (see B. J. L. Berry, *Market Centers*, pp. 59 ff. for a discussion of this model). The manner in which the parish model develops from one phase to the next recalls the packing of "cellular hexagonal territories" in P. Haggett, "Network Models in Geography," and in Chorley and Haggett, *Models*, pp. 648-49, Fig. 15.22. The parish model is assumed to predict the development of the administrative network of the diocese, which in turn reflects the character of the settlement pattern; it is in itself neither an economic model nor a demographic one.

[14] The probable sequence of foundation of the parish centers is determined through the comparison of certain factors, of which the more important are direct documentation, dedications (patron saint), and toponyms. Factors such as ecclesiastical patronage, relationship to Roman and later routes, archaeological data, physical location, and distance to adjacent parishes of known date are treated as secondary variables. Weighing these indications and working back from the earliest verified date, each parish center is assigned an "earliest expected date." Arranged in chronological groups, a series of "time-slice" distribution maps can be constructed, as in Figs. 5-11. In these the degree of assurance of a parish's existence is expressed by a scale of probability: hypothetical (25% probability); possible (50%); probable (75%); and certain, i.e., documented (100%). This method is based on M. Chaume, "Les plus anciennes églises de Bourgogne," *Annales de Bourgogne*, 8 (1938), 201-29 and his "Pour la recherche des anciens

260

vocables d'église," *Annales de Bourgogne*, 12 (1940), 41-44; and Roblin, *Le terroir de Paris aux époques gallo-romaine et franque*, pp. 151-93. Allowance for Chaume's rather over-optimistic reliance on saint's names has been made through the use of other additional factors and the probability scale.

[15] The basic sources for the area are: J.-G. Bulliot, *Essai historique sur l'abbaye de Saint-Martin d'Autun*, 2 vols. (Autun: Dejussieu, 1849); A. de Charmasse, *Cartulaire de l'église d'Autun*, 3 vols. (Autun and Paris: Dejussieu and Pédone, 1865 and 1900), *Cartulaire, de l'evêché d'Autun*, (Autun and Paris: Dejussieu, 1880) and his "Origine des paroisses rurales dans le département de Saône-et-Loire," *Mémoires de la Société Éduenne*, n.s., 37 (1909), 33-121; U. Chevallier, *Chartularium prioratus Beatae Mariae de Paredo Monachorum* (Montbeliard: Hoffmann, 1891); A Déléage, *Recueil des actes du prieuré de Saint-Symphorien d'Autun de 696 à 1300* (Autun: Taverne and Chandioux, 1936). Also of importance are Courtépée and Béguillet, *Description generale et particulière du Duche de Bourgogne*, 3rd ed., 4 vols. (Avallon: F.E.R.N., 1967); J.-F. Baudiau, *La Morvan*, 3rd ed., 2 vols. (Paris: Guenegaud, 1965); Chaume, *Origines*; and A. Déléage, *La vie rurale en Bourgogne jusqu'au début du onzième siècle*, 3 vols. (Mâcon: Protat frères, 1941).

[16] For examples of the use of Thiessen polygons, see Hodder and Orton, *Spatial Analysis in Archaeology*, pp. 59 ff., 78 ff., and esp. 187 ff. A comparison of Thiessen polygons drawn around the parishes of c. 1300 with the actual boundaries of those parishes shows a very close resemblance. As 85% of the parishes c. fourteenth century also existed in the eleventh century, the hypothesized boundaries shown in Fig. 5 are probably quite accurate. The pattern is well-packed. The average contact edge count is 5.47, and this is well along the way to the hexagonal arrangement of the thirteenth century. Conversely, the shapes of the territories tend toward elongated rather than regular forms, an indication that while a hexagonal administrative relationship had been arrived at in relation to adjacent parishes, the actual configurations of the parishes conform to other factors; see A. R. H. Baker, "Some Shape and Contact Characteristics of French Rural Communes," in *L'habitat et les paysages ruraux d'Europe* (Liège: Univ. de Liège, 1971), pp. 13-23. Thiessen polygons must, however, be used with caution, for the shapes of site territories are dictated by many more factors than simply the distance to neighboring sites. Just the same, it is interesting to note that each succeeding "generation" of new parish foundations tended to appear along the edges of the Thiessen polygons of the preceding generation.

[17] The distribution of these parishes is very close to the patterns known from the documented contemporary cases of the dioceses of Tours and Auxerre; see C. E. Stancliffe, "From Town to Country: The Christianization of the Touraine 370-600," *Studies in Church History*, 16 (1979), 43-59; and Chaume, *Origines*, vol. 2, ch. 2, pp. 799-803 and his "Paroisses rurales," pp. 65-66.

[18] For a discussion of site catchment, see D. C. Roper, "The Method and Theory of Site Catchment Analysis: A Review," in Schiffer, *Advances*, vol. 2, pp. 119-40; and J. Francis and G. A. Clark, "Towards a Model of Subsistence and Settlement," in G. A. Clark, *The North Burgos Archaeological Survey: Bronze and Iron Age Archaeology on the Meseta del Norte*, Anthropological res. papers

19 (Tempe, AZ: Arizona State Univ., 1979), pp. 210-11. Despite the problems with site catchment analysis, I have employed it in a modified fashion in this study because of what I believe is its applicability to medieval settlement forms; see B. K. Roberts, *Rural Settlement in Britain*, Studies in Historical Geography (Folkestone, Kent, and Hamden, CN: Dawson and Archon, 1977), pp. 85-99, Figs. 19 and 22. Two examples of the use of this method are A. Ellison and J. Harriss, "Settlement and Land Use in the Prehistory and Early History of Southern England: A Study Based on Locational Models," in Clarke, *Models*, pp. 911-62; and G. Barker, "Early Neolithic Land Use in Yugoslavia," *Proceedings of the Prehistoric Society*, n.s., 41 (1975), 85-104.

[19] See Hodder and Orton, *Spatial Analysis in Archaeology*, pp. 155-74, esp. 163 ff., where the drawbacks are outlined: "Trend surface analysis is the name . . . for methods of smoothing the values of some mapped variable. A generalized surface is derived from, or fitted to, the mapped data and two components or trends extracted—that of a regional nature, and local fluctuations" (p. 155). A different approach, the contoured density map, is of similar use; a good example is found in C. Thomas, *Christianity in Roman Britain to A.D. 500* (Berkeley and Los Angeles: Univ. of California Press, 1981), Figs. 14-16. Both are employed in the study of which this paper is a summary.

[20] Clarke, *Analytical Archaeology*, p. 444.

[21] B. J. L. Berry, *Market Centers*, pp. 59 ff.

[22] Smith, "Economic Systems," vol. 1., pp. 34 ff.

[23] P. Haggett, *Locational Analysis in Human Geography* (London: Edward Arnold, 1965), p. 19.

[24] For a good example of the possibilities of this type of inquiry, see C. Phythian-Adams, *Continuity, Fields and Fission: The Making of a Midland Parish*, Leicester Univ. Dept. of Eng. Hist. Occ. Papers, 3rd ser., 4 (Leicester: Leicester Univ. Press, 1978).

CASTLE AND COUNTRYSIDE: CAPALBIACCIO AND THE CHANGING SETTLEMENT HISTORY OF THE *AGER COSANUS*

STEPHEN L. DYSON

My intention here is to describe the history of settlement in the *Ager Cosanus*, the territory of the ancient Roman colony of Cosa, as it has been reconstructed by the Wesleyan survey team. Emphasis will be on the Middle Ages, which are the concern of this volume; however, in order to place medieval patterns in context, one must first consider the long-term relationship between human communities and the region, and, therefore, a brief history of Roman Cosa will precede my discussion of the medieval period.

According to ancient sources, Cosa was an Etruscan city. Decades of excavation by the American Academy in Rome have failed, however, to turn up any substantial traces of Etruscan occupation at the site, a hilltop in Ansedonia generally linked to Roman Cosa[1] (see Fig. 1 at end of essay). The Etruscan center may have been located elsewhere, perhaps at modern Orbetello. Archaeological excavation and survey have demonstrated that the four- to five-hundred square kilometers of land set aside as the *territorium* of ancient Cosa was sparsely inhabited when the Romans arrived. The latest evidence from excavations at Capalbiaccio may force some re-evaluation of this point, about which I will withhold discussion until later.

The Romans founded Cosa in 273 B.C. on a coastal point some one-hundred miles north of the city now known as Ansedonia.[2] Founded to watch over the recently-rebellious Etruscans and, more importantly, the inhabitants of the major center at Vulci, Cosa was a Latin colony. Its population of several thousand families was settled partly in the city and in greater numbers in the surrounding countryside. Excavations by the American Academy have shown that, although the urban center prospered in the second and first centuries B.C., the city suffered some disaster toward the end of the first quarter of the first century B.C., and, while occupation continued at the site until the end of the fourth century A.D., the city never recovered its former vigor.[3]

Literary evidence for Cosa's transition from Antiquity to the Middle Ages is very limited. Religious legends suggest some occupation during the Carolingian period,[4] probably centered on the settlement of Succosa, which grew up below the town, between the small harbor which served the area and the line of the Via Aurelia, the Roman trunk road. The monastery of the Tre Fontane near Rome claimed the zone and continued to play an important role in the medieval history of Cosa.[5]

By the twelfth century, written documentation is more abundant. The center of Orbetello had probably been continuously inhabited from the Etruscan era, through the Roman period, into the Middle Ages. In the thirteenth century, it became a commune.[6] In the territory of the old Roman colony were established several castles or fortified centers, including one on the *capitolium*, or religious center, of the old Roman colony, which recall the process of *incastellamento* in southern Lazio described by the French medievalist Pierre Toubert.[7] This castle-dominated landscape can still be seen in the first views we have of the Cosa area—the maps in the Vatican's sixteenth century *Galleria delle Carte Geografiche*.

Politically, the Cosa area was a border zone in which the diverse interests of the Papal States—Orvieto, Siena, and even Pisa—came into conflict; political uncertainty allowed local magnates to establish at least a temporary hold over the area. In spite of these inevitable difficulties, the area seems to have enjoyed a reasonable degree of prosperity in the twelfth and thirteenth centuries. In the fourteenth century came the economic decline and depopulation for which, traditionally, malaria has been blamed.[8] Certainly, throughout the nineteenth century, the malarial swamps kept most people out of the area, particularly during the summer months.[9] However, fourteenth-century accounts clearly place more of the blame for this decline on growing political insecurity.[10] By the fifteenth and sixteenth centuries, most of the castles had been dismantled or abandoned, and the area gradually assumed the deserted appearance described by eighteenth and nineteenth century travellers.[11]

This brief history of the rise and fall of Cosa has been assembled from the sources and from excavations at the ancient city site. Before turning to the ways in which the Wesleyan survey has modified this picture, some general observations on the geography of the area should be made. The landscape around Cosa is extremely varied (see Fig. 2). A reasonably wide coastal plain along which the Via Aurelia passed borders the territory on the southwest and provided fertile farmland and access to the sea. It was also dotted with coastal swamps which could become a breeding ground for the mosquito. The northern border of the colony, formed by the Albegna River, provided a communication route to the interior. Several other highly fertile valleys linked the coast with the hill country behind, and even today they provide some of the best farmland in the area. The northeast, however, is hilly and sometimes rugged; the land is relatively poor in quality and the ground cover often dense.

One may observe, in the twentieth-century pattern of settlement in the *Ager Cosanus*, two distinct landscapes—the first is the early modern, the second a post World War II development. To the former, the city of Orbetello represents continuity. Toward the interior, the fifteenth-century hilltop city of Capalbiaccio reflects an inland shift of population during the later Middle Ages. Topographic maps of the 1930s show its farmsteads still grouped in a late-medieval pattern: a number are clustered along the line of the Via Aurelia, especially near its juncture with the road to Orbetello. Another concentration of settlements is to be found in the northeast highlands, where the elevation and distance from the coast provided protection from malaria, piracy, and passing armies. Complementing these survivors of the Middle Ages are the ruins of several castles, monasteries, and hermitages.

The second landscape, a post-World War II development, uncannily reproduces the pattern of the Roman period. The Italian government undertook extensive land reforms in the area after the war, creating numerous small farmsteads,[12] the locational pattern for which is very close to that of the Roman farms and very different from the settlement structure of the medieval countryside. Furthermore, the coastal region has, in recent years, become a popular vacation spot, and the Ansedonia area is crowded with sumptuous summer homes—an interesting parallel to the phenomenon found during the Roman period when several large pleasure villas were built below the city.

In 1974, Wesleyan University began a systematic survey of the Cosa area with the aim of producing a settlement history based on

265

archaeological evidence. Our model was the series of surveys undertaken by the British School at Rome around Veii, the results of which have been summarized in Timothy Potter's *The Changing Landscape of South Etruria*.[13] For nearly three seasons we have investigated by car and on foot all accessible areas of the *Ager Cosanus*. Among many advantages offered by the area for such a survey is the quality of farmland: extensive tilling of the land by mechanical means has resulted in the type of deep soil disturbance so useful for the survey archaeologist. Our inventory of nearly 150 sites, while not massive, is still a great improvement over few more than a dozen known when our work began; our methods and results have been summarized in previous publications.[14]

The survey showed that for areas presently under cultivation, Roman sites are most dominant; almost no Etruscan sites were turned up, although a few Etruscan tombs have been recorded in the past. The Roman evidence was of special interest, since it related to the question of the decline of the Roman small farmer in the wake of the Hannibalic War and the rise of the large slave estates. In the past, this development has often been associated with the Cosa region, particularly since Tiberius Gracchus, while passing along the Via Aurelia, supposedly drew inspiration for his reforms from the deserted, slave-dominated landscape he saw from the road.[15]

Contrary to previous research linking the desertion of the area around Cosa to the second century B.C., our survey demonstrated that, in actuality, settlement was relatively dense at this time, with a mixture of medium and small estates. Later in the century, large villas appeared, but these were probably resort estates mainly confined to a limited coastal area and did not threaten the demise of smaller farms (see Figs. 3 and 4). Some consolidation of farm holdings did take place in the early Empire, but the area continued to support a healthy mixture of agricultural estates.

In the second century A.D. the rapid process of desertion began, which, by the late third century A.D. had spread not only to farms and other small estates but to the largest villas as well. Excavations at Le Colonne and Sette Finestre suggest that these large villas were, for the most part, in ruins early in the century.[16] To date, archaeological research cannot supply the reasons for the rapid desertion of the countryside in a period well before barbarian pressures were felt in Italy. One is therefore tempted to look to the spread of malaria as a factor, particularly since all socio-economic groups seem to have joined in the flight.

Survey evidence for the medieval period in the Cosa region is sparse. Almost no true medieval sites were found in the lowland agricultural zones; in the interior, a few ruined early modern farmhouses were discovered. If any deliberate attempt was made to resettle the *Ager*

Cosanus in the early medieval period, such as happened around Veii, we have not found the traces.[17] However, the survey did investigate the major standing medieval ruins, most of which are located on hills, well above the zone of cultivation. These sites are usually unploughed and are often covered with thick vegetation that makes normal survey impossible. Nevertheless, since they were an important part of Cosa's settlement history, we felt that our research would not be complete until at least one site had been cleared, mapped, and selectively excavated.

The site selected was a hilltop settlement known as Capalbiaccio, in many respects the medieval equivalent of Roman Cosa. Located on a hill 4.5 km. from the sea, at an elevation of 231 m., it commands a view of the coastal plain and two of the larger valleys which lead into the interior. The elevation provided some protection from malaria, while the inland location decreased the danger of sudden pirate raids.

The plan of Capalbiaccio differs from other, smaller castles and watchtowers scattered about the *Ager Cosanus* (see Fig. 5). The outline of the fortifications is oval in form, and there is a wall that bisects the enclosed area, which measures roughly 94 x 180 m. Both aerial photographs and detailed ground surveys clearly show that the smaller section contains no internal buildings, while the larger part is crowded with structures. Thus, Capalbiaccio appears to have been more of a fortified village than a military outpost.[18] The distribution of structural surface remains suggests that a small community permanently inhabited one part of the fortress, while the other section was left free as a place of refuge for men and beasts in times of temporary danger. Subsequent archaeological investigations, however, have shown that the evolution of the settlement and its defense system was far more complex.

Documentary evidence for Capalbiaccio is sparse; the site is mentioned for the first time in 1161. It is tempting to connect its foundation with *incastellamento*, the process of concentrating population in controllable fortified centers known to other areas in medieval Italy.[19]

Our intention was to reconstruct in detail a history of the site and, thus, to illuminate the material aspects of medieval community life in this part of central Italy. Unfortunately, the difficulties of the site, with its heavy cover of underbrush and thick layers of rubble from the fallen walls, and our limited financial resources, forced us during this phase to limit excavation to what seemed key areas.

One puzzling aspect of the fortification system at Capalbiaccio was a break in the central area of the division wall (see Fig. 6). Wall foundations and mounds of earth suggested that there had been a gate in the area which had been leveled when the site was abandoned. However, when this section was excavated, the remains of a small church were

267

discovered. This structure was probably the church of S. Frediano, mentioned as being located at Capalbiaccio[20] (see Fig. 7). Although churches built into walls are known from other medieval Italian sites,[21] in this case the church clearly preceded the fortification system, and the building of the wall led to the destruction of the church: foundations of one cross wall were built across the entrance of the church, and in the apse area, the division wall abutted the church apse. Although construction of the division wall clearly came after the building of the church, the next question was whether this was true for the rest of the fortification system.

It was possible that the division wall was a secondary addition to the circuit of walls and that the outer fortifications had been built when Capalbiaccio was first settled. However, careful study of the juncture points of outer fortifications and the division wall shows that they were in fact contemporary: the construction of the walls appeared to postdate the foundation of the settlement. To test further this relation between the fortifications and the buildings within the circuit, we excavated one large building (J on Fig. 4) which abutted the outer wall in the northwest area. The soundings showed clearly that the west wall of building J had been destroyed when the fortifications had been started. Other evidence suggests that the attempt to build the very ambitious defense system represented the very last phase of occupation at Capalbiaccio but that it was never completed. Today the outer circuit has a very disjunctive quality: the division wall is preserved to nearly its original height, and certain segments of the outer wall are almost totally intact. These sections are located at key positions around the perimeter of the hill and provide excellent observation points. The parts in between are usually not preserved much above the foundations.

One explanation for this discrepancy, that later inhabitants of the area robbed the stone for building purposes, is insufficient. Between the sixteenth century and the 1950s, few people lived in the area. Since stone is abundant close to the zone of settlement, there is little reason to assume that people went up in great numbers to rob material from Capalbiaccio. A more logical explanation is that the fortification was never finished. The great division wall was complete enough to provide not only a good lookout but also to give the impression, to anyone coming in from the sea or coastal plain, of massive fortification. Other wall sections were constructed at key intervals, but the connecting parts were never completed. Before the possible events behind this aborted fortification scheme are discussed, it seems appropriate to review briefly the history of the earlier, unfortified community.

There is no reason to doubt documentary evidence that Capalbiaccio was settled in the twelfth century, although most of the pottery recovered from the excavations dates from the thirteenth through the early sixteenth centuries. The central features of this early community would have been the church and the large keep tower (P on Fig. 5), the remains of which are still among the most impressive on the site (Fig. 8). The variety in the construction details of individual buildings suggests a gradual expansion of the community. This reconstruction of a largely open settlement dependent for its protection on the central keep tower, its natural location, and perhaps some ditches and banks not yet discovered, greatly varies from theories of the evolution of fortified settlements in Italy as proposed by such scholars as David Andrews.[22] However, most of the analysis of building typology has been based on examination of standing structures and has not been tested by excavation. Clearly, Capalbiaccio has shown the importance of both archaeological investigation and examination of above-ground features.

The decision to adopt a more ambitious scheme of fortification at Capalbiaccio came relatively late and may have resulted, in part, from a disaster that eliminated the keep tower as a fortification. Large sections of the tower are scattered around the site today, as if thrown down by a very powerful force. An earthquake is the only reasonable cause for such destruction. The Capalbiaccio region is still active geologically, and there have been earthquakes in the general area in recent years.[23] The smaller buildings do not show the same degree of destruction, but they could have been repaired more quickly and easily than the tower.

At present we do not have any stratified deposits which allow us to date the construction of the outer walls. We do have a key reference that traces the abandonment of the site to 1417, when the Sienese, who controlled the area by that time, ordered the demolition of Capalbiaccio.[24] Pottery and coins found at the site, however, show that occupation continued until the early sixteenth century. Among the artifacts was a series of coins from Perugia which can be dated to the 1480s. As Capalbiaccio is well removed from Perugia and was historically more dependent on Siena and Rome, the number of Perugian coins is interesting and points to patterns of contact and influence that require more investigation.

Why, then, was the fortification plan abandoned when only partially completed? In part, this was probably due to the widespread abandonment of *castella* in the fifteenth and sixteenth centuries. For Capalbiaccio, the observations of Judith Hook on the changes in Sienese military policy seem relevant.[25] She observes that for such fifteenth- and sixteenth-century city-states as Siena, new and more expensive fortification systems were urgently needed to meet the changes in siege tactics produced by the introduction of artillery, at a time when the financial

269

position of these outdated political units was becoming increasingly precarious. Although it is tempting to associate the decision to stop construction of the already-outmoded fortifications of Capalbiaccio to these developments, the decision to leave the site may have had more local causes. Security in the area was not improving, and presumably the problem of malaria was increasing. Cosa was quickly slipping into the wilderness condition described by George Denis in the early nineteenth century.

Before some closing observations, the cycle of settlement at Capalbiaccio, and in the *Ager Cosanus* in general, should be taken back to its Etruscan origins. I have noted above the lack of Etruscan sites in the lowland areas. However, deep soundings in two of the buildings at Capalbiaccio revealed clear traces of an Etruscan occupation, including *bucchero* pottery. At present, we cannot determine how extensive the settlement was, but the findings suggest that we must seek our missing Etruscans on the high places, in sites which were later inhabited during the Middle Ages; this pattern of Iron Age settlement on the heights, a move during the *Pax Romana* down to the more accessible agricultural areas, and then a return during the Middle Ages to the high points, is one that is found elsewhere on sites in Europe.

Here, an effort to profile one small part of the Italian peninsula which played an important role during the Roman Republic and an increasingly marginal one during the Empire and the Middle Ages has been made. For both periods, the reality of settlement history as revealed by archaeology is more complex than the documents suggest. I have also attempted to show the relative value of survey versus excavation in illuminating that history: for the Roman period where the settlement pattern is closely related to areas of modern cultivation, survey is a most effective technique. David Andrews and other scholars working out of the British School at Rome as well as the older topographers such as G. and F. Tomassetti have shown how much is to be learned about the settlement patterns of the Middle Ages from the careful examination and recording of standing monuments. Excavations at sites such as Capalbiaccio show that much is to be learned by selective digging—not only about the material history of a community, but also about its structural evolution.

One final observation about this project is in order, especially in this period of rising costs and limited funding. Any archaeology is expensive relative to other historical investigatory techniques. However, the Wesleyan Cosa project has been run at a minimal cost and, in addition to its research goals, has provided valuable field training for students in archaeology.[26] Emphasis on survey and on carefully-defined excavation goals has kept the cost down. The potential of such projects is, we feel, worth consideration by others interested in investigating the landscape history of Europe and the Mediterranean.

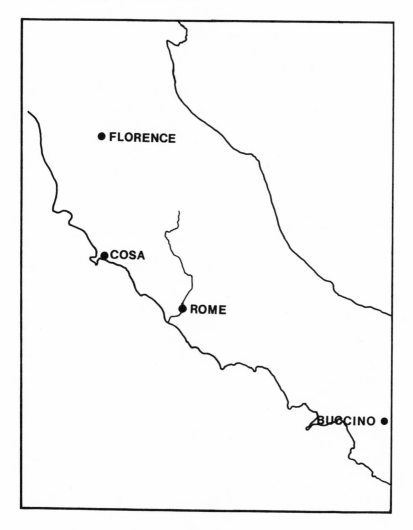

Figure 1
Cosa and Italy

271

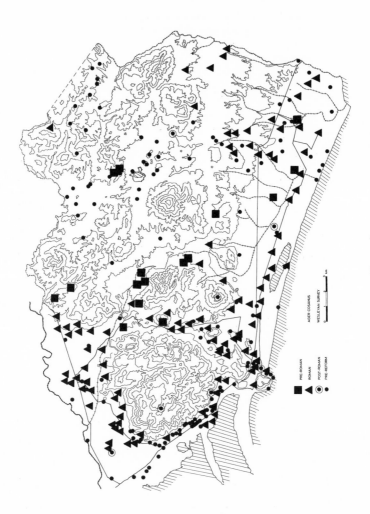

Figure 2
Archaeological Sites in the *Ager Cosanus*

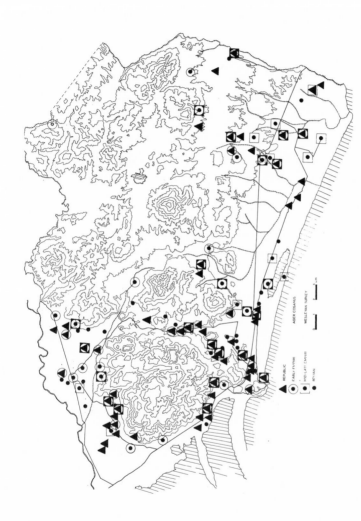

Figure 3
Roman Period Sites in the *Ager Cosanus*

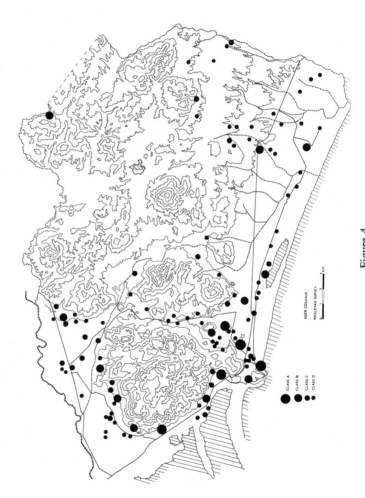

Figure 4
Variation in Villa Size in the *Ager Cosanus*

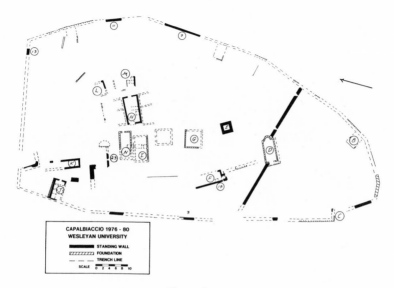

Figure 5
The Plan of Capalbiaccio

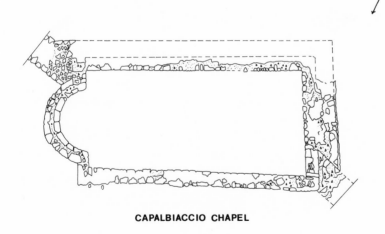

CAPALBIACCIO CHAPEL

Figure 6

Figure 7
View of Capalbiaccio Chapel

Figure 8
The Keep Tower at Capalbiaccio

NOTES

[1] The best account of Cosa and its excavations is now F. E. Brown, *Cosa: The Making of a Roman Town* (Ann Arbor: Univ. of Michigan Press, 1980). It contains a full bibliography of previous work.

[2] *Cosa: The Making of a Roman Town*, pp. 1-30; E. T. Salmon, *Roman Colonization Under the Republic* (Ithaca: Cornell Univ. Press, 1970), pp. 29-39.

[3] *Cosa: The Making of a Roman Town*, pp. 72-76; R. T. Scott, "A New Inscription of the Emperor Maximinus at Cosa," *Chiron*, 11 (1981), pp. 309-14.

[4] The written evidence for the history of the Cosa area during the Middle Ages has been collected and analyzed by Cardarelli. For his reconstructions see R. Cardarelli, "Confini fra Magliano e Masiliana; fra Manciano e Montuto Scerpenna Stachilagi; fra Tricosto e Ansedonia; fra Orbetello e Marsiliana; fra Port Ercole e Monte Arsgentario (28 dicembre 1508 - 2 marzo 1510)," *Bollettino delle Societe Storice Maremmana*, 1 (1924), 131-42, 155-86, 205-24; 2 (1925), 3-36, 75-128, 147-213; and, for the reference to the Carolingian period, (1925), 89-92.

[5] R. Cardarelli (1925), 88, 96-100.

[6] R. Cardarelli (1925), 117-28.

[7] For the whole question of *incastellamento* in Lazio see P. Toubert, *Les structures de Latium medieval* (Rome: Ecole Française de Rome, 1973).

[8] R. Cardarelli (1925), 147.

[9] G. Dennis, *Cities and Cemeteries of Etruria*, 3rd. ed. (London: J. Murray, 1883), ch. 42.

[10] R. Cardarelli (1925), 160-61.

[11] R. Cardarelli (1925), 147-88.

[12] For the routine and process of this reform, see C. Retzleff, *Kulturgeographische Wandlungen in der Maremma* (Kiel: Selbstverlag des geographischen Instituts der Universität Kiel, 1967).

[13] T. Potter, *The Changing Landscape of South Etruria* (New York: St. Martin's Press, 1979).

[14] The results of this survey have been summarized in S. L. Dyson, "Settlement Patterns in the Ager Cosanus: The Wesleyan University Survey, 1974-1976," *Journal of Field Archaeology*, 5 (1978), 251-68; S. L. Dyson, "Settlement Reconstruction in the Ager Cosanus and the Albegna Valley: Wesleyan University Research, 1974-1979," in *Archaeology and Italian Society*, ed. G. Barker and R. Hodges, BAR International Series 102 (Oxford, 1981), pp. 269-74; and S. L. Dyson, "Survey Archaeology: Reconstructing the Roman Countryside," *Archaeology*, 34 (1981), 31-37.

[15] Plutarch, *Tiberius Gracchus* 8.7; D. B. Nagle, "The Etruscan Journey of Tiberius Gracchus," *Historia*, 25 (1976), 487-89.

[16] For the recent work on Sette Finestre see A. Carandini and S. Settis, *Schiavi e Padroni nell' Etruria Romana* (Bari: De Donato, 1979). The information on the villa at Le Colonne is based on the Wesleyan University excavations at the site which now is in process of publication.

[17] For the resettlement efforts in the area around Veii, see T. Potter, *The Changing Landscape of South Etruria*, pp. 138-67.

[18] The best recent study of medieval fortification in central Italy is D. Andrews, "The Archaeology of the Medieval Castrum in Central Italy," in *Archaeology and Italian Society*, pp. 313-34. Other useful articles are: A. W. Lawrence, "Early Medieval Fortifications near Rome," *Papers of the British School at Rome*, n.s. 19 (1964), 89-122; and D. Andrews, "Medieval Masonry in Northern Lazio: Its Development and Uses for Dating," in *Papers in Italian Archaeology*, vol. 1, ed. H. Mc. Blake, T. W. Potter, and D. B. Whitehouse, BAR International Series 41 (Oxford, 1978), pp. 391-422.

[19] See R. Cardarelli (1925), 95 for first references to Capalbiaccio, or Tircoste as it is called in the medieval texts.

[20] R. Cardarelli (1925), 96.

[21] D. Andrews, "The Archaeology of the Medieval Castrum in Central Italy," 318-19.

[22] D. Andrews, "Medieval Masonry in Northern Lazio," and "The Archaeology of the Medieval Castrum in Central Italy."

[23] My own hypothesis on an earthquake causing the destruction at Capalbiaccio was supported by on-site studies during the 1980 field season by Professor Jelle de Boer of the Wesleyan Earth and Environmental Sciences Department.

[24] R. Cardarelli (1925), 157-59.

[25] J. Hook, "Fortifications and the End of the Sienese State," *History*, 62 (1977), 372-87.

[26] The survey and excavations were conducted by Wesleyan University, in cooperation with the American Academy in Rome. The surveys were conducted by the author, together with teams of two to five undergraduates. Undergraduates (about fifteen per session) were used to carry out the excavations at Capalbiaccio). Funding came from Wesleyan and in 1978 from the National Endowment for the Humanities. Total annual budget for the project reached $17,000 in the final year.

PART V:
CONTEXT AND CONCERNS

CURRENT RESEARCH CONCERNS IN MEDIEVAL ARCHAEOLOGY IN WEST GERMANY

WALTER JANSSEN

Definition of Medieval Archaeology in West Germany

In West Germany, medieval archaeology is considered a historical discipline contributing to the study of the Middle Ages.[1] Defined chronologically, it includes both the migration period (Frühgeschichte) which stretches from the end of the Roman Empire, in the middle of the fifth century, to the end of the Merovingian dynasty in the Frankish kingdom, in the middle of the eighth century, and the medieval period proper, up to the Reformation.

Traditionally, the study of the migration period has concentrated almost exclusively on grave goods, which has resulted in a narrow formulation of problems and interpretations. A new generation of archaeologists, recognizing these methodological limitations, is now reassessing mortuary practices in a broader framework that includes the study of rural settlement systems, and integrates ongoing research on early medieval towns, churches, and fortifications. Archaeology is now altering the social and economic history of the migration period with models of settlement, agricultural production, exchange, defense, and ritual.

Burials with grave goods, typical of the migration period, began to disappear in Germany at the turn of the eighth century, as Christianity penetrated the countryside. The changes in mortuary practice and the loss of this typical archaeological source mark a practical divide between early and later medieval archaeology in Germany. The age of exploration and the formation of the early-modern world system mark another division between later medieval and post-medieval archaeology. The changing configuration of imports and the new commodities of everyday life characteristic of early modern exchange systems resulted in the restructuring of household inventories which archaeologists excavate and study. In relying on criteria of "materielle Kultur" or "Sach kultur des Mittelalters" to provide endpoints to their study, medieval archaeologists circumvent the traditional discussions among historians over when the Middle Ages ended. The line of continuity in material culture between the twelfth and the fifteenth century is unbroken and very strong in the German evidence. A real caesura is not visible until the end of the fifteenth or the beginning of the sixteenth century.

Medieval archaeology in West Germany requires definition not only with respect to chronology but also in its relationship to other disciplines, especially history, prehistory, and the history of art.[2] Art historians, for example, might argue that the creation of a specialized discipline of medieval archaeology is redundant, since they have used excavation as a method of investigation from the eighteenth century. Research in medieval archaeology since World War II has taken its own path and has demonstrated that an art historical approach alone, which confines itself to problems of style and architecture, is far too narrow. Medieval archaeology incorporates all of material culture as its subject matter, and its scope is, therefore, much wider than an art historical, or even a traditional economic historian's, approach.

A historian might object that the sheer quantity of written sources for the Middle Ages renders archaeological research an interesting but auxiliary exercise. First, such a statement does not account for the unequal quality and quantity of medieval documentation and, more importantly, for its paucity in the early medieval period. No series of documents, not even the well-preserved runs of court rolls and account rolls, can offer the temporal depth that archaeology brings to the study of material culture.

Medieval documents do not take material culture and human ecology as their explicit subject matter, as archaeology does. Information about these aspects of human life can be painstakingly reconstructed by the historian and can complement, but not substitute for, the systematic study that medieval archaeology makes of such subjects. Furthermore,

282

documents were produced by leading social groups; other communities are only reflected through them. Archaeology is able to recover embedded aspects of everyday life of these communities and contributes to a more direct and fuller understanding of them.

The contributions that medieval archaeology can make do not pertain to all fields of medieval studies in the same way. It can suggest new linkages between material culture and symbolic culture, but it cannot uncover the theoretical premises of theological, philosophical, or political systems. Medieval archaeology is most effective when studying the history of: medieval settlement and settlement systems; agriculture and the landscape; crafts and industry; religion, cults, and burial practices; urban development, demography, and exchange systems; protection, defense and war; and civilization, when medieval archaeology views all these areas of study as dynamic processes of human culture.

In summary, the discipline of medieval archaeology can contribute to the study of the Middle Ages in different ways. It can supplement, challenge, or contradict interpretations of written sources. It may constitute an interdisciplinary contribution to the study of the Middle Ages or its own full source in the study of medieval communities when other sources are absent.

History of Medieval Archaeology in Germany

Research in medieval archaeology began in Germany in 1933 when the pioneering medieval archaeologist, Paul Grimm from Halle, published his studies of the medieval pottery of the Harz region of central Germany.[3] Through his research, the attention of archaeologists was drawn to medieval pottery for the first time. Paul Grimm gave another pioneering impulse to medieval archaeology with the publication (1938-39) of the first excavation of a rural settlement of the medieval period— the deserted village of Hohenrode.[4] These two publications marked the birth of medieval archaeology as a discipline in Germany.

During World War II medieval archaeology suffered a complete setback, although, paradoxically, damages caused by the war were an important condition for its later progress as a discipline. When rebuilding began after the war, it became abundantly manifest that medieval layers, structures, and finds underlay towns, villages, farms, churches, monasteries, and other kinds of sites. The administration and services for the rescue and protection of ancient monuments treated these medieval discoveries as a part of the national heritage and tried to excavate them

283

and protect them. Thus, the foundations of medieval archaeology in Germany were, in fact, formed through practical necessity and action rather than through intellectual discussion and theorizing in the university. The historical origins of the discipline may account for the diverse standards for medieval archaeology in the different Bundesländer of the Federal Republic, to which the administration of rescue archaeology and the protection of monuments is delegated by law.

In the last decade, medieval archaeology has made substantial progress as a coherent discipline. In 1973, the publication *Zeitschrift für Archäologie des Mittelalters* was launched.[5] It is independently edited by Heiko Steuer and me, since some central German institutions of prehistory and protohistory refused to support this new undertaking. The journal is not only a scientific success; it is also faring well commercially. Academically, medieval archaeology is also making great strides. There are now two official chairs in medieval archaeology (Kiel-Schleswig-Holstein; Bamberg-Bavaria). The chair at Würzburg, officially one for pre- and proto-history, has been dedicated for several years to specialized study of the Migration and Merovingian periods. Medieval archaeologists also occupy governmental positions involved with the supervision of rescue archaeology and the protection of national monuments. In Lübeck,[6] Münster,[7] and Stuttgart,[8] publication series have been set up by departments devoted to the conservation of national monuments.[9]

Fields of Medieval Archaeology in West Germany

Towns

Medieval archaeologists classify West German towns into two basic categories as far as their origin is concerned: (1) towns of Roman origin and (2) towns without Roman roots.[10] Towns with Roman origins include Xanten (*Ad Sanctos*); Neuss (*Novaesium*); Cologne (*CCAA*); Trier (*Augusta Treverorum*); Mainz (*Mogontia cum*); Regensburg (*Castra Regina*); and others. A small group of towns in this category are characterized by a shift in occupational locus. These towns did not develop directly at the location of the Roman town or settlement, but in an area adjoining it.[11] Xanten and Bonn *(Bonna)* are typical examples. The most ancient nucleus of medieval Xanten[12] was a late Roman cemetery located south of the Roman town (*Colonia Ulpia Traiana*). On this cemetery site an early church, a Merovingian cemetery, and, later, a Carolingian monastery, were founded. These sacral elements are indicative of an early medieval settlement in the vicinity. At Bonn[13] a similar development of the medieval town from a late Roman cemetery can be traced. Towns with such a shift of locus do not reveal Roman features in their medieval town plan, since the later town is not identical with the Roman one; it is only influenced by the nearby Roman settlement.

Most of the medieval towns with Roman origins did incorporate Roman urban cores into their later development, as, for instance, Cologne, Trier, Mainz, Regensburg, and others. Towns of this type display many elements of continuity between Roman and medieval phases: Roman town walls were preserved for centuries; the pattern of roads and town quarters did not change; town gates, roads leading out of the city, water supplies, harbors, and so forth were maintained; even Roman urban plots were perpetuated into the medieval period; civic buildings and *cultus* sites remained in use during the early and later medieval periods.

Medieval archaeologists are now engaged in building up models for the development of towns between the end of the Roman period and the later Middle Ages. Work at Trier has uncovered evidence for some of this process.[14] During the post-Roman centuries the urban core of Trier contracted markedly. Habitation during the migration period was concentrated in a village-like settlement and in the vicinity of the cathedral of later Roman origin. Since the time of the last Roman emperor, the bishop of Trier exercised not only ecclesiastical but also secular rule in Trier. The continuity of this leadership is evidenced by the complete list of bishops of Trier—a list without gaps from the late Roman to early medieval period.

The material embodiment of this political power can be seen in the cathedral precinct constructed under Bishop Henry (956-64). The precinct was designed not only for clergymen in service of the cathedral but also for merchants, artisans, and other secular people. Excavations at several places along the substantial wall reveal that a marketplace was founded just outside its perimeter at the time of the wall's construction. This new nucleus with its own parish church (St. Gangolf) served as a focal point for the development of medieval Trier. After a period of growth, this area was fortified by a new town wall constructed around 1100 under the reign of Archbishop Bruno. At this time the medieval town was still only half of the size of the Roman *Augusta Treverorum*.

Development in Cologne may be compared to Trier.[15] A small population was resident there during the migration period. Some civic and religious buildings show evidence of continuous use from the late Roman period. A royal dynasty of the Merovingians, dated by written sources to the early sixth century, may have founded a residence and religious center in Roman buildings located near the cathedral and in the

285

cathedral itself.

The outlines of development in early medieval Cologne have been much more fully explored than its later medieval growth. Excavation within medieval quarters did not take place until 1972 when Hugo Borger took over the leadership of the Römisch-Germanisches Museum in Cologne. Much of his work in St. Alban's quarter, the so-called Quatermarkt, is still unpublished, but the interim results suggest the following.

Roman buildings in the heart of Cologne were used continuously from the Roman period up to the tenth century. Renewal and development in the town did not take place before the Ottonian period, when new rectangular buildings in the Quatermarkt were constructed. This activity must be seen in the context of development initiated by Archbishop Bruno, brother of Emperor Otto I. Under Ottonian patronage, the new town wall was constructed, which encompassed a larger urban area than had the Roman wall and incorporated a number of early medieval suburban churches into the tenth century town area. The harbor on the Rhine that fronted the Roman town had been in continuous use since the Roman period and served as an important export harbor for the medieval pottery industry undergoing growth and development in the rural areas outside of Cologne. Cologne's economic power coupled with an increasing population caused rapid expansion of the town during the twelfth century. Under the rule of Archbishop Philipp von Heinsberg (1167-91) a new town wall had to be built. This town wall continued its existence into the nineteenth century.

As in Trier, the bishop of Cologne wielded religious and temporal power from the early medieval period. The cathedral stood as the spiritual and political center of the town. By the thirteenth century this power was challenged by urban residents. In 1288 the conflict was settled at the battle of Worringen; the archbishop left the town and took up residence in smaller neighboring centers, leaving the burgesses of Cologne more or less independent and self-administering for centuries.

Ecclesiastical towns such as Trier and Cologne served as the model for a group of new towns founded by the Carolingians in conquered border areas, particularly in Saxony in the ninth century. Bishoprics such as Münster, Osnabrück, Minden, Paderborn, Verden, and Hamburg-Bremen[16] were established by Charlemagne to foster Christianization. They were implanted into settlements already developing into town-like sites. Archaeological investigation has demonstrated that these sites were not simply agricultural. They served as important economic centers for exchange and craft production and may be regarded as inland parallels to such early medieval coastal trading centers as Dorestad[17] in Holland, Haithabu[18] in Schleswig-Holstein, or Birka[19] in Sweden.

In Münster/Westfalia,[20] excavations carried out by Wilhelm Winkelmann have succeeded in explaining the process of implantation in some detail. There is archaeological evidence for Saxon settlement at Münster dating to the seventh and eighth centuries. An earthen fortification consisting of a rampart and ditch was constructed around A.D. 800. This earthwork continued in use until about 1100 when it was refurbished and transformed into a real town wall. A Carolingian enclosure of about eight ha. was established in 792-93 by the missionary Liudger who was later ordained as the first bishop of Münster in 805. Inside this monastic enclosure, archaeological remains of civil settlement have also been found. These consist of small plots measuring seven to eight m. by eleven to fourteen m., with houses of wooden construction of about four by six m. in size. These houses were occupied by artisans and merchants. The monastery church, which later became the bishop's cathedral, along with this settlement, formed the nucleus of the medieval town.

Similar developments have been traced in Hamburg[21] through excavations carried out by Reinhard Schindler and Dietrich Bohnsack. They have uncovered an old earthwork consisting of a rampart with an external ditch. The earthwork, measuring 115 by 120 m., was constructed in the Carolingian period at the beginning of the ninth century. In 834 the well-known missionary Anskar became the first bishop of the newly established bishopric of Hamburg. His cathedral was founded just outside of the old earthwork, called the *Hammaburg*, which offered direct protection to the cathedral. In the area west of the *Hammaburg*, the traces of a merchant and artisan settlement with its own harbor have been excavated. In the tenth century, Hamburg expanded rapidly. A larger fortification was necessary, and it was constructed as an earthwork with rampart and ditch cutting off the whole spur of land lying between the river Kleine Alster in the north and a channel in the south. The *Heidenwall*, as it was called, was needed to protect early Hamburg against raids made by Danes and Slavs. In 1962 the *domus lapidea* of the residence of the eleventh century bishop of Hamburg was excavated. It was a strong stone tower of circular shape measuring nineteen m. in diameter with walls four m. thick. This keep, constructed under the rule of Archbishop Bezelin (1035-43), is the earliest of its type in northern Germany.

This discussion of town archaeology in West Germany has concentrated on aspects of developmental phases of medieval urban centers.[22] These phases are not expected to behave in a synchronic fashion. Towns in former Roman provinces passed through different stages of development earlier and more quickly than those towns beyond the frontier of the Empire. In addition to questions of chronology and geography, archaeologists are also engaged in the study of the economic and social principles of town development. The role of exchange, rural development, artisan production, social stratification, communication, and food distribution are all of interest to the medieval urban archaeologist. In the space of a summary, it is not possible to illustrate in detail the major research programs at Haithabu, the early medieval emporium, and at Lübeck, headquarters of the medieval Hanse, which have been explicitly designed to address these broad issues of urban development. The reader is referred to the end notes for information about these projects.

Rural Settlement

The application of archaeological techniques to the study of medieval settlement began with Paul Grimm's pioneering project at Hohenrode in the years before World War II.[23] At Hohenrode, Grimm uncovered occupation dating to two phases: a slavic-germanic phase (eighth-eleventh centuries) and a germanic phase (twelfth-fourteenth centuries). Approximately twenty houses of different sizes, construction, and function were excavated. Houses used as permanent dwellings consisted of several rooms: kitchen, sleeping rooms, and dwelling rooms. The size of the dwelling houses measured on average twelve to fifteen m. by six to eight m. Smaller houses measuring four to five m. by five to six m. served as granaries or storehouses. Firehouses or cooking houses were also associated with dwelling structures. Groups of buildings were bounded by fences, suggesting that farms were the functional economic unit. The settlement had no church. A spring in the center of the settlement furnished the fresh water supply. A rich inventory of pottery, iron tools, and other materials helped to establish the chronology of the Hohenrode occupation and pointed to the potential of archaeology in contributing to the understanding of the material world of the villager. The excavations also yielded evidence for settlement contraction during the fourteenth century—a new source of evidence for the study of the later medieval demographic crisis.

From 1959-61, I myself excavated the medieval village of Königshagen in the Harz area.[24] As the suffix "-hagen" suggests, the foundation of the village took place during the twelfth century, probably on royal ground in an area of forest clearances. A fortified stone house, the seat of a noble, formed the nucleus of the village, which was surrounded by a circle of small dwelling houses occupied by the colonizing community. In a later period several farms were constructed outside the fortification. Most of them consisted of clusters of timber or half-timber buildings bordering on an internal yard. As the settlement began to develop, a church became necessary. It was created by transforming the stonehouse: a choir and a western annex were constructed, thus transforming a noble's house into a village church. At the east end of Königs hagen, a local pottery production site was excavated. It produced the pottery used by the peasants of the village. From the pollen profile from Königshagen, it is possible to reconstruct some of the local agricultural activities. Grain was cultivated, and the terraces of the Königshäger Feld, preserved on the slopes of the valley, are further evidence of this activity. Cattle breeding was practiced and increased in importance towards the end of the occupation of the site in the fourteenth century.

A remarkable layer consisting of burnt clay, charcoal, and other charred material, was found in nearly all of the sections excavated at Königshagen. This layer suggests that the village was burnt down and destroyed, most likely during a local war which took place about 1413-20. Apparently the inhabitants fled and never returned. They went to the neighboring village of Barbis, where they constructed new farms and houses and continued to use their old fields from their new location. Founded in the middle of the twelfth century, Königshagen is a typical creation of the medieval clearing period: deserted at the beginning of the fifteenth century, it belongs to the peak period of later medieval settlement desertions which has played such a large role in discussion of the later medieval economic and agrarian crisis.

The excavations at Königshagen initiated a new phase of archaeological research in rural settlement in all parts of Germany. In southwest Germany, Günther Fehring has excavated the deserted settlements of Unterregenbach[25] and Wülfingen.[26] In Unterregenbach, he uncovered a large basilica with a crypt dating from the first half of the eleventh century, a parish church (St. Veith) from the middle of the same century, and stone buildings serving as principal residence of the local noble family. A farming complex adjoined the noble residence. The masterful publication of this project, incorporating the field results with specialist reports and including a study of the historical documentation, is a model of the interdisciplinary cooperation and broad concerns of current projects in medieval archaeology.

The rural site of Wülfingen is published nearly completely. The site shows permanent occupation from the seventh to the thirteenth centuries and is a good example of the many deserted villages in Germany with early medieval origins. Its -ingen ending places it in a group of place-names (-ingen, -dorf, -heim, -hoven) with strong associations to early medieval settlement. These old villages participated in the process of desertion on the same scale as the villages founded in the clearance period (eleventh-twelfth centuries) with the suffices -rode, -scheid,

-hagen.[27]

Another type of medieval settlement under study is characterized by short-term occupation. One of these, the eighth-century settlement of Warendorf in Westfalia, has been excavated by Wilhelm Winkelmann.[28] He uncovered a large village consisting of many different types of houses and farms. Although the economic base was primarily agricultural, archaeological traces of craft activity were also found—weaving, metallurgy, woodworking, and so forth.

The archaeological study of medieval settlement is just beginning, and it would be premature to generalize about its findings at the moment. It is useful, however, to outline the main problems in medieval settlement studies which are under discussion right now. The origins of the village as a medieval settlement type are controversial. One group of experts denies the existence of villages in the early medieval period. According to them, rural settlement consisted of isolated farms or small groups of farms. Population studies of migration cemeteries in southwestern Germany which suggest a low density of population tend to support this view.[29] The temptation with this argument is to assume that low density of population must be distributed in dispersed settlement patterns. Unfortunately, none of these isolated farms has been excavated. The opposition maintains that village settlements were present in the early Middle Ages, and large villages can, in fact, be found in the first five centuries A.D. in many parts of central Europe. Excavation of Roman and migration period settlements do, in fact, indicate that villages were wide spread. Research at a regional scale that combines settlement studies with cemetery studies are crucial for resolving this debate.

Another problem under discussion concerns the rhythms of settlement expansion, contraction, and desertion. Archaeological data for settlement contradict the traditional assumption of agricultural historians who regard the later medieval settlement desertion as unique and explain it by evoking the later medieval settlement economic depression.[30] Archaeological results show very clearly that in central Europe several periods of desertion are observable before the late Middle Ages. Large numbers of desertions may be found during the fourth and fifth centuries; the eighth and ninth centuries; the eleventh and twelfth centuries; and even in the late nineteenth century.[31] With its time-depth perspective, medieval archaeology has introduced a new dimension to the study of settlement desertion. Desertion is more fruitfully viewed as a settlement process and not as an event unique to any particular period.

A third problem in rural settlement studies concerns the economic structure of medieval villages. Excavated settlements reveal the traces of a range of craft activities from pottery production to bone working carried

290

out in a rural context.[32] In the present discussion on the role of rural craft and industry, two forms of activity are distinguished: "hauswerk," which means that the craft output was exclusively geared to supply inhabitants of rural settlement with products necessary for daily life, without the production of surplus. The other type of economic activity involved surplus production of goods within rural settlement areas. In the Cologne area we know several villages where masses of medieval pottery were produced: Badorf, Walberberg, Pingsdorf, Brühl, Frechen, Siegburg, and Katterbach. These are all well-known centers for the production of pottery on an industrial scale. These communities must have existed exclusively for the production of ceramics, thus requiring that food supply for this non-agrarian but rurally based part of the population be organized systematically. Even within the countryside, communities could be differentiated into agricultural and industrial producers. The study of industrialized rural settlement is a major contribution to medieval economic and social history.

Sites of Production

In 1955 the Swedish archaeologist Dagmar Selling published a book entitled *Wikingerzeitliche und frühmittelalterliche Keramik in Schweden*,[33] in which she concluded that a greater part of medieval pottery in Sweden had been imported from the Rhineland. Imported wares from the Rhineland have also been found at other North Sea emporia including Dorestad, Kaupang,[34] Bergen,[35] and Haithabu.[36] Over the past three decades production centers in the Rhineland have been investigated by medieval archaeologists in order to determine under what economic, technical, and social conditions production was carried out. Agglomerations of pottery kilns have been excavated at Katterbach located twenty miles northeast of Cologne and in Walberberg, Badorf, Pingsdorf, south of Cologne, and in Siegburg in the same region.[37] The kilns studied belonged to different periods, thus allowing the course of technical improvement over time to be traced out in detail. It is now known that a revolution in kiln techniques occurred during the eleventh and twelfth centuries as the low-fired kilns from the Carolingian period were replaced by a new type of kiln which allowed the use of much higher temperatures during firing. Greater control over technology and improved wares ushered in a new period of prosperity for Rhenish pottery production.

The excavation of these kilns and several heaps of pottery waste have also provided a body of data concerning types and forms of ceramics

291

over time. This combination of information makes it possible to reconstruct the sociology of production and consumption. On the basis of studies of Rhenish ware, it can be established that producers and consumers of pottery were different groups—producers lived in the countryside, whereas consumers inhabited towns and emporia in widespread parts of medieval Europe. The production of Rhenish ware was performed by professional potters and their assistants; small thumb impressions on the pots indicate the participation of women and children in production. The construction of the kiln also required expert, experienced labor. Pottery products were standardized in form, type, size, decoration, and function in response to the volume and demands of the market. The distribution of pottery was dependent on a group of professional merchants resident in towns. Transport of this bulky commodity was only profitable by ship, and the harbor at Cologne served as the center for the distribution of Rhenish ware.

Comparable work has been carried out by medieval archaeologists in the study of iron ore production. A mining village in the Siegerland region in Altenberg[38] has been fully excavated, and bog iron production centers in the Schleswig-Holstein[39] and Hannover[40] areas have also been studied. The techniques of open-cast mining have been investigated in Bavaria near Kelheim,[41] where a mining area of the La Tène period (second-first centuries B.C.) was exploited again in the Middle Ages.

Residences, Seats, Palaces

The medieval German Empire was characterized by a plurality of political power that differed from the more centrally organized kingdoms of France and England. Princes, archbishops and bishops, electors, and other authorities participated in the rule of kings and emperors. The material world of residences and palaces reflects this complex, political authority. There are residences of the archbishops of Cologne, Trier, and Mainz, who were electors at the same time; powerful dukes like Henry the Lion built their own residences. The king and emperor had a series of residences called Königs- or Kaiserpfalzen. A substantial number of royal residences have been excavated, and their archaeology is striking for its variability both through time and across regions. It is not possible, however, to find one model of royal residences to which all examples belong, and only an impression of royal residences of the Carolingian and post-Carolingian period will be offered here.[42]

Aachen (*Aquis Grani*) was the most important imperial residence in western Germany.[43] More than thirty kings were crowned there during the Middle Ages, and the imperial residence is one of the best preserved in Germany. Excavation has been underway at Aachen since the nineteenth century. Although earlier work was motivated by the art historical question of style and chronology, it is now possible to reconstruct the concept and material manifestation of a Carolingian *palatium*. At Aachen the palatial chapel, the famous octagon, and the imperial palace, the *aula regia*, were essential to the *palatium* concept and were both symbolically and materially intertwined. The *aula regia*, which is structurally contained today by the town hall, was only reconstructable through archaeological investigation. It was originally composed of a large rectangular hall with two apses in the long walls and a third apse in one of the small walls. There was an annex at the eastern front, and the strong Granus tower was also part of the Carolingian plan. The *aula regia* and the palatial chapel were connected by a long passageway which allowed the emperor to enter the chapel at the first floor level. As far as can be ascertained today, the imperial residence at Aachen was not fortified, in contrast to such later residences from the tenth and eleventh centuries as Werla and Tilleda, which were fortified by earthworks and walls.

One of the most important achievements of medieval archaeology in recent years are the results of Wilhelm Winkelmann's excavations of the imperial complex at Paderborn, where he uncovered an *aula* and church with auxiliary buildings—none of which had been preserved at ground level.[44] Without excavation, the setting of the imperial assemblies held in Paderborn in 777, 785, and 799 could not have been known. The imperial *aula* at Paderborn was a large rectangular hall measuring thirty-one m. in length and ten m. in width. The imperial church, on a grander scale, measured fifty-two m. long and eighteen m. wide. Both the hall and the church were destroyed several times during periods of Saxon unrest, but after each episode the buildings were newly erected and their functions in the imperial complex preserved. The Carolingian tradition at Paderborn was perpetuated by succeeding kings. During the eleventh and twelfth centuries it was visited by kings at least twenty-one times. After destruction by fire around 1000, a new and larger (55 m. by 16 m.) imperial *aula* was built slightly north of the former one, and construction of the cathedral, which is still standing today, began. Dwelling structures, a monastery, and two chapels completed the imperial complex.

In the eastern part of Germany, a very different type of royal residence was under construction during the tenth century. The royal Tilleda complex, a gift of Otto II (973-83) to his wife Theophanu, was excavated by Paul Grimm and represents another phase of his pioneering activities in medieval archaeology.[45] The site, which is situated on the plateau of a narrow mountain spur, continues the tradition of prehistoric fortification which frequently utilized such topography. The Tilleda spur was cut off from the rest of the mountain by triple ranges of rampart and ditch. The transverses of these three fortifications divided the spur into three areas, all of which were occupied. The outermost tip of the spur was used for the royal residence itself, including a royal hall, church, and dwelling buildings. This area, known as the Hauptburg, served as the main fortification and place of residence. The Vorburg extended west from this and contained 120 houses of different sizes, construction, and function as well as a great number of pits of various form and function. Fireplaces inside the houses attested to their permanent use for dwelling purposes. Other buildings were used for storage. A third group of structures served as workshops for various artisans: weavers, iron and bronze workers, and textile workers. The excavation of the settlement and royal residence at Tilleda sheds much light on the economic basis of royal residences, which included not only adjoining royal estates, but the production of artisans as well.

Churches and Monasteries

The excavation of churches and monasteries has received a great deal of attention in medieval archaeology in West Germany, and it is impossible even to begin to summarize results here.[46] It is worthwhile, however, to emphasize that the goals of more recent studies have not only chronology and architectural style as research interests but also the economic and social contexts of religious settlements.

Fortifications and Castles

In this field of research, medieval archaeology deals with two different traditions. The large earthen ringworks of the early medieval period continued in the tradition of prehistoric fortification, especially with their use of topographical setting.[47] Castles, in contrast, served not only defensive purposes in a variety of topographical settings but also as dwellings and seats for ruling houses.[48] Both types of fortifications have been excavated in Western Germany. I confine myself here to mentioning two castles which have been excavated over the last two years. One of them is the Tomburg near Bonn, a seat of the Rhenish Count Palatine of the eleventh and twelfth centuries.[49] The castle was situated on top of a mountain peak of volcanic origin. Below the medieval layers, remainders

294

of a late Roman castle, probably a *burgus*, protecting an important road,were also uncovered. The timber-constructed castle of Haus Meer near Neuss, built on an old course of the Rhine, is my second example.[50] The dynasty that constructed the castle was one of colonizers in the area. During its final period, this primitive castle was used as a cloister by Prémontre nuns. The project at Haus Meer is important, since it was carried out with an interdisciplinary team of archaeologists and natural scientists. This type of collaboration is one of the most exciting directions in medieval archaeology today.

Conclusions

The research summarized here reflects a robust disciplinary situation for archaeology in West Germany, one which is surpassed only in Great Britain and in Scandinavia. Although an enormous amount of data is already available in medieval archaeology, the aims and directions of this young discipline are still very much under discussion. In the next years, theoretical and methodological reflection on the fundamental questions medieval archeology would like to ask should be undertaken in as broad an interdisciplinary setting as possible.

NOTES

I am deeply indebted to Kathleen Biddick, who was so kind as to help with the written version of my lecture.
   [1] E. Cinthio, "Medieval Archaeology as a Research Subject," *Meddelanden från Lunds Universitets Historiksa Museum* (1962-63), 190-95; H. v. Petrikovits, "Vorwort," in *Kirche und Burg in der Archäologie des Rheinlandes, Kunst und Altertum am Rhein*, no. 8 (Düsseldorf: Rheinisches Landesmuseum Bonn, 1962), pp. 5-7; W. Bader, "Zu einer Archäologie des Mittelalters," in *Kirche und Burg*, pp. 11-12; O. Meyer, "Mit Spaten und Feder—Wende in der Methode der Mittelalter- Forschung," *Varia Franconiae Historica*, vol. 1 (1981), 9-11; M. de. Bouard, *Manuel d'Archéologie Médiévale: De la Fouille à l'histoire* (Paris: C.D.U. SEDES, 1975), pp. 9-18; P. Grimm, "Der Beitrag der Archäologie für die Erforschung des Mittelalters," in *Probleme des frühen Mittelalters in archäologischer und historischer Sicht*, ed. H. Knorr (East Berlin: Akademie Verlag, 1966), pp. 39-74; E. Nickel, Die Erforschung Magdeburgs als Beispiel des Zusammenwirkens von Archäologie und der nur auf schriftlicher Überlieferung beruhenden Geschichtsforschung," in *Probleme des frühen Mittelalters*, pp. 75-83; H. Borger, "Möglichkeiten und Grenzen der Archäologie des Mittelalters, dargelegt am Beispiel Xanten," *Frühmittelalterliche Studien*, 2 (1968), 251-77; and H. Jankuhn, "Umrisse einer Archäologie des Mittelalters," in *Zeitschrift für*

Archäologie des Mittelalters, 1 (1973), 9-19.

[2] W. Janssen, "Methoden und Probleme archäologischer Siedlungsforschung," in *Geschichtswissenschaft und Archäologie*, ed. H. Jankuhn and R. Wenskus, Vorträge und Forschungen, vol. 22 (Sigmaringen: Jan Thorbeke Verlag, 1979), pp. 101 ff.

[3] P. Grimm, "Zur Entwicklung der mittelalterlichen Keramik in den Harzlandschaften," *Zeitschrift d. Harzvereins für Geschichte und Altertumskunde*, 66 (1933), 1-38.

[4] P. Grimm, "Hohenrode, eine mittelalterliche Siedlung im Südharz," *Veröffentlichung d. Landesanstalt f. Volkheitskunde zu Halle*, 11 (1939), 1-56; and his "Phosphatuntersuchungen in der Wüstung Hohenrode bei Grillenberg, Kr. Sangerhausen," *Ausgrabungen und Funde*, 16 (1971), 43-49. See also K. Baumgarten, "Ethnographische Bemerkungen zum Grabungsbefund," *Ausgrabungen und Funde*, 16 (1971), 49-53.

[5] *Zeitschrift f. Archäologie des Mittelalters*, ed. W. Janssen and H. Steuer, vol. 1 (1973) through vol. 10 (1982); vol. 11 (forthcoming).

[6] *Lübecker Schriften zur Archäologie und Kulturgeschichte* (Amt f. Vor- und Frühgeschichte, Bodendenkmalpflege der Hansestadt Lübeck), ed. G. P. Fehring (Bonn: Habelt), vol. 1 (1978) through 7 (1983).

[7] *Denkmalpflege und Forschung in Westfalen* (Landschaftsverband Westfalen-Lippe), ed. D. Ellger and U. Lobbedey (Bonn: Habelt). The series started with vol. 1 (1979) and has now been published through vol. 3 (1981). It will continue.

[8] *Forschungen und Berichte der Archäologie des Mittelalters in Baden-Württemberg* (Landesdenkmalamt Baden-Württemberg), ed. D. Lutz, vol. 1 (1972) through 8 (1983).

[9] A handbook of medieval archaeology for Germany would be desirable. See n. 1 for reference to the French handbook for medieval archaeology.

[10] For an introduction to German town archaeology, see *European Towns: Their Archaeology and Early History*, ed. M. W. Barley (London: Academic Press, 1977), esp. ch. 8, "Northern Germany," by U. Lobbedey and ch. 11, "Urban and Rural Settlement in the Frankish Kingdom" by K. Böhner. See also *Vor- und Frühformen der europäischen Stadt im Mittelalter*, ed. H. Jankuhn, W. Schlesinger, and H. Steuer, 2 vols, Abhandlungen der Akademie der Wissenschaften in Göttingen (Göttingen: Verlag Vandenhoeck und Ruprecht, 1973-74).

[11] The problem of continuity: H. v. Petrikovits, "Das Fortleben römischer Städte an Rhein und Donau im frühen Mittelalter," in *Aus der Schatzkammer des antiken Trier. Festgabe des Rheinischen Landesmuseums Trier zum 150-jährigen Bestehen der Gesellschaft für nützliche Forschungen*, 1801-1951, 1st ed., 1951 (2nd ed., Trier: Paulinus Verlag, 1959), pp. 74-84; K. Böhner, "Die Frage der Kontinuität zwischen Altertum und Mittelalter im Spiegel der fränkischen Funde des Rheinlandes," in *Aus der Schatzkammer*, pp. 85-109.

[12] H. Hinz, *Xanten zur Römerzeit*, 4th ed. (Duisburg Ruhrort: Renckhoff, 1971); and F. W. Oediger, *Beiträge zur Frühgeschichte des Xantener Viktorstiftes*, Rheinische Ausgrabungen, 6 (Bonn: Rheinisches Landesmuseum Bonn, 1969).

[13] E. Ennen and D. Höroldt, *Kleine Geschichte der Stadt Bonn* (Bonn: Stollfuss Verlag, 1967); H. Lehner and W. Bader, "Baugeschichtliche Untersuchungen am Bonner Münster," *Bonner Jahrb.*, 136-37 (1932), 1-211; H. v. Petrikovits, "Zur Zeitstellung der ältesten frühchristlichen Kultanlage unter dem Bonner Münster," *Kölner Jahrb.*, 9 (1967-68), 112-19; H. Borger, "Zur Neugliederung der Stadt in ottonisch-staufischer Zeit auf Grund archäologischer Quellen," in *Kiel Papers: Symposium des Sonderforschungsbereichs 17, 'Skandinavien und Ostseeraumforschung,'* ed. H. Hinz (Neumünster: Wacholtz Verlag, 1972), pp. 9-20; and K. Böhner, "Bonn im frühen Mittelalter," *Bonner Jahrb.*, 178 (1978), 395-426.

[14] R. Schindler, "Trier in merowingischer Zeit," in *Vor- und Frühformen der europäischen Stadt*, vol. 1, pp. 130-51; E. M. Wightman, *Roman Trier and the Treveri* (London: Hart-Davis, 1970); K. Flink, "Bemerkungen zur Topographie der Stadt Trier im Mittelalter," in *Landschaft und Geschichte: Festschrift f. Franz Petri* (Bonn: Röhrscheid, 1970), pp. 222-36; and E. Ewig, *Trier im Merowingerreich: Civitas, Stadt Bistum* (Trierer Zeitschrift f. Geschichte u. Kunst der Trierer Landes u. Nachbargebiete, 21 [1952] and Trier: Paulinus Verlag, 1954).

[15] H. Hellenkemper, "Zu archäologischen Untersuchungen in rheinischen Stadtkernen. Ausgewählte Bibliographie," in *Kiel Papers*, pp. 21-22; H. Steuer, *Die Franken in Köln* (Köln: Greven, 1980); O. Doppelfeld, "Das Fortleben der Stadt Köln vom 5. - bis 8. Jahrhundert," *Early Medieval Studies*, 1 and *Antikvarisk Arkiv*, 38 (1970), 35-42; and O. Doppelfeld, "Köln von der Spätantike bis zur Karolingerzeit," in *Vor- und Frühformen der europäischen Stadt*, vol. 1, pp. 110-29.

[16] See Lobbedey in *European Towns*, n. 10 above.

[17] W. A. van Es, "Die neuen Dorestad-Grabungen 1967-72," in *Vor- und Frühformen der europäischen Stadt* (see n. 10) vol. 1, pp. 202-17; and W. A. van Es and W. J. H. Verwers, *Excavations at Dorestad I: The Harbor: Hoogstraat I*, Nederlandse Oudheden, 9 (Amersfoort: B.R.O.B., 1980).

[18] K. Schietzel, "Stand der siedlungsarchäologischen Forschung in Haithabu—Ergebnisse und Probleme," in *Berichte über die Ausgrabungen in Haithabu*, 16 (1981), includes bibliography.

[19] E. Schieche and B. Arrhenius, "Birka," in *J. Hoops Reallexikon der Germanischen Altertumskunde*, ed. H. Jankuhn et al., vol. 3, 2nd ed. (Berlin: de Gruyter, 1978), pp. 23-28, with bibliography.

[20] W. Winkelmann, "Ausgrabungen auf dem Domhof in Münster," in *Monasterium*, ed. A. Schröer (Regensberg: Münster in Westfalen, 1966), pp. 25-54; and U. Lobbedey, in *European Towns* (n. 10).

[21] R. Schindler, *Ausgrabungen in Alt-Hamburg* (Hamburg: Heimatbücher, 1957); and D. Bohnsack, "Das Fundament eines steinernen Rundturmes (11th century)," *Château Gaillard*, 2 (1967), 1-6.

[22] E. Ennen, *Die europäische Stadt des Mittelalters*, 3rd ed. (Göttingen: Vandenhoeck und Ruprecht, 1979), trans. N. Fryde as *The Medieval Town*, vol. 15 of *Europe in the Middle Ages, Selected Studies* (New York: North Holland Publ. Co., 1979); and H. Borger, "Bemerkungen zu den "Wachstumstufen"

einiger mittelalterlicher Städte im Rheinland," in *Landschaft und Geschichte*, pp. 52-89.

[23] See n. 4 above.

[24] W. Janssen, *Königshagen. Ein archäologisch-historischer Beitrag zur Siedlungsgeschichte des südwestlichen Harzvorlandes* (Hildesheim: A. Lax, 1965); his *Zur Typologie und Chronologie mittelalterlicher Keramik aus Südniedersachsen* (Neumünster: Wacholtz, 1966); and, for a survey of excavations of medieval rural sites, his "Dorf und Dorfformen des 7. bis 12. Jahrhunderts im Lichte neuer Ausgrabungen in Mittel- und Nordeuropa," in *Das Dorf der Eisenzeit und des frühen Mittelalters: Siedlungsform, wirtschaftliche Funktion, soziale Struktur*, 3rd ser., no. 101, ed. H. Jankuhn, R. Schützeichel, and F. Schwind (Akademie der Wissenschaften in Göttingen, 1977), pp. 285-356. See also G. P. Fehring, "Zur archäologischen Erforschung mittelalterlicher Dorfsiedlungen als archäologisches Problem," *Zeitschrift f. Agrargeschichte und Agrarsoziologie*, 21 (1973), 1-35.

[25] G. P. Fehring, *Unterregenbach: Kirchen, Herrensitz, Siedlungsbereiche*, 3 vols., *Forschungen und Berichte der Archäologie des Mittelalters in Baden-Württemberg*, 1 (1972).

[26] G. P. Fehring, "Grabungen in Siedlungsbereichen des 3. bis 13. Jahrhunderts sowie an Töpferöfen der Wüstung Wülfingen am Kocher," *Château Gaillard*, 3 (1969), 48-60; M. Schulze, "Die mittelalterliche Keramik der Wüstung Wülfingen am Kocher, Stadt Forchtenberg, Hohenlohekreis," *Forschungen und Berichte der Archäologie des Mittelalters in Baden-Württemberg*, 7 (1981), 5-148; and her "Die Wüstung Wülfingen in Nordwürttemberg," *Offa*, 39 (1982), 235-43.

[27] For the problem of desertions from an archaeological point of view see W. Janssen, "Methodische Probleme archäologischer Wüstungsforschung," *Nachrichten der Akademie der Wissenschaften in Göttingen, Phil.-Hist. Kl.* no. 2 (1968), pp. 29-56; W. Janssen, "Mittelalterliche Dorfsiedlungen als archäologisches Problem," *Frühmittelalterliche Studien*, 2 (1968), 305-67; and his *Studien Zur Wüstungsfrage im fränkischen Altsiedelland zwischen Rhein, Mosel, und Eifel nordrand*, 2 vols. (Köln: Rheinland Verlag, 1975).

[28] W. Winkelmann, "Eine westfälische Siedlung des 8. Jahrhunderts bei Warendorf, Kr. Warendorf," *Germania*, 32 (1954), 189-213; his "Die Ausgrabungen in der frühmittelalterlichen Siedlung bei Warendorf, Westfalen," in *Neue Ausgrabungen in Deutschland*, ed. W. Krämer (Berlin: Gebr. Mann, 1958), pp. 492-517; and his "Archäologische Zeugnisse zum frühmittelalterlichen Handwerk in Westfalen," *Frühmittelalterliche Studien*, 11 (1977), 92-126.

[29] See K. Böhner, "Urban and Rural Settlement," in *European Towns*; and his "Die Frage der Kontinuität," see n. 11 above.

[30] W. Abel, *Die Wüstungen des ausgehenden Mittelalters*, 3rd ed. (Stuttgart: Gustav Fischer, 1976).

[31] For new aspects of desertion see: W. Janssen, "Dorf und Dorfformen," n. 24 above; and E. Ennen and W. Janssen, *Deutsche Agrargeschichte. Vom Neolithikum bis zur Schwelle des Industriezeitalters* (Wiesbaden: Franz Steiner, 1979), pp. 160 ff.

[32] See "Das Handwerk in vor- und Frühgeschichtlicher Zeit," vol. 1, *Historische und rechtshistorische Beiträge und Untersuchungen zur Frühgeschichte der Gilde*, ed. H. Jankuhn, W. Janssen, R. Schmidt-Wiegand, H. Tiefenbach, Abhandlungen der Akademie der Wissenschaften in Göttingen (Göttingen: Vanderhoeck & Rupprecht, 1981); vol. 2, *Archäologische und rechtshistorische Beiträge* (1983). As far as craft activities in rural settlements are concerned, see W. Janssen, "Gewerbliche Produktion des Mittelalters als Wirtschaftsfaktor im ländlichen Raum," in above, vol. 2, pp. 317-94; see also his "Die Bedeutung der mittelalterlichen Burg für die Wirtschafts- und Sozialgeschichte des Mittelalters," vol. 2, pp. 261-316.

[33] Stockholm: V. Pettersons, 1955.

[34] C. Blindheim, Kaupangunderso/gelsen avsluttet," *Viking*, 33 (1969), 5-40; and C. Blindheim and R. L. Tollnes, *Kaupang: Vikingetines handelsplass* (Oslo: Mortensen, 1972).

[35] A. E. Herteig, *Kongers havn og handels sete* (Oslo: Aschehoug, 1969); and W. Janssen, "Mittelalterliche deutsche Keramik in Norwegen und ihre Bedeutung für die Handelsgeschichte," in *Studien zur europäischen Vor- und Frühgeschichte, Festschrift f. H. Jankuhn*, ed. M. Claus, W. Haarnagel and K. Raddatz (Neumünster: Wachholtz, 1968), pp. 200-08.

[36] W. Hübener, *Die Keramik von Haithabu* (Neumünster: Wachholtz, 1959); and K. Weidemann, "Importkeramik aus Haithabu. Ausgrabung 1963-64," *Berichte über die Ausgrabungen in Haithabu*, 4 (1970), 46-52.

[37] U. Lobbedey, *Untersuchungen mittelalterlicher Keramik vornehmlich aus Südwestdeutschland* (Berlin: de Gruyter, 1968); K. Böhner, "Frühmittelalterliche Töpfereien in Walberberg und Pingsdorf," *Bonner Jahrb.*, 155-56 (1955-56), 372 ff; W. Janssen, "Badorf," in *J. Hoops Reallexikon*, pp. 593-97; his "Der Karolingische Töpfereibezirk von Brühl-Eckdorf, Kreis Köln," *Neue Ausgrabungen und Forschungen in Niedersachsen*, 6 (1970), 224-39; and W. Lung, "Zur vor- und frühgeschichtlichen Keramik im Kölner Raum," *Kölner Jahrb. f. Vor- und Frühgesch.*, 4 (1959), 45-65.

[38] *Die Bergbausiedlung Altenberg*, ed. Verein Altenberg e. V. (Altenberg: Landeskonservator Westfalen-Lippe [Münster-Westfalen], 1979), with contributions by M. Lúsznat, U. Lobbedey, C. Dahm, G. Weisgerber, and F. R. Kühn.

[39] H. Hingst, "Vor- und frühgeschichtliche Eisenverhüttung in Schleswig-Holstein," in *Neue Ausgrabungen in Deutschland*, pp. 258-67.

[40] G. Schulz, "Die Kartierung mittelalterlicher und frühneuzeitlicher Eisenschmelzplätze in der Wietze-Niederung bei Isernhagen, Kr. Burgdorf," *Neue Ausgrabungen und Forschungen in Niedersachsen*, 7 (1972), 308-33; and her "Ausgrabung eines Eisenschmelzplatzes (12-15 Jahrh.) in der Wietze-Niederung bei Isernhagen, Kreis Burgdorf (Platz 42), *Neue Ausgrabungen und Forschungen in Niedersachsen*, 8 (1973), 91-125.

[41] K. Schwarz, H. Tillmann, and W. Treibs, "Zur spätlatènezeitlichen und mittelalterlichen Eisenerzgewinnung auf der südlichen Frankenalb bei Kelheim," *Jahresberichte d. Bayerischen Bodendenkmalpflege*, 6-7 (1965-66), 35-66.

[42] For a good introduction to the problem, see *Deutsche Königspfalzen. Beiträge zu ihrer historischen und archäologischen Erforschung*, vols. 1-3, Max

Planck-Institut für Geschichte in Göttingen (Göttingen: Vandenhoeck und Ruprecht, 1963, 1965, 1979).

[43] W. Kaemmerer, "Die Aachener Pfalz Karls des Grossen in Anlage und Überlieferung," in *Karl der Grosse, vol. I*, ed. H. Beumann (Düsseldorf: Schwans, 1965), pp. 322-48; W. Sage, "Zur archäologischen Untersuchung karolingischer Pfalzen in Deutschland," in *Karl der Grosse, vol. III*, ed. W. Braunfels and H. Schnitzler (Düsseldorf: Schwann, 1965), pp. 323-35; L. Hugot, "Die Pfalz Karls des Grossen in Aachen. Ergebnisse einer archäologisch-topographischen Untersuchung des Ortes und der Pfalz," in *Karl der Grosse, vol. III*, pp. 534-72; and L. Falkenstein, "Zwischenbilanz zur Aachener Pfalzenforschung, Kritische Bemerkungen zu Forschungsberichten über die Aachener Pfalz im Sammelwerk *Karl der Grosse-Lebenswerk und Nachleben*," *Zeitschr. d. Aachener Geschichtsvereins*, 80 (1970), pp. 7-71.

[44] W. Winkelmann, "Die Königspfalz und die Bishofspfalz des 11. und 12. Jahrhunderts in Paderborn," in *Kaiserpfalz Paderborn*, ed. Erzbischöfliches Generalvikariat Paderborn, Presse und Informationsstelle (Salzkotten: Meinwerk Verlag, 1978).

[45] P. Grimm, *Tilleda, Eine Königspfalz am Kyffhäuser. Teil 1: Die Hauptberg*, Deutsche Akademie d. Wissenschaften zu Berlin. Schriften d. Sektion f. Vor- u. Frühgeschichte, 24 (Berlin: Akademie Verlag, 1968); and his "Beiträge zu Handwerk und Handel in der Vorburg der Pfalz Tilleda," *Zeitschrift f. Archäologie*, 10 (1976), 261-306.

[46] A useful introduction to church archaeology is given by H. Borger, *Die Abbilder des Himmels in Köln, Kölner Kirchenbauten des Mittelalters*, vol. 1 (Köln: Greven, 1979). Important for the history of the bishop's church: O. Doppelfeld and W. Weyres, *Die Ausgrabungen im Dom zu Köln*, Kölner Forschung, 1 (Mainz: Zabernverlag, 1980). See *Der Trierer Dom*, ed. F. J. Ronig, Rheinischer Verein f. Denkmalpflege und Heimatschutz (Neuss: Gesellschaft f. Buchdruckerei AG Neuss, 1980) for a series of reports on the excavations in the Cologne cathedral.

[47] R. v. Uslar, *Studien zu frühgeschichtlichen Befestigungen zwischen Nordsee und Alpen*, Bonner Jahrb. Beih. 11 (Köln: Bohlau, 1964).

[48] M. Müller-Wille, *Mittelalterliche Burghügel ("Motten") im nördlichen Rheinland*, Bonner Jahrb. Beih. 16 (Köln: Böhlau, 1966); and W. Janssen, W. Meyer, O. Olsen, J. Renaud, H. Schneider, and K. W. Struve, *Burgen aus Holz und Stein*, Schweizer Beitr. z. Kulturgesch. und Archäologie des Mittelalters, 5 (Olten und Freiburg im Breisgau: Walter, 1979). A forum for archaeological research on medieval castles is formed by the international colloquium *Château Gaillard*, which takes place every two years in one of the countries of Western Europe. See the colloquium reports: *Château Gaillard. Etudes de Castellolgie Européene*, vol. 1 (1964) through vol. 11 (1982).

[49] W. Janssen, "Die Tomburg bei Rheinbach, Landkreis Bonn," *Château Gaillard*, 4 (1968), 163-78.

[50] W. Janssen and K.-H. Knörzer, "Die frühmittelalterliche Niederungsburg bei Haus Meer, Stadt Meerbusch, Kreis Grevenbroich," *Schriftenreihe d. Kreises Grevenbroich*, 8 (1971), 7-186.

CONTRIBUTORS

WALTER E. BERRY, Department of Art History at University of Missouri, Columbia

KATHLEEN BIDDICK, Department of History at University of Notre Dame, Notre Dame, Indiana

JANET E. BUERGER, George Eastman House in Rochester, New York

WILLIAM S. COOTER, Department of Meteorology at University of Oklahoma, Norman

PAMELA CRABTREE, The University Museum at The University of Pennsylvania, Philadelphia

CAROLE L. CRUMLEY, Department of Anthropology at the University of North Carolina, Chapel Hill

STEPHEN L. DYSON, Department of Classics at Wesleyan University, Middletown, Connecticut

HAROLD S. A. FOX, Department of English Local History at the University of Leicester, Leicester, England

DAVID HALL, The Fenland Project, Department of Archaeology at Cambridge, England

RICHARD HODGES, Department of Prehistory and Archaeology at the University of Sheffield, Sheffield, England

WALTER JANSSEN, Institut für Archäologie, Sowie Vor-und Frühgeschichte at the Universität Würzburg, West Germany

GLANVILLE R. J. JONES, Department of Geography at the University of Leeds, Leeds, England

OLIVER RACKHAM, Corpus Christi College in Cambridge, England

WILLIAM H. TEBRAKE, Department of History at the University of Maine, Orono, Maine